KT-472-652

The Best of JAZZ
2

The Best of JAZZ

2: Enter the Giants

Humphrey LYTTELTON

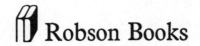

Robson Books

FIRST PUBLISHED IN GREAT BRITAIN IN 1981
BY ROBSON BOOKS LTD., BOLSOVER HOUSE,
5/6 CLIPSTONE STREET, LONDON, W1P 7EB.
COPYRIGHT © 1981 HUMPHREY LYTTELTON.

*Grateful acknowledgement is made to Jazz Music Books
for the photographs which appear in this book.*

British Library Cataloguing in Publication Data
Lyttelton, Humphrey
    Enter the giants. – (The Best of Jazz; 2)
1. Jazz music – United States
I. Title   II. Series
    785.42'0973   ML3561.J3

    ISBN 0–86051–107–3

All rights reserved. No part of this publication may be
reproduced, stored in a retrieval system, or transmitted
in any form or by any means, electronic, mechanical,
photocopying or otherwise, without the prior permission
in writing of the publishers.

Printed in Great Britain by
Mackays of Chatham Ltd

Contents

Introduction

WHEN I EMBARKED upon this series of *Best of Jazz* books, the plan seemed quite simple. They would constitute an exhaustive guide to the important performances committed to wax during the era of the 78 r.p.m. record. Volume One started with a confession that the plan had already gone awry. So many new pieces of information and intriguing lines of thought emerged from my early researches that, before I knew it, I had rattled off over five thousand words on the Original Dixieland Jazz Band alone, signifying that the book as originally conceived would end up occupying two feet of shelf space and weighing half a hundredweight! In the end, a slimmer volume appeared dealing with the recordings of just sixteen key figures in jazz development between 1917 and 1930.

Even with this drastic change of plan, the progression to Volume Two seemed logical—we would look at roughly the same number of influential musicians from the period, spanning 1931 to 1944, which has been historically designated as the Swing Era. Off I went with an optimistic clatter of the typewriter only to discover, just about as quickly, that I was in trouble again. The reasons are probably more obvious to you, dear reader, than they were to me when I set off. The disastrous slump in the recording industry that signalled the end of the first Jazz Age was not long in recovering, and to the domestic output of the major recording companies in America were added supplementary lists aimed at the growing overseas market, not to mention contributions from small, independent companies that sprang up as the ranks of avowedly specialist jazz enthusiasts swelled.

Amidst all this activity, the development of jazz accelerated. Musicians such as Louis Armstrong, Sidney Bechet, Duke Ellington and Coleman Hawkins, fully discussed in Volume One, continued to grow in style and to impress and influence their fellow-musicians. They could not simply be filed away in a drawer marked 'The Twenties'. There were other musicians concerning whom I deferred discussion in the first book because they recorded most prolifically during the Thirties. So as the reader will discover, investigation into the origins and influence of such men as Fats Waller, Jack Teagarden, Johnny Hodges and Benny Carter stretch back to the earliest day of the period already covered. And, of course, new musicians came up thick and fast on the heels of the first wave of originators, many of them initiating their own secondary strands of influence. Before Fats Waller had been neatly wrapped up, it became apparent that we were in for another change of plan.

The title *Enter the Giants* adequately describes my revised scheme for this second volume. Though great and influential soloists did emerge during the Twenties, they were discussed in the context of equally important ensembles—the King Oliver Creole Jazz Band, the Louis Armstrong Hot Five, Jelly Roll Morton's Red Hot Peppers and so on. As the Thirties dawned and with it the growth of published and widely-disseminated jazz criticism, it became more usual for jazz to be discussed in terms of the great individuals, sooner or later to be dubbed 'jazz giants'. Jazz writers and fans tend to be generous to the point of profligacy in bestowing gianthood upon their idols, and I have had to devise some way of limiting the field. Consequently, this book will embrace some of those who exerted the strongest influence on their own and subsequent periods. Those who are left out—and Benny Goodman and the guitarist Charlie Christian are two who will spring to mind—will be deferred to the third volume. This will discuss the bands, large and small, formal and transitory, which provide the landmarks in the progress towards the twin phenomena, Traditionalism and Modernism, that dominated the minds of jazz followers as the era of the '78s' came to a close. If, at the end, the three volumes point the way to a sound basic collection of masterpieces from the first three decades of jazz and at the same time constitute what I described in the introduction to Volume One as 'a rough and ready history' of that period, I shall be happy enough.

As before, I cherish the hope that this volume will have something of interest to the newcomer and the old hand in jazz. I aim to initiate, rather than impose, critical thoughts, and to this end kites are flown, hobby-horses are mounted and bees are given untrammelled access to bonnets, without too much concern for any disagreement they may arouse. On the other hand, care has been taken to ensure, I hope, that facts are correct and that theory can always be supported by aural evidence.

The books from which I have gleaned information and quotations are listed in a bibliography at the end. Any quotation which is not individually acknowledged will derive from a source already introduced in the same chapter. As before, Leonard Feather's *Encyclopedia of Jazz* and John Chilton's *Who's Who in Jazz* have been constantly at my elbow, as have the discographies of Brian Rust. My renewed thanks to all of them.

Bearing in mind that many readers will not be adept at reading music, I have once again tried to describe the nuances of the music under discussion in onomatopaeic and descriptive terms rather than with musical examples. This becomes harder and less precise as jazz increases in complexity, but I have done my best, and the reader will at least have fun 'doodle-doodling' to himself and banging on the table-top! Those readers who *do* read music but are not well up in jazz will derive enormous help, as I have done, from the paperback called *Teach Yourself Jazz Piano* in the well-known instructional series. It is by the trombonist and pianist, Eddie Harvey, an old friend and colleague of mine to whom I am indebted for much technical help.

Finally, I must express the hope, perhaps less confidently than in Volume One, that the reader will be able to buy or borrow the recordings cited. This time there are sometimes more than one per musician. All of them have been reissued in fairly recent times in various collections, but even so the listing of catalogue details could well send the reader off on a fruitless errand or direct him to a deleted album when a newer one is freshly available, so I have avoided it. We will draw a veil over the motives of those listeners to my weekly BBC record programme who begged me, within a few weeks of publication, to feature on the air all the examples cited in Volume One! *Honi soit*—as the man said.

Louis Armstrong

LOUIS ARMSTRONG DIED in July 1971, within two days of his seventy-first birthday. Three years earlier, he had visited Britain to play a two-week season at the Variety Club in Batley, Yorkshire, blowing well enough on the good nights to reward the hundreds of devotees who made the pilgrimage to hear him. From this point his playing career stretched back, virtually uninterrupted, beyond the earliest days of recorded jazz. There were no periods of idleness or obscurity, no times when changing musical fashion threw him temporarily off course, no occasions, despite shoddy and slapdash accompaniment and sorties deep into the hazardous territories of commerical show biz, when his trumpet playing fell far below the high standard of honesty and integrity which he set himself in the Twenties.

It is a record unrivalled in all of jazz. And it seems to have been achieved by dint of a deep-seated instinct for survival. This drove him along a path of apparent ruthlessness which contrasts strangely with the surface image of a cheerful, warm-hearted and, in his early days, insouciant man. King Oliver, Fletcher Henderson and Lil Hardin Armstrong, Louis's second wife, all had a decisive influence on his rise to pre-eminence in the Twenties—and all were abandoned, conclusively but with a surprising absence of rancour, when they had ceased to be of use to him. Lil Armstrong seems to have viewed the ultimate break-up of their marriage, which took place around 1930, with a resigned sense of the inevitable. 'You don't need me now you're earning a thousand dollars a week. We'll call it a day,' was how, in her recollection, she concluded the matter. Jazz critics over the years have been slower to resign themselves to what they have regarded as a divorce, of a more generally distressing kind, between Louis Armstrong and the jazz ideals to which he appeared to have been wedded in the days of the famous Hot Five recordings. I say 'appeared to be' because we always have to remember that it took little more than three weeks, spread over three or more years, to commit to posterity the much-admired recordings by Louis Armstrong and his Hot Five. The band had no existence outside the studio, and for the rest of the time, Louis was enjoying himself hugely in his publicized role of 'The World's Greatest Trumpet Player', performing with bands of all sizes in cabaret, between shows in a movie house and for dancing. His own conception of his role in life was based as much on these performances as on what he regarded as high-jinks with his old New Orleans chums in the Hot Five.

Nevertheless, it is true that, during the Twenties, Louis brought about a single-handed musical *coup* that revolutionized jazz and influenced thenceforward every branch of the music from solo improvisation to big band arranging. It is also true that the retrospective wailing and gnashing of teeth over Louis's post-1930 career that peppers the jazz histories is so much baying at the moon. In asking that Louis should have continued to blaze the trail while the rest of the jazz world stood still, the writers have called for a superman, not a human being with finite resources of creative energy. When they suggest that he somehow abandoned high artistic principles for the fleshpots of commercial entertainment, they wilfully turn a blind eye to the professional life that he was actually leading in the Twenties. And, in imagining that his adoption of a solo career was a surrender to some egotistical urge, they have failed to accept that, as British writer Victor Schonfield has pointed out in a strongly argued review of Louis's music between 1925 and '30, Louis's style ever since his recording of 'Cornet Chop Suey' in 1926 had 'reduced everyone else to the level of accompaniment and riveted all the attention on his trumpet.'

The Hot Five and Hot Seven era ended with the last small-group recordings in 1929, by which time Louis, with Earl Hines at his shoulder, had risen clear of the collectively improvised New Orleans-style ensemble. Acknowledged masterpieces such as 'Tight Like This', 'Muggles' and 'West End Blues' were essentially solo-and-accompaniment performances in which Louis and Earl Hines starred while the other horn men played a valuable but less dramatic supporting role. While in Chicago, Louis had made several recordings in the bigger-band setting in which he did his regular cabaret and theatre work, but the few titles made with the Carroll Dickerson and Erskine Tate orchestras give no more than a glimpse at the manner in which he was earning his every-day living. There are plenty of eye-witness accounts, however, to indicate quite clearly that his emergence as a showman-trumpeter in front of a band was a more gradual process than the discographies, with their sudden jump from quintet to big band, suggest.

In March 1929, Louis made a brief sortie to New York, playing a couple of dates with Luis Russell's Band and doing a recording session which included the extraordinary jam-session performance of 'Knockin' a Jug' (discussed in the chapter on Jack Teagarden) and two sides made with a contingent from the Russell band. 'Mahogany Hall Stomp' may be said to be an extension of the sort of informal small-group recordings that Louis had been making in Chicago. With New Orleans men Pops Foster, Paul Barbarin and guitarist Lonnie Johnson in the rhythm section, the music has a more relaxed, down-home flavour than some of the frenzied, up-tempo work of the latter-day Hot Fives, but the fact that Albert Nicholas's clarinet is conspicuously absent in the ensembles means that the Armstrong trumpet, prominent on the top of a trombone and saxophone ensemble, is once again virtually producing a solo with backing.

It is the other title recorded on the same day which gives an insight into the near future. The tune is the Jimmy McHugh–Dorothy Fields song 'I Can't Give you Anything but Love', which had been written the year before for the all-black review, *Black-birds of 1928*. Louis had recorded popular songs before—indeed, much of the material recorded by the Hot Five had come straight from the floorshow at the Sunset Café, where Louis worked at nights. And the recordings that he made with Bessie Smith, Clarence Williams and others were nothing if not commercially orientated towards a mass audience. But the style of show-business that Louis had experienced in his developing days was a chummy, happy-go-lucky, parochial affair compared with New York in the late Twenties. Hollywood and talking-pictures had yet to assert themselves as a musical influence, and it was on Broadway and in the lavish Harlem tourist traps that stars were made. Furthermore, the rapid growth of radio and the juke-box industry had begun to expand the empire of Tin Pan Alley worldwide. To Louis, even on that short first visit, the atmosphere must have been awe inspiring—and challenging.

His response was foreshadowed in the recording of 'I Can't Give you Anything but Love'. Here for the first time is Louis Armstrong shouldering the responsibility for the whole performance. I have to dissent from the view of several writers who have suggested that the extraordinary vocal chorus represented Louis Armstrong's way of showing his contempt for the 'Tin Pan Alley slop' that he was called upon to deliver, rather in the way that Fats Waller would later guy the lyrics of sentimental songs. In Louis, such a demonstration, however subtly concealed, would have been entirely out of character. This was a man who, according to his wife Lil, would prowl around their house in Chicago worrying about his ability to deliver the high notes that his audience expected; who had, on two occasions in the previous year, accompanied the commercial singer, Lily Delk Christian with manifest warmth and wholeheartedness, in songs whose syrupy lyrics make the Fields-McHugh favourite sound positively frigid; and who had just embarked on a love affair with the sweet music of Guy Lombardo's Royal Canadians which was to baffle earnest jazz students for years to come. Is it conceivable that, on a visit to New York that was presumably aimed at getting a toe-hold in that city, such an experienced professional would subvert the whole exercise in defence of some high artistic principles? It seems more probable that the eccentricity of this vocal refrain, with its melodramatic wailing and grunting, arose from Louis Armstrong's uncertainty about how to treat these new 'pretty' songs.

Louis was a singer before he ever touched a trumpet. Before he reached his teens, he was roaming the streets of New Orleans with a youthful quartet. In his autobiography, *Treat It Gentle*, Sidney Bechet recalled: 'It was Bunk Johnson who was the first to make me acquainted with Louis Armstrong. Bunk told me about this quartet that Louis was singing in. "Sidney," he said, "I want you to go hear a little quartet, how they sing and harmonize". He knew I was crazy about singing harmony ... They were real good—they had a way. There was a little fellow singing there, Little Mack was his name, he was the lead. And Louis, he sang tenor then.' Whenever Louis himself recalled those days in an interview, he would sing a snatch of lyric with great feeling and tenderness.

When Lil Armstrong recorded her reminiscences for Riverside Records, she recalled another aspect of Louis's musicality. It was at a time when she was beginning to push Louis to leave King Oliver and go out on his own. 'I could hear Louis coming home whistling for, oh, much more than a block away. He had the most beautiful shrill whistle, and all those riffs that he later made in his music, he used to whistle them—such beautiful riffs and runs and trills and things, you know—and I said to myself, "Maybe one day that guy'll play like that." Just crazy thoughts, you know, but it turned out all right!' The nearest Louis came to whistling on record was on three occasions, with King Oliver and with his own Hot Five, when he recorded solos on the slide, or Swannee, whistle. Despite the obvious inadequacy of the instrument with its sliding pitch that makes it virtually impossible to play the notes perfectly in tune, Louis as always threw himself heart and soul into the solos in 'Sobbin' Blues', 'Buddy's Habit' and 'Who's It?' So unashamedly sentimental are the results that, for many years, discographers were reluctant to believe that it was Louis at all, ascribing the solos to drummer Baby Dodds.

The picture that emerges is of a man with a strong, well integrated and rapidly expanding musical conception that expressed itself through whatever medium he chose. His love of singing did not find regular expression in his professional life until he returned to Chicago after the Fletcher Henderson engagement. Neither Oliver nor Henderson encouraged it, although fellow-Hendersonians have testified that Louis constantly badgered Henderson to allow his voice an airing and was rewarded with the chance to bellow a few ribald, vaudeville-style lines at the end of 'Everybody Loves My Baby'.

Because the singing appeared late in the day, it has been customary for writers to say of Louis that he sang exactly as he played the trumpet. Chronologically, it is almost certainly more accurate to say that, when he took up the cornet, he played exactly as he had sung with his roving quartet. But such chicken-and-egg discussion is irrelevant. Either way, the music was always the same. One of his earliest vocals with the Hot Five, in the 'Heebie Jeebies' of 1926 vintage, makes the point perfectly. This is as good a moment as any to bury, beyond reach of disinterment, the legend enthusiastically propagated by Louis himself that, half-way through the vocal chorus, he dropped the songsheet and, in carrying on wordlessly, invented 'scat-singing'. For one thing, he had already sung a complete lyric, such as it was, word perfectly when amnesia struck so conveniently at the very outset of the second chorus. For another, it is not conceivable that the primitive recording equipment would have continued to pick up Louis's voice if, as is alleged, he was floundering about the studio floor trying to grab the errant piece of paper. It was a good story, and it may have been that Louis, or someone at the recording studios, felt that it was necessary to put it about to explain a style of wordless singing which, though not invented by Louis, was new to the record-buying public. In a similar instance in a 1930 recording of 'I'm a Ding Dong Daddy', Louis repeated the trick, interjecting the line 'an' I done forgot the words' into a section of scat-singing that was clearly planned and premeditated.

The important thing about this interjection, the scat syllables that surround it and, indeed, the words of any song which Louis sang, is that they were all subordinated to the musical sense of what was, in effect, an instrumental solo without the instrument. The lyrics of 'Heebie Jeebies' are far short of intellectual in the first place. Louis divests them of any verbal sense they might have, flattening out their silly syncopation and replacing it with the relaxed, rhythmically charged phrasing that distinguishes his opening statement on cornet. The result, paradoxically, is to make the song seem much less nonsensical that it does in its natural state. In writing about Bessie Smith in *The Best of Jazz* Volume

One, I pointed to the phenomenon of jazz vocalizing through which, by making the words subservient to an overall rhythmic and melodic conception, consummate jazz singers like Bessie, Louis and Billie Holiday have fed back into a song a higher emotional content than its words are able to sustain. In Louis's vocal, the words 'Come on And do that dance' sound more like an urgent and irresistible entreaty than a jaunty invitation.

Where Louis Armstrong's singing diverged from his cornet playing in the early days was in quality and warmth of tone. We need not attach too much importance to this, recording equipment at the time demanding a degree of voice projection which Louis, a totally untrained singer, could only achieve by shouting. As it improved, so did he and, as the Hot Five years passed, his voice, while losing none of its expressive outer crust, acquired a more tender and attractive central tone. By the time he came to record 'I Can't Give you Anything but Love', trumpet and voice were as compatible as their physical characteristics would allow.

It follows that, for an explanation of Louis's somewhat eccentric vocal rendering of the Fields-McHugh song, it would be safer to refer to his trumpet playing of the period than to read into it implications of musical or literary criticism which were quite uncharacteristic of him. The striking thing about Louis Armstrong's playing in the latter days of the small-group recordings was its huge emotional range. If we pick out some famous titles at random—'Basin Street Blues', 'Save it Pretty Mama', 'Muggles', 'Tight Like This', 'St James Infirmary'—we find no two performances exactly alike. One is dramatic, the next tender, the third imbued with the simple strength of the blues and so on. There could be no greater contrast than between the stately, controlled melancholy of 'St James Infirmary' and the style of 'Tight Like This', without doubt the most intense and emotionally highly-charged passage of jazz improvisation that had up till then been captured on record. In each instance in which Louis sings, the vocal either matches or complements the trumpet playing.

The singing on 'I Can't Give you Anything but Love' takes its mood from the trumpet playing, with various grunts and gasps put in to simulate the violent and distorted notes which burst from the horn. If the one mocks the Tin Pan Alley product, then so must the other, and that is inconceivable. What perhaps makes the version seem satirical to us (but not to the contemporary record-buying public, with whom it was a hit) is the unduly heavy emotional weight which Louis piled upon a rather frail little love song. So far from trying to be funny or derisive, he seems to me to have carried forward the tragic mood of 'Tight Like This' on to a vehicle which would barely take it.

If I am right in this belief, then Louis very quickly acquired a sense of balance. After a brief return to Chicago, he travelled to New York with Carroll Dickerson's Orchestra for a more protracted stay. A study of his subsequent career that relied solely on recording details might lead one to think that, when the Carroll Dickerson Orchestra broke up, Louis embarked upon a new role as a bandleader. The truth is that at no time during the subsequent forty-odd years did he show any inclination to shoulder the responsibility of leadership, and the various organizations that recorded under the name 'Louis Armstrong and his Orchestra' during the Thirties, turn out on close inspection to have been either assembled or actually led by others. In all but nominal respects, the career that he embarked upon from the middle of 1929 onwards was one of virtuoso solo artist.

In this capacity, Louis became more and more closely involved with popular entertainment. While the Carroll Dickerson Orchestra was fulfilling a cabaret residency at Connie's Inn, Louis 'doubled' as featured soloist in a review called *Hot Chocolates* staged by the Inn's Connie Immerman at the Hudson Theatre. The music for this review was written by Fats Waller and his lyricist, Andy Razaf. It is ironical, in the light of all the retrospective criticism levelled at Louis for his alleged defection to commercialism at this stage, that his belated arrival on that scene at the age of twenty-nine should have been in collaboration with another respected jazzman who had been immersed in Harlem showbiz for the past four or five years. There have been plenty of jazz historians ready to lament Louis Armstrong's choice to begin recording the popular songs of the day. Few, if any, have come forward to berate Fats Waller for writing them! But that is another story, and it will be taken up in the chapter on Fats himself.

A more justifiable source of regret is the undoubted deterioration, once Louis had moved to New York, in the quality of his accompaniment on record. Here again, history has tended to put this down to some sort of artistic dereliction of duty on the part of Louis Armstrong himself. The judgement ignores the fact that every black artist and band had, since recording became a major industry in the middle Twenties, been tugged this way and that by the ebb and flow of commercial tides. In an interview recorded for Riverside records in 1956, Coleman Hawkins looked back on the Fletcher Henderson Orchestra of that period and said, 'That was during the time when Fletcher was . . . exchanging arrangements with other bands and getting to sound too much like other bands . . . all the big time bands.'

The big time bands were those of Jean Goldkette and Paul Whiteman, and a cursory browse through the Fletcher Henderson output in the late Twenties and early Thirties will reveal plenty of examples of their direct influence. But Henderson was not the only one. In *The Best of Jazz* Volume One, in writing about the influence of white musicians such as Bix Beiderbecke and Frankie Trumbauer on their black contemporaries, I noted that it had infiltrated, through the arranger and alto saxophonist Don Redman, into the Louis Armstrong small-group recordings in which he took part. Two records—'Symphonic Raps' and 'Savoyager's Stomp'—made in 1928 by Carroll Dickerson's Orchestra with Louis and Earl Hines to the fore, again show that the orchestrator, possibly Redman, had an ear cocked in the direction of the successful white orchestras, especially in the rocking two-beat of the middle-tempo 'Savoyager's Stomp'. The clarinettist and tenor saxophonist Jimmy Strong, much maligned for having failed to maintain the earthy, New Orleans tradition of Johnny Dodds in Louis's Hot Five recordings, shows himself here and in other solos to have anticipated Lester Young by several years in his admiration of Frankie Trumbauer.

This was the band which, without Earl Hines who stayed on in Chicago, travelled to New York with Louis Armstrong in mid-1929. There, according to Mezz Mezzrow in his book *Really the Blues*, they found the Harlem juke boxes pouring out the saccharine music of Guy Lombardo's Royal Canadians. Louis had fallen in love with this band when it played a season in Chicago the previous year. But even without this startling fact, it would have been surprising if a band which had already toyed with the cute, ear-catching rhythmic 'effects' of the successful white arrangers had turned a totally deaf ear to the success, *among black audiences*, of Lombardo.

The trouble is that, while the influence of Whiteman and Goldkette had been, at best, stimulating and, at worst, harmless, that of Lombardo was wholly deleterious. The hallmark of the Royal Canadians was a repetitive formula in which brass and reed sections took turns to churn out the melody. The band proudly featured a saxophone section, dominated by the oily vibrato of Guy's brother Carmen, whose phrases rose and fell dramatically, like the bosom of a silent movie heroine in distress. Someone, no doubt with Louis Armstrong's acquiescence, decided that this sort of backing was ideal for projecting Louis as a successful recording star. It didn't happen all at once, and in most of the bands assembled around him, there were some saving graces. In the Dickerson Orchestra, for instance, both Jimmy Strong and trombonist, Fred Robinson, prove themselves, when comparisons with Johnny Dodds and Kid Ory are put aside, to be capable and attractive soloists. On drums, more felt than heard in the imprecise recordings of the time, there was the great New Orleans drummer, Zutty Singleton, laying down a propulsive rhythm that would have given the Royal Canadians hysterics.

And there was Louis. As a trumpet player he was now at the height of his powers. Jazz was rich in trumpet men by the end of the Twenties. Bix Beiderbecke, Tommy Ladnier, Jabbo Smith, Henry Allen, Cootie Williams, Bobby Stark and Rex Stewart were all making important, individual and indispensable contributions at the time. But as a jazz virtuoso, Louis, with his combination of burnished copper tone, majestic range, unerring rhythmic sense and massive warmth of feeling, stood head and shoulders above them all. Gone were the occasional over-ambitious flights of fancy, the notes that tripped themselves up in the rush of ideas, and the slight tenseness that can be felt in some of the wilder exchanges with Earl Hines. There is a feeling of intense exhilaration in the playing, stemming from complete instrumental command.

The programme of recording popular songs, on which Louis embarked with the version of 'I Can't Give you Anything but Love', cast a revealing spotlight on an aspect of his playing which had always been present, though never before illuminated with such clarity. This was his instinct for re-phrasing a slender and repetitive melody so as to strengthen its line, broaden its emotional range and endow it with rhythmic characteristics of which it was entirely innocent when it rolled off the Tin Pan Alley assembly line. The first sessions that Louis undertook on his return to New York in the summer of 1929 included four numbers from the Fats Waller show *Hot Chocolates*. Two of them, 'Sweet Savannah Sue' and 'That Rhythm Man', were up-tempo romps of no great distinction. But Louis also recorded his feature in the show, 'Ain't Misbehavin' ', and a song which was sung on stage by Edith Wilson, 'Black and Blue'. Much retrospective abuse has been hurled at 'Black and Blue' for its lyric by Andy Razaf. Certainly, the line 'I'm white inside' is unlikely to commend itself to modern thinking. But in fairness it should be said that the song showed a certain unique courage in suggesting, through the Tin Pan Alley medium, that being black in the America of 1929 was not all a matter of strumming banjos down on the levee or beating ecstatic feet on the Mississippi mud. Louis Armstrong's statement of the melody on trumpet divests its minor-key melancholy of any hint of self-pity, redistributes the repetitive four-note phrases of the tune so that they lose their predictable symmetry and, in the second eight bars, replaces the actual notes of the tune with arpeggios that somehow contrive to suggest both the melody and the harmony. One has only to hear the saxes, in the final eight bars of this opening chorus, playing the tune 'as written' to see what a transformation Louis wrought. The same sort of enhancing treatment is given to 'Ain't Misbehavin' '. Fats Waller was a jazz musician as well as composer, and he knew as well as anyone how to interpret and expand upon the notes and chord symbols outlined in a song copy. For this reason, his tunes, however hurriedly they may have been dashed off, always had a solid structure on which the interpreter could build.

But as Louis's career as an itinerant soloist and prolific recording artist progressed, he was called on to tackle songs which often fell

far below Waller's unassuming standards. The effect he had on
them can only be described as magical. No great effort in the
direction of window-dressing arrangement or routining is apparent
in the recordings, which mostly follow the same casual and unambitious pattern. In this respect, early jazz writers who referred
to Louis Armstrong's solo performances as 'concerto style' implied
a relationship between Louis's trumpet and the accompanying
orchestra which did not exist. On a preponderant number of
records, all the orchestra is asked to do is supply either sustained
chords or else blurting explosions of sound on the first and third
beats of the bar which, in orchestral terms, do no more than apply
the principle of full employment to the 'stop chords' which a
rhythm section can provide on its own. And yet those writers
were not entirely wrong. For all the sloppiness of the arrangements and the inadequacy of most of the bands, Louis did somehow bestow a certain grandeur on the proceedings, piercing the
turgid tapestry of sound with dazzling threads of gold that pull it
all together into the semblance of opulent splendour. A musician
with a greater sense of his own artistic importance might sound
to us as if he were fighting against, or at least attempting to ignore,
the uninspiring accompaniment. Louis sounds inspired because
that is exactly what he was. Hard as it is for us to accept, he was
in his element luxuriating and stretching himself on that bed of
foam-filled Lombardo-esque saxophones.

The period is full of striking performances. In his recorded
'Musical Autobiography' made in 1956, Louis recalled having
heard a trumpeter called B. A. Rolfe, 'a man that inspired me to
play high notes. I never heard a man stand up and play what he
played on a trumpet in my life. He stood up and played a tune
called "Shadow Land" an octave higher! It inspired me so, I went
down to the studio the following week and made "When You're
Smilin'"'.' The first half of 'When You're Smilin'' is undiluted
Lombardo, right down to a middle-eight on quavering violin.
Louis may well have imagined that his vocal and high-note
trumpet solo were continuing in the same vein. Certainly, neither
offers the slightest evidence of tongue-in-cheek. If it was his wish
to flatter Messrs B. A. Rolfe and Guy Lombardo by imitation,
then it was happily thwarted by his inability to produce the cheaply

ingratiating commercial style. Freddy Fisher's fatuous tune, which has since found its true niche in popular music history as the 'get off' number for generations of stand-up comics, acquires on Louis Armstrong's entrance a massive dignity far above its station. It is one of countless examples of Louis salvaging a crumpled scrap of musical ephemera from history's waste-paper basket and re-instating it as something of value.

I have chosen as a masterpiece from this period a song written by Carmen Lombardo which the lovers of 'sweet' music will always associate with the Royal Canadians. Their first record of 'Sweethearts on Parade', made in 1928 (the year of publication), is surprisingly 'hot' in flavour, but subsequently the tune was given the standard Lombardo treatment in which the cloying melody was passed from section to section while those instruments not otherwise employed filled in with coy bugle-call effects. When Louis recorded the tune in December 1930, he was in California playing an engagement at the Sebastian New Cotton Club in Culver City. The backing orchestra had included, on earlier recordings, the fine trombonist, Lawrence Brown, who shared solo spots with Louis. By December he had gone, and the band, now led by a young saxophonist called Les Hite, boasted only one name familiar to jazz lovers, that of the teenage drummer, Lionel Hampton. Despite this, Louis sounded happy enough with the band for one of his biographers, John Chilton, to be able to cite the twelve consecutive recordings which Louis made in California as the best possible example of Louis's amazing consistency at this time. He himself would in later years react to anyone who raised an eyebrow at his enthusiasm for Guy Lombardo by pointing the doubter firmly in the direction of 'Sweethearts on Parade'.

To be sure, there is plenty of evidence of Lombardo-ish intent from the outset, what with the heaving bosom of the saxophone section and tinkerbell interjections from the upper end of the piano keyboard. But solid four beats in the bar from the banjo—and how often does one thank Providence for a banjo?—and some crisp accents from Lionel Hampton provide welcome rhythmic muscle that leaves Louis Armstrong's muted trumpet free to outline the melody in quite a free fashion. The arrangement is

curiously ambiguous in that four bars of trumpet over a sustained
tonic F chord lead straight into the theme without a break and,
since that starts on an F chord too, confuse the listener as to
when the tune actually begins. If the arranger assumed that Louis
would help by stating the tune note for note, he was led sadly
astray. What Louis does is to toy with the bugle-call motif of the
Lombardo version over the introductory chords, but in a rumina-
tory rather than militaristic way, carrying the idea through into
the first two bars of the tune. All in all, six bars go by without
Louis playing one note that falls outside the major chord harmonics
of a bugle. If one didn't know him to be a totally intuitive improviser, one might say that he was deliberately translating the
martial overtones of the song's title into music in a subtle and
witty fashion.

Instant composition of this kind abounds in the opening chorus.
The bugle-call idea is not entirely abandoned until the seventh
bar of the tune, when Louis, who has already established a feeling
of total relaxation by spacing measured, on-the-beat phrases
around long gaps of bare accompaniment, abandons the beat altogether and drapes thirteen notes lazily across two bars as if
stretching himself in preparation for more strenuous exertions
ahead. For the next eight bars he addresses himself more purposefully to the actual notes of the tune, though once again he wanders
off, in the second half of the section, into areas unimagined by
Carmen Lombardo, this time introducing blues inflexions with a
characteristic minor third in bar six and, in bar seven, the anticipation by a bar and a half of the F seventh chord leading into the
middle-eight.

Early in the middle-eight there is a typical Louis touch which
shows how independent his musical conception was of the things
going on around him. He hurries the first phrase ('I'd love to join
their fun' in the lyric) and delays the second ('but they bar me'),
giving himself time to insert a note in between, the sole purpose
of which is to suggest a harmony that he hears in his mind. The
note, an A flat, belongs to an F diminished chord which he clearly,
and rightly, thinks should link the B flat of the first two bars with
the F of the third, but which has occurred neither to the composers
nor to Les Hite's arranger. Louis was not a trained harmonist like

some of the improvisers who were to follow him, but his references to harmony, usually in the form of single guiding notes or rapid descending arpeggios, often suggested fresh harmonic routes that gave added subtlety to a tune.

About the vocal chorus, I would like to make one central point. Here is a perfect example of the unity of conception between Louis Armstrong's playing and singing. All along the way, extra syllables and phrases are added to the lyric, starting with the word 'Oh' that precedes the opening 'Two by two' and going on to the carelessly articulated 'baby' after the words 'they go marchin' through'. If one interprets these odd sounds verbally, they will probably seem irrelevant, sloppy, humorous or even grotesque. But they are not there to convey a literal meaning, but to complete and fill out musical phrases for which the lyric is inadequate. One extreme example occurs at the end of the second eight-bar section, on the reprise of the words 'Sweethearts on Parade'. In literary terms, Louis makes a dog's breakfast of the actual words, which emerge as 'Oooh, sweethearten . . . earts on parade'. But the musical phrase to which these dismembered syllables are put, delivered in that gruff, pained voice, convey a feeling of loneliness far beyond the sentimental intentions of the lyricist. Once again, we come back to the paradox underlying great jazz singing—that by torturing, smothering and mutilating the actual words in the service of purely musical ideas, the singer will put back into the song a greatly enhanced emotional meaning.

With the words out of the way, there is a rather flabby and fumbling call to arms on the alto saxophone, and then Louis sallies forth, with Lionel Hampton faithfully and attentively at his elbow, on a triumphal march that completely transforms the wistful mood of the song. After two identical declamatory phrases, Louis hammers out a rhythmic pattern on one note to which Hampton adds some quick-witted complementary accents in an exhilarating exchange which reminds one of the way Lionel Hampton has often attacked single notes with the mallets since he graduated to vibraphone. It soon transpires that with this heightening of the rhythmic tension, Louis is winding himself up for a leap into the stratosphere. One of the charges laid against Louis in this period is that he too often fell back on reworking material that had burst into life during the spontaneous improvisation of the Hot Five sessions. Leaving aside the possibility that they may have burst into life on the bandstand of the Sunset Café during a dance routine, the important question is whether the phrase sounds fresh and fits logically into its new context. Louis had used the two bars borrowed from Alphonse Picou's clarinet variation in 'High Society' on previous occasions, notably in the 1928 recording of 'Squeeze Me'. To my ears the 'Sweethearts on Parade' break is more fluent and successful, the familiar passage, condensed into one bar, being effortlessly carried on to form a perfectly balanced break.

What happens immediately after this break throws further light on the advanced rhythmic—and technical—ideas which can still be found lurking in seemingly casual Louis Armstrong performances. Most of the unorthodox effects—the long upward glissando, the rapid 'shake', the dying fall at the end of a note—which Louis introduced or perfected, were made by hand, e.g. by shaking the instrument, manipulating the valves and so on. But at the mouthpiece end, too, where the combination of lip, tongue and mouthpiece actually produces and pitches the note, he was busy breaking rules. No lover of his work on popular ballads in the Thirties will need to be reminded of the strange, flagging articulation which gave such expressiveness to the legato phrases. Where the normally tongued note is attacked with a crisp 'too too' sound, Louis contrived to soften the attack into something like 'phloo phloo'. What he did was to use the tongue, not to articulate the notes separately, but to give them a gentle push slightly ahead of the beat. This technique of using the tongue for rhythmic emphasis rather than straightforward attack was to prove indispensable to Dizzy Gillespie years later when he came to introduce more complex rhythmic patterns into the trumpet solo.

But we do not need to wait for Dizzy for an example. In the passage in 'Sweethearts on Parade' immediately following the 'High Society' break, Louis plays a phrase that sounds simple enough—indeed, for its first bar, it appears to sit rather squarely on the beat. But if we listen closely to the apparent crotchets or quarter notes on the first and third beats, and again on the first beat of the second bar, we find that they are articulated *twice*, albeit barely perceptibly. To establish the exact value and context of the notes, we have to remind ourselves that Louis Armstrong's phrases were built, not on the one-and-two-and-three-and-four rhythm of early jazz, but a one-and-a-two-and-a-three-and-a-four rhythm in which the four crotchets to the bar of conventional four-four time were broken up into four sets of quaver triplets— 'da da da, da da da, da da da, da da da'. If we take the 'double' notes to which I have drawn attention as representing the first two notes of a triplet, with the silent third note represented by a hyphen, we find that what Louis actually plays in this phrase would not be out of place in the complex, cross-rhythmic context of an African drum ensemble—'da da -, da - da, da da -, da - da, da da -' etc. Being Louis, with the solo responsibility of taking care of all the rhythmic variation himself, he finishes the four-bar phrase with broad notes that are seemingly stretched at random across the beat, but which in fact imply a three-four rhythm straddled over bars two and three. To the layman whose mind is reeling under this barrage of technicalities I would say—relax, in the assurance that the feeling of elation, buoyancy and swing which you receive from this and similar Louis passages have their origins in a brilliant rhythmic conception which is all the more remarkable in that it was never exploited or shown off for its own sake.

Having expended such enthusiasm on two or three bars which are by no means the most spectacular in the solo, I can only leave the listener to explore for himself the secrets of the remaining highspots—the searing break that ends the second eight-bar section, the opening of the middle-eight in which the upward trend of the song's melody is consummated with a high note that takes off and explodes like a rocket, scattering notes in all directions; the break coming out of the middle-eight which once again puts a familiar Armstrong phrase to new and spectacular use, and the return to the bugle-call motif at the end, which is saved from banality when Louis stifles almost to extinction the final note of the second phrase in order to give passionate weight to the final martial notes. Behind many of Louis Armstrong's finest performances, a great drummer will be found beavering away, often in acoustically unflattering circumstances. It is not overgenerous to add the teenage Lionel Hampton to a list that includes Baby Dodds, Zutty Singleton, Chick Webb and Sid Catlett. Here and on the other recordings made in Los Angeles during this period, Louis seems to respond to Hampton's crisply timed accents like a sprinter leaping from the starting-gun.

To me, and I hope to the reader, it seems grotesque that a performance such as 'Sweethearts on Parade' should ever be relegated, with expressions of faint praise tinged with reproach, to the mere middle reaches of Louis Armstrong's achievement. Had his entire output in the Twenties been, through some catastrophe, totally lost to posterity, the recordings which he made in the early Thirties would surely have established him immediately as a giant. Indeed, for many fans and musicians, it was just these recordings, and the public performances from which they were distilled, that initiated what can only be described as idolatry.

Nor did the magic end there. When I 'discovered' Louis as a schoolboy, the records which I and my friends bought belonged to a much-maligned series issued, in the middle and late Thirties, on the British Decca label. How we enthused over such gems as 'Struttin' with some Barbecue', 'I Double Dare You', 'Jubilee' and 'Swing that Music', bewildered by constant assertion by the pundits of the musical press that these represented a betrayal of Louis's previous standards! Louis Armstrong, the great survivor, had by this time put his career under the total protection of Mr Joe Glaser, a strong man before whose flinty gaze such pressing problems as intrusive gangsters, importunate managers, turbulent womenfolk and marauding rivals all faded away. It may have been the persistent challenge from fellow-trumpeters trying on every occasion to pit their talents against those of the champion that, together with the unwelcome attentions of the underworld which saw in him a hot and negotiable property, sent him fleeing to Europe in 1932 and again, for a longer spell, in 1933. There, for the best part of two years, he spent his resources, both onstage and off, with furious abandon, fronting a band in a variety act that outraged the regular theatre-goers and startled even the avowed jazz lovers with its display of unbridled power and ferocious energy. It was the last the world was to see of Louis the carefree and profligate spender of his talents. When he returned to America in January 1935, beset by unresolved lawsuits and a troublesome lip, it is as if Fate, in the incarnate form of Joe Glaser, put a restraining hand on his shoulder. From now on the trumpet playing, still majestic in its tone, range and technical command, would be less volatile, more considered. As his career broadened into films, comedy and increasingly commercial recording, the material and the quality of the backing would more and more often give the purist cause to wince. But the cooler approach, in which Louis seemed to be re-examining and refining his earlier discoveries, produced, in circumstances as widely different as a collaboration with the Mills Brothers and a reunion with his old colleague, Sidney Bechet, much commanding and moving stuff. Had I the luxury of a volume the width of a London omnibus, I could pick more than one masterpiece from this period for illuminating analysis. But new names and fresh innovators claim attention, and I must move on.

Fats Waller

IN THE STORY of twentieth-century popular music, Louis Armstrong and Thomas 'Fats' Waller share a unique position. Acknowledged and revered by fellow-musicians and *cognoscenti* as masters in the esoteric field of jazz, they found their way separately and by rather different routes into the affections of a wide public that knew nothing about jazz and regarded them as lovable and talented entertainers.

Of the two, Fats was the more unlikely contender for the role. True, he had an infectious and accessible piano style, an outgoing personality and a line in irreverent clowning which in his childhood 'slayed' his school friends and often turned aside adult wrath. But he showed none of Louis Armstrong's powerful urge for survival in the entertainment world. Appetites as gargantuan as his massive frame were indulged without thought of the consequences, which not infrequently involved engagements either missed altogether or in which the star attraction was found, at curtain-up, taking a recuperative nap under the piano. His assets as a radio performer, quickly recognized by a Cincinnati radio producer in 1932 and later followed up in New York, were offset by his penchant for provocative and risqué ad-libbing, one outrageous bout of which prompted a radio announcer to close a show with the words 'And now it's time to say goodbye to Fats Waller and his music . . . and if it wasn't time, it would be a good idea'. Indeed, the very factors which earned the recordings by Fats Waller and His Rhythm a cult following all over the world in the late Thirties—the mocking of sentimental lyrics, the stentorian off-the-cuff commentary, the atmosphere of inspired chaos—flew in the face of show-business protocol, by which artists were expected to sell the song first, themselves afterwards.

With the bracketing together of Louis and Fats in this context more interesting comparisons emerge. In the hagiography of jazz, Louis Armstrong is usually depicted as a Hamlet who resolutely pursued the path of clown. Fats Waller, on the other hand, is drawn in the more conventional image of the light entertainer inside whom a serious and frustrated artist was screaming to be let out. No doubt there has been some wishful thinking in this respect by jazz commentators raised in the European tradition of 'high culture' and disappointed with heroes who do not always behave as 'great artists' should. But allowing for this, there remains weighty evidence from those close to Fats to support the picture of a thoughtful and sensitive musician trapped within a restricting musical environment. His son Maurice Waller, in a book about his father (*Fats Waller* by Maurice Waller and Anthony Calabrese) recalls an interview Fats gave after his return from Europe in 1938.

'When a reporter asked him about the difference between American boogie and the music preferred in Europe, the hamming ceased. "For years I've been trying to sell the idea of softer stuff over here. I used to tell 'em down at Victor I ought to tone it down, but they'd just say, 'No, go ahead and give 'em that hot primitive stuff.' Dad wasn't just attacking boogie woogie this time. Fats Waller was going through something of a transition. He was becoming more introspective, considering his achievements and potential as a composer. He constantly talked about his admiration for George Gershwin's "Rhapsody in Blue" and "Concerto in F". He was introducing more and more classical themes into his music.'

Eugene Sedric, the tenor-player with Fats on most of the rumbustious recordings in the Thirties, gives a colleague's opinion. 'He wanted to do great things on the organ and piano, which he could do. There were many times when . . . he felt like himself and wanted to play great. But when he played as musically as he could, many people in the audience would think he was laying down and they'd yell, "Come on, Fats!" He'd take a swig of gin or something and say resignedly, "Aw right, here it is." Fats really was a great artist . . .'

It sounds a familiar story, not unlike the one which, for many years, was repeated about Bix Beiderbecke. Detailed biographies of Beiderbecke eventually established that what drove him to drink was not the frustration of a dedicated jazz musician forced to earn his bread in the commercial Whiteman orchestra, but the confusion of a musician with doubts as to the validity of his jazz work and an innate inability to fulfil higher ambitions. Similar thoughts arise about Fats Waller, demanding consideration if his standing as a jazz musician is to be accurately assessed. It will help if we briefly summarize his development from musically precocious child to world-renowned entertainer, a story well documented and authenticated in at least three full biographies.

One point of some significance which emerges from all these biographies is the prodigious ease with which Fats seems to have assimilated keyboard technique. At the age of six he was a regular visitor to an upstairs neighbour's apartment which, unlike the Wallers' own overpopulated place (Fats was one of the five survivors from a family of eleven) boasted an upright piano. His childish skill at picking out tunes induced his parents to acquire an instrument of their own, on which they fondly believed that either Tom or his sister, Naomi, would lay the foundations for a career as concert pianist. Edward and Adeline Waller were quite typical of the strict, strait-laced, church-loving families who were in the van of the black migration into Harlem. Edward Waller had built up a haulage business which kept the large family adequately fed and clothed, but it was the church which was central to their lives. As soon as he was able to wheeze out simple chords on the harmonium, little Thomas Waller was recruited into the street-corner meetings at which Edward preached and Adeline sang the hymns. It is not hard to imagine the family scenes and upheavals when Thomas's predilection for 'the devil's music'— that is to say, all music associated with secular entertainment— led him into the decidedly unholy realms of nightlife which were blossoming rapidly not more than a block or two from the Wallers' sedate area.

The first haunt to which Fats—he earned the nickname as a

schoolboy—was attracted was a movie house called the Lincoln Theatre. It was not the films that attracted him, but the accompanying piano music played by a Miss Mazie Mullins, who must rank with Duke Ellington's early teacher, Mrs Clinkscales, as one of the unsung—and unconscious—heroines of the jazz story. Day after day Tom Waller bought a ticket and took a seat as near as possible to the pit, where he could watch and listen. Then he would go home and try to reproduce what he had heard on the piano. Since it is alleged that he weighed over fourteen stone (two hundred pounds) by this time, it is hardly surprising that Miss Mullins began to notice the huge boy in short trousers watching every move of her fingers. She invited him into the pit to sit alongside her, and within days, so the story goes, she was allowing him to take over for short spells while she took a breather. The Lincoln Theatre boasted an expensive pipe organ too and, even more incredibly, Fats was soon taking his turn on this more complex instrument, to such good effect that he was given the job permanently.

The Lincoln Theatre was no backstreet flea-pit. As well as movies, it presented live shows at weekends, and the finest black musicians and vaudeville artists would appear there, drawing an audience that would often contain white composers such as George Gershwin and Irving Berlin as well as theatrical bookers and agents. In the light of this, Fats Waller's success story might seem hard to swallow. But the reader should be warned that short pants have played a prominent and often misleading role in jazz legend. Careful scrutiny of the relevant dates suggest that, if the eye-witness accounts are true, male juveniles in America were condemned to a longer spell in truncated leg-wear than their counterparts in modern times. For, short pants or not, Fats was fifteen years old when he gained professional access to the Lincoln Theatre organ. Even in the full biographies, the nine years or so between the Waller family's acquisition of a piano and Fats's professional début are condensed and vague. We know that after early abortive piano lessons, he studied piano and violin at school, and that the religious activity of his parents in the local community provided him with access to both piano and organ in the church. He learned to read music and this, combined with an

acute ear which enabled him to reproduce in rough and ready
fashion whatever music he heard, would have furnished him with
some kind of a repertoire. Although it would not have been jazz
in any currently accepted sense, his music was seemingly su-
fficiently tainted with inflaming syncopation for it to cause the
schism within the Waller family.

So it was no fumbling beginner who insinuated himself into the
professional ambience of the Lincoln Theatre. But there was one
area in which his basic musical education was incomplete. Fats
Waller's impressionable adolescence coincided with the rapid
growth of Harlem from a quiet and rather stuffy suburb into a
teeming urban community. The centre of black entertainment
shifted from the rough San Juan Hill area known as The Jungles,
where pianists such as James P. Johnson and Willie 'The Lion'
Smith had achieved renown, to almost within earshot of the
Waller home. From basements and store-fronts, piano music
wafted into the street continuously, and Fats took it in greedily.
He was too young to go into the clubs and cabarets, so actual
tuition in this field of piano playing was harder to acquire.

One of the lesser lights among the Harlem pianists was Russell
Brooks, whose younger brother, Wilson, had been one of Fats's
school cronies. In 1920, when Fats was sixteen, his mother died
suddenly, her heart failing under the cumulative strain of child-
bearing, obesity and diabetes. Despite the frequent hostilities
with his father regarding his devotion to the 'music from the
devil's workshop', Fats had enjoyed a warm and secure family
life. With Adeline's death, it came to an end. Not long afterwards,
still in a state of shock, Fats left home and it was to the Brooks
household that he gravitated. They took him in and it was agreed
with Edward Waller that it would be best for him to stay with
them.

A new phase in his career began. For one thing, the Brooks
family owned a player-piano, the forerunner of the phonograph
and record-player as a mechanical disseminator of music, and just
as important to the young musical explorer. When a paper roll
was inserted in the instrument and the automatic mechanism
brought into play, rectangular holes cut in the paper in appropriate places to correspond to musical notes would activate the

piano in such a way that the keys would be automatically depressed as if manipulated by ghostly hands. To Fats, the great boon of this apparatus was not only that it brought him close to the music of idols such as James P. Johnson, but that, by slowing down the machine at certain points and fitting his fingers into the depressed keys, he could learn the fingering of complex chords which his ear could not identify. (It would have been a few years earlier that Duke Ellington, back home in Washington, D.C., learned James P. Johnson's 'Carolina Shout' by exactly the same method).

The Brooks family's player-piano advanced Fats Waller's career in a far more important, if indirect, way. Russell Brooks, who lived away from home, came by to see his mother one day and came upon Fats teaching himself 'Carolina Shout' from the piano roll. He was so impressed by the boy's keenness that, the next time he saw James P. Johnson, he persuaded him to give Fats a hearing. James P. did not normally undertake piano tuition, but when Fats played for him, the combination of precocious talent and the big, suppliant brown eyes conquered him as swiftly as it had Mazie Mullins at the Lincoln Theatre.

The relationship between James P. Johnson and Fats Waller reminds one strongly of that between King Oliver and Louis Armstrong in New Orleans, as recalled by Louis. The Johnsons took Fats under their wing, Lillian Johnson making an important contribution to his career by sending him out to buy his first pair of long pants. James P. Johnson initiated Fats into the art and technique of compulsive swinging which lies at the heart of Harlem stride piano. The pupil made such rapid progress that Johnson soon began to take him around the nightspots as his protégé, encouraging him to get up and play.

Time came when Fats had to be introduced to James P. Johnson's friend and principal rival, Willie the Lion Smith. The meeting was at a club called Leroy's, the most prestigious venue for the Harlem pianists. Willie the Lion recalled in his autobiography *Music On My Mind*, 'Leroy Wilkins was . . . a stickler for high-toned manners and good conduct. He was the first cabaret man to insist on the proper clothes for the floor managers, the waiters, and the musicians. On weekends *everybody* had to wear tuxedos, including the customers.' Into these showbiz surroundings walked Fats in the wake of James P. As was customary, his long trousers were unpressed and spotted with grease and, according to Willie the Lion's memory, he was sucking a toffee apple. When the Lion caught sight of them, it was Johnson who got the mauling. 'Who the hell's the punk kid with you?' roared the Lion. 'Fats Waller—' 'Fats Waller? He looks more like Filthy Waller!' It is a measure of the respect which Fats earned that night through his piano playing that the nickname stuck. The Lion bestowed permanent nicknames only upon his closest friends—some time earlier, James P. Johnson had been dubbed 'The Brute', allegedly because of the big, hairy overcoat that he used to wear. It was only a matter of months before the Lion, the Brute and Filthy were roaming the Harlem piano haunts together, a triumvirate of invincible keyboard masters.

We can get an idea of Fats Waller's style at this period through his first solo recordings, made for the Okeh company in 1922. 'Muscle Shoals Blues' is not a very reliable guide since it was a publisher's tune that Fats was hired to play, with an eye to the newly discovered market for the blues in the black community. The stiffness of the performance suggests that Fats was paying diligent attention to the sheet-music. The biographies by Fats's manager of later years, Ed Kirkeby, and by his son, Maurice Waller, both tell, in first-hand, fly-on-the-wall style how Fats, called on to provide something for the B side of the record, immediately improvised a piece which he called, on the spur of the moment, 'Birmingham Blues'. It is an improbable story. The very completeness of the tune, furnished with a verse and recollected in every detail for three choruses, suggests that it was a piece that Fats had already composed with some thoroughness and that perhaps only the title was an off-the-cuff invention.

Comparison of 'Birmingham Blues' with James P. Johnson's 'Carolina Shout', recorded the previous year, shows the two pianists very strongly in a master-and-pupil relationship. Johnson was totally in command of all his effects and variations, which included a bass line which was rich in invention and right-hand figurations which flowed smoothly and with assurance. Fats Waller was already taking advantage of the ten-note reach afforded by his huge hands, but the excessive use of broken tenths in the left hand, with much too heavy an emphasis on the upper 'thumb' note, produces a cumbersome rhythm. In the second and third choruses there are examples of the frisking about at the treble end of the piano which was to become one of the most exhilarating ingredients of his later style. But here again, the fingering is not properly mastered and there is some uncertainty as to how to match the treble figures with the movement of the bass. Despite these youthful deficiencies, it is clear to the listener that, in Willie the Lion's words, 'The kid's got it.'

The story behind Fats's first recording opportunity is characteristic of him and throws some light on his attitude to music. He had been befriended by Clarence Williams, the pianist from New Orleans who had established himself in New York as composer, publisher, leader of studio bands and all-round entrepreneur. Anxious to help the promising young musician, Williams persuaded the Okeh recording company to use him as accompanist to the blues singer, Sara Martin. When he called Fats to tell him of the date, the reply he got was something less than grateful. 'I don't need the money, and I don't want to accompany anybody.' Williams gave him a lecture on his responsibilities as a professional musician and Fats finally agreed. However, it was to no avail—the session came and went without Fats putting in an appearance, and Clarence Williams deputized for him, launching himself on a lucrative studio career in the process.

In effect, though Fats Waller and James P. Johnson remained firm friends and associates, it was Clarence Williams who acted as the chief catalyst in the next phase of Fats's career. He was impressed by the ease with which Waller seemed able to trot out catchy melodies, and urged him to bring some in for publication. In the first batch was the 'Wildcat Blues', Sidney Bechet's performance of which, with a band led by Clarence Williams, was the subject of a chapter in *The Best of Jazz* Volume One. This was followed by 'Squeeze Me', a tune which Fats is alleged to have developed from a rude ditty called 'Boy in the Boat' that was much in demand at rent-parties when the merry-making had ripened. It has always seemed a somewhat irrelevant piece of historical information, since no one has been able to glean any clear indication of how the original tune went, other than that it was in limerick form—which 'Squeeze Me' is not, except possibly in the first two lines of the verse. It is marginally more interesting to note that the harmonic basis of Fats's piece—a rotating sequence of three chords relieved by modulation at the half-way and concluding marks—occurs in the second strain of a James P. Johnson composition called 'Fascination'.

However it came into being, 'Squeeze Me' was a hit for the Clarence Williams publishing firm and established Fats in the song-writing business. In those days, this was a casual, none-too-scrupulous activity that suited Fats well. He had married his first wife, Edith, on the rebound from the shock of his mother's death, and his first son, Thomas Jnr., had followed soon afterwards. There were mouths to feed, rent instalments to pay and, when a manifestly incompatible partnership inevitably dissolved, alimony payments to be found. Publishers would pay from twenty-five to fifty dollars for a song, often buying tunes which had already been sold to a rival down the street. Copyright went to the first firm to print the song, so it was a fair gamble. As for the composer, all that was left for him, after pocketing the cash, was the satisfaction of seeing his name on the song-copy or, not infrequently, the frustration of seeing someone else's name on it!

In their book, Maurice Waller and Anthony Calabrese list thirty-eight known Waller compositions, published and unpublished, in the year 1924 alone. Many of these were written in partnership with Andy Razaf, a young poet and lyricist with whom Fats struck up a partnership after a casual meeting, and who was later to acquire fame largely on the basis of his work with Fats. I say 'later' because the fact is that, despite quite prolific songwriting activity, with or without Razaf, few if any of the pieces written in the five years between 1924 and 1929 mean anything today in popular music terms, and only a handful survive in the affections of jazz enthusiasts. Collectors' pieces such as 'I'm Goin' Huntin'' and 'Georgia Bo Bo' recorded by Louis Armstrong and 'The Stampede', 'Whiteman Stomp' and goodness knows what others played by Fletcher Henderson's Orchestra (Fats is said to have sold one job lot of nine tunes, including 'The Stampede', to Henderson for the price of twelve hamburgers) attest not only to the facility with which Fats turned out original melodies but also to Clarence Williams's readiness to put them about and get them recorded.

It was not until the late Twenties that Fats Waller the composer was swept into the big time on the crest of a wave. In the years since Fats had made his precocious début at the Lincoln Theatre, Harlem had blossomed as an entertainment centre. Jazz history, justifiably absorbed in extracting and isolating the jazz essence from the rest of the great musical cocktail in which it spent its early years, gives us a lop-sided view, suggesting that, while first New Orleans and then Chicago nurtured the very finest musicians, New York was a late developer in assimilating the new music. But if we take black music and dance as an entity of which jazz was a part, then there is no denying that Harlem from the early Twenties onwards was burgeoning with talent.

Behind the handful of names that Tin Pan Alley, Broadway and Hollywood have helped to immortalize—Florence Mills, Bill 'Bojangles' Robinson, Bert Williams, Ethel Waters—there existed a regular army of hoofers, singers, comedians and musicians, all contributing to a rich entertainment scene which was one of the attractions which brought hordes of white New Yorkers with money to spend into night-time Harlem. Another reason, related to the first, was the growing fascination with Negro culture among New York intellectuals, with the 'liberal' journalist and author, Carl Van Vechten, as the movement's chief propagandist. Paternalistic and selective as it was (Harlemites with neither talent nor beauty derived little warmth from it), it did contribute a lot to creating the Harlem which, to a wide-eyed Duke Ellington on his arrival in 1923, looked 'like the Arabian Nights'.

The third attraction was very much more down to earth. Joel Vance sums it up succinctly in his biography, *Fats Waller—His Life and Times*. 'With the hedonistic defiance of Prohibition among whites, there came a taste for the exotic, the taboo, and the generally frowned upon.' He might have added 'the dangerous', too, for the elegant and lucrative tourist traps, ready outlets for the illicit liquor trade, soon came under the control of 'downtown' gangsters. The former proprietors who yielded gracefully to the take-over were often left in charge as front-men and managers. One who did not was Barron D. Wilkins, brother of the owner of

Leroy's and himself a frequent employer of the Harlem stride men in his ritzier establishment, Barron's. In 1926, he was knifed to death by a professional hit-man called Yellow Charleston.

Jazz, as represented by the Harlem pianists, was at the very centre of all this activity. As Willie the Lion Smith wrote about the clubs in which he and James P. and Fats played, 'The pianist had duties and responsibilities. He played solo piano, accompanied the singers, directed whatever band was on hand, and watched the kitty to be sure no one cheated on tips ... The piano was *it*! The man in charge ... he had to be an all-round showman and it helped if he could both dance and sing. It was like being the host at a party, you were expected to greet everyone who entered to establish favourable feelings.' As the shows became larger and more lavish, the pianist was also expected to write the songs. *Shuffle Along*, the first all-Negro show to make a surprise impact on Broadway in 1920, had songs written by Eubie Blake. Three years later, James P. Johnson gave the decade its theme tune— 'Charleston'—among the songs he wrote for the review *Runnin' Wild*. A rival show *Go-Go* in the same year had music by Luckey Roberts.

In the mid-Twenties Fats Waller, busy in an unspectacular and diffuse way with resident theatre work, vaudeville touring, a sojourn in Chicago and sporadic radio shows, made tentative inroads into this field with two shows written for the Lafayette Theatre. Neither *Tan Town Topics* nor *Junior Blackbirds* rates more than a footnote in the showbiz history of the times, though the first provided Fats and his collaborator, Spencer Williams, with a nationwide hit in the now forgotten 'Senorita Mine'. Equally obscured beneath the dusts of time is a song called 'Willow Tree' with which Fats and Andy Razaf scored a success in *Keep Shufflin'*, a Broadway review to which James P. Johnson also contributed, and in which they made a personal appearance, playing the entr'acte music on two pianos.

But Fats's real chance came through two old associates, Connie and George Immerman, for whose delicatessen store he had worked some years before as an errand boy. The Immermans had entered the show-business world when they opened a club called Connie's Inn in premises next to the Lafayette Theatre. In 1928, they decided to cash in on the vogue for all-Negro reviews with a show called *Load of Coal*, for which Fats and Andy Razaf wrote some songs. 'Zonky' and 'My Fate is in your Hands' were successful featured songs, but a third 'Honeysuckle Rose', was relegated to the backing for a soft-shoe dance by the chorus, and had to wait some fifteen years before it became one of Fats's most popular compositions and a favourite work-out for jamming musicians the world over.

Load of Coal was followed at Connie's Inn by *Hot Chocolates*, for which Waller and Razaf wrote even more numbers—twenty in all. The chronology of *Hot Chocolates* is somewhat confused in the Waller biographies which give the impression that Louis Armstrong's band (the Carroll Dickerson team from Chicago), newly arrived in New York, were booked from the outset. The facts seem to be that the review opened as a Connie's Inn floor-show in the early summer of 1929, without Louis Armstrong or his band. On 20 June, with a strengthened cast and some new tunes added, it opened at the Hudson Theatre on Broadway. A review in the *New York Telegram* began: 'With most of its gold teeth and no little of its tediousness removed, Connie's new tanskin revel is a far better show than it was a couple of weeks ago in the Bronx Windsor Theatre. Nowadays, at the Hudson, *Hot Chocolates* is faster, funnier and a good deal franker.' This indicates that the arrival on Broadway was by a rather more devious route than the potted histories suggest. Another source of confusion is the fact that the show never actually left Connie's Inn for Broadway. As soon as the curtain came down at the Hudson, the cast would hotfoot it back to Harlem to perform a curtailed version at the club. It was here that Louis Armstrong's band, booked for a four-month season from 24 June, would have first made a supporting appearance in the show. Within days, Louis himself was picked out of this floorshow version and added to the theatre cast. A review of the show prior to his joining noted: 'There is a song called "Ain't Misbehavin'"' on which much reliance is placed. Almost everybody in the show sings it at one time or another, and as there are a good many in the show, the song gets sung pretty often.' With Louis Armstrong's arrival, yet another performance of it was added—this time the definitive one.

If the above appears to indulge in some nit-picking about the exact sequence of events surrounding *Hot Chocolates*, there is a purpose to it. In the prevailing fashion for 'tanskin revels', *Hot Chocolates* would probably have enjoyed ephemeral success without Louis Armstrong. But, as I have noted in the chapter on Louis, he was at this time poised for take-off into a new phase in his career. Ever since the Dreamland Ballroom in Chicago had billed him as 'The World's Greatest Trumpet Player', Louis had enjoyed a reputation as a virtuoso performer which spread, through his series of spectacular recordings on the Okeh 'race' label, to black audiences across America and to musicians and record collectors across the globe wherever jazz itself had taken root. With the maturing of his talent for singing into a style which could encompass popular songs, and the application of his phenomenal trumpet technique and range to a new repertoire of gallery-fetching effects, he was ready to reach a wider audience that was less concerned with the musical refinements than with the overall entertainment value. It has become a platitude to say that a great many of Tin Pan Alley's more run-of-the-mill products from 1929 onwards had a long life and a distinction above their true station in life bestowed upon them by Armstrong performances.

In July 1929, Louis recorded four of the tunes from *Hot Chocolates*—'Ain't Misbehavin' ', 'Black and Blue' (sung in the show by Edith Wilson), 'Sweet Savannah Sue' and 'That Rhythm Man'. The two latter, plus some other rhythm numbers from the show, were recorded around the same time by Duke Ellington. (Apart from 'Ain't Misbehavin' ', which became a standard fixture in his repertoire, and a piano solo version of 'Sweet Savannah Sue', Fats did nothing in his own recording sessions to plug the tunes from the show, a fact which is less surprising when we learn that, with characteristic irresponsibility, he had sold them all in one job lot to the publisher and band-agent Irving Mills for the derisory sum of five hundred dollars.) But it was the Armstrong recordings which were significant. As popular songs divorced from the context of the *Hot Chocolates* revue, 'Sweet Savannah Sue' and 'That Rhythm Man' had no great distinction, the former in particular harking back stylistically to the 'Peg o' my Heart' type ballads of at least fifteen years earlier. Nevertheless, the power and personality of Armstrong's versions are such that, almost certainly, some band somewhere in the world is still trotting them out nightly in response to popular request. But it was 'Ain't Misbehavin'' and 'Black and Blue', the two songs added to *Hot Chocolates* to strengthen its Broadway production, which were projected by Louis Armstrong into their rightful place among the evergreen standards of popular music, hoisting their composer up with them.

So, by 1929, Fats Waller's career had blossomed along what, for Harlem 'stride' men, had become conventional lines. He had recorded piano solos of his own compositions (and, in the early days, some piano rolls, too). He had done his stint as accompanist for blues singers and had popped up on sundry band recordings. He had become a local celebrity on the rent-party circuit, had toured in vaudeville and had made a successful breakthrough into the wider area of show-business represented by Broadway reviews. He had also broken new ground of his own with his recorded work on pipe organ, presumably reflecting the kind of music which he played during his long residencies at the Lincoln and Lafayette Theatres. The jazz fraternity has not, on the whole, shown much enthusiasm for these, and it is doubtful if posterity will revise the verdict that, attractive and impressive as they are beside other Wurlitzer performances of the period, they fall down as jazz simply because of the instrument's tonal and mechanical shortcomings.

Mike Lipskin, an authority on Harlem 'stride' piano and a one-time pupil and protégé of Willie the Lion Smith, has written about Fats: 'His being a star was a kind of accident. Nobody had any idea that he was going to be that big, least of all him. He never looked for it; it just happened to him. If it hadn't happened to him, he could still have earned a very good living as a sideman on record dates, even without the songs he wrote. He could read, he was a good arranger, he could make guys want to play on a session —make them happy while they were doing it—and they had to record a lot of junk material . . . Nobody could have heard of the famous Fats Waller, and he would still have been one of the busiest musicians in the country . . .'

Let us stay in the realms of supposition and imagine that Fats's career ended abruptly in 1929. What would our judgement be today on his contribution to jazz? That he had already made his mark on jazz history is clear. Tunes like 'Squeeze Me', 'Honeysuckle Rose', 'Ain't Misbehavin'' and 'Black and Blue' were destined, through the recordings by Louis Armstrong alone, to survive as 'standards'. Solo piano recordings such as 'Valentine Stomp', 'Numb Fumblin'', 'Handful of Keys', 'Smashing Thirds' and 'African Ripples' would have been enough to single him out as a stride pianist of enormous power and potential. He was already a more modern player than both Willie the Lion Smith and James P. Johnson, whose work always bore rhythmic traces of their ragtime origins. With Fats, the forward momentum of stride was streamlined and interior sprung, assisted by a keyboard technique that outstripped that of his mentors. For instance, he exploited his enormous hands to devise a bass pattern involving left-hand intervals of tenths moving smoothly upwards and downwards in parallel, a rich harmonic ploy which was later developed by Art Tatum. The piano compositions (the personal rags which were an obligatory part of the stride man's armoury) had a new look about them, too. By 1929, when Fats recorded his most important batch of solos, ragtime was a thing of the past, and the pattern of sixteen-bar march-like themes on which most of James P. Johnson's compositions were based, had begun to sound old-fashioned. The new popular music was based predominantly on themes of thirty-two-bars' length, arranged either as variants of the time-honoured ABAC format, as in Jimmy McHugh's 'I Can't Give you Anything but Love' (1928) or in the AABA form popularized by George Gershwin and exemplified in his 'Oh, Lady Be Good' (1924). These are the twin formulae which came most naturally to Fats and formed the basis of his most successful pre-1930 solos.

Let us take an example. 'Handful of Keys' was first recorded in 1929 and, strictly speaking, falls outside the brief of this volume. But in this instance, time is irrelevant. Had Fats conceived the piece in 1939, it would have sounded no different, so characteristic is it of his style at any period. A mood of boisterousness is established at the outset with the frisky, kitten-on-the-keys-type introduction, and then we are off at full steam ahead. The opening theme conforms to a familiar Waller pattern, a two-bar figure repeated, with minor harmonic variation, to cover an eight-bar section. The format of this opening theme is AABA, so that after the eight-bar section is repeated, it gives way to a 'middle-eight' before returning. What gives the piece such a rollicking start is the rhythmic interplay between right and left hand. Even when overt clowning was kept in check, humour was never far below the surface in a Fats Waller performance. Here it is exemplified in the way the upward octave run in the right hand skips away from the heavy first bass beat of the bar as if challenging it to desert its solid regular metre and take off in pursuit. The left hand resolutely spurns all such temptation, its firmness accentuated by the 'broken tenth' which Fats uses in place of a single bass note on the first and third beats of the bar. In simple terms, this means that the little finger strikes a keynote in the bass, the thumb the third note of the octave above. This tenth is 'broken' by the thumb note being struck fractionally after the lower note, and with rather more force, so that what gives the listener his sense of the direction in which the bass harmonies are moving is not the root notes of the chords but notes in effect a third above—the E in the case of a C chord. It is an effective device, heavily exploited in ensuing years by Earl Hines, and varied with great subtlety by Art Tatum and Teddy Wilson.

The middle-eight B section of this first theme is based, as countless middle-eights have been since, on the corresponding section of George Gershwin's song, 'I Got Rhythm', and this emphasizes the popular song origins of Fats's thematic material. Unlike the bars that surround it, this middle-eight has no mandatory 'tune'. In subsequent performances of the piece, Fats played it differently. (Indeed, there is one 1939 Musak recording, a rare example of Fats sounding patently too drunk to play, in which he substitutes the middle-eight chords from his own 'Honeysuckle Rose' in fuddled error). The vagueness of this middle section enables him to introduce into his party piece some straightforward jazz improvisation, an element which, so far as one can tell from recordings, was new to such stride performances. In the first chorus, he pounds out a simple melodic line of the kind which Andy Razaf would have had no difficulty in equipping with words, had he been called on to do so. Fats comes out of this section with a favourite device, a series of phrases covering two beats with a little triplet 'turn' on the first beat. In the second chorus, in which Fats follows his customary pattern of repeating the first main theme in the piano's upper register, this curlicue triplet motif rebounds from Fats's subconscious to become a skittish variation covering the whole middle-eight bars.

After the two opening choruses there is a four-bar interlude leading into a new theme in a new key. This is a straightforward thirty-two-bar harmonic theme, a first cousin once-removed of the harmonic basis of the trio in 'Tiger Rag' or, going back still further into popular music, of Hughie Cannon's hit of 1902, 'Won't You Come Home, Bill Bailey'. Once again, there is no dominant melody to this section. As in much of James P. Johnson's work, we have a basic harmonic framework on which complex rhythmic patterns are superimposed. This brief secondary theme is stride piano *par excellence*. In its first eight bars there is exhilarating interplay between pumping, on-the-beat notes in the bass and ahead-of-the-best phrases in the right hand. For the next eight bars the harmonic sequence is followed with the outline of a melody expressed in percussive chords again struck ahead of the beat and culminating in a typical Wallerism, a descending scale in the bass in which the right hand is brought in to double the notes, so that the pianist is literally drumming on the keys. The second half of the chorus shows how Fats's method differed from that of James P. Johnson, whose carefully worked out scheme of things would have demanded a reprise of the rhythmic pattern of the first eight bars. But Fats in full flight seldom concerned himself with such niceties of construction. Stomping chords devolve into another device which Fats inherited from Johnson and developed along his own lines. Basically, it is a pattern in which changing thirds played by the inner fingers of the right hand are rocked between appropriate notes played by little finger and thumb. No need to search around for an onomatopaeic aid to describe the effect. Fats provides one himself in the ribald verbal coda to his recording of 'Dinah' which starts 'Oh, ji-bee-ji-bye-ji-bee-ji-bee-ji-bo'. If one takes the long syllables to be thirds with appropriate harmonic variation and the 'ji' syllables to be notes above and below them played alternatively with little finger and thumb, we get a rough idea of a device with which Fats would often link his phrases or, on occasion, build a whole chorus.

The rest of the thirty-two-bar section in 'Handful of Keys' is made up of the sort of declamatory phrases which a trumpet player or a blues singer would use in similar harmonic circumstances. This is Fats expressing himself in orchestral rather than pianistic terms, and shows how simple he must have found it to churn out easily adaptable themes for Fletcher Henderson's use. In general, this thirty-two-bar section provides a strong contrast to the busy scampering of the opening theme. Having served this purpose, it is not developed. A brisk modulation takes us back to the opening theme, the rising scales of which Fats spreads in the first eight bars over three octaves. The fact that he doesn't repeat this happy notion in the second eight bars, as James P. Johnson would undoubtedly have done, stresses again the different approach of the two men. Fats is impatient with structural symmetry, eager all the time to push the performance on to a higher momentum. After a powerfully rhythmic middle-eight, he doesn't return to the theme but replaces its decorative line with a variation which is purely rhythmic. We can see why. Stride pianists liked to refer to their most spectacular keyboard inventions as 'fingerbusters', and Fats was on the run-up to his. He doesn't re-state the theme but literally submerges it in variation in which the left hand suddenly abandons its 'oom-chah' role to join in the fun.

The final 'fingerbuster' represents the kind of technical gymnastic display which the Harlem ticklers used to hold in reserve for the moment when an importunate rival needed to be put to rout. Following the harmonies meticulously, he spatters the keyboard with staccato phrases like a machine-gunner raking the field with fire. Fats used basically the same device in a contemporary solo which he called 'Smashing Thirds', and the words describe it perfectly. A less thoughtful player than Fats—or indeed Fats himself in his more abandoned moments—might have barged on through the middle-eight with sustained impetuosity. But with a brilliant stroke, he interrupts the forward movement with two breaks involving reflective broken chords that contrive to increase, rather than relieve, the tension. There is only one way to end the piece, and that is in the grand, ride-out style of Louis Armstrong, right hand punching out trumpet phrases across the beat. The coda, a descending bass figure combining the 'drumming' technique described earlier with James P. Johnson's 'interrupted bass', is an instrumental foreshadowing of those manic verbal overflows with which Fats's later commercial recordings would often career to a halt.

Earlier, I summed up Fats Waller, the pianist, at this stage in his development as a stride man of enormous power and potential. Before we go on to see the extent to which that potential was resolved, it is necessary to examine more closely my assertion that Fats Waller was a more 'modern' player than either James P. Johnson or Willie the Lion Smith. First, we must clear our minds of any suggestion that to be 'more modern' implies superiority. On more than one occasion in *The Best of Jazz* Volume One, I made the point, apropos of jazz rhythm, that new discoveries do not (or should not) devalue or render permanently obsolete all that went before. The piano pieces which James P. Johnson and, to a lesser extent, Willie the Lion recorded stand today as gems of keyboard composition. Indeed, Johnson is still shamefully underrated in this respect. But times were changing. Radio began to rival the piano as the chief agency of home entertainment. Through the Thirties, those families who still gathered round the piano of an evening would prop up on the music rack, not keyboard pieces specially written for the piano, but the published sheet music of the popular songs which were plugged on the radio and on gramophone records. By 1929, when Fats recorded the great majority of his solo pieces, the rich vein of keyboard composition that had started with the first published ragtime piece thirty-two years earlier had been worked out. The thrilling improvisational flights of Louis Armstrong and those exponents of every instrument who came under his influence engendered in musicians and audiences alike an impatience with the orderly and restrained dispensation of theme and variation which characterized the music of the ragtime players and their immediate descendants—and, to some extent, the band music of Jelly Roll Morton and King Oliver. It is no coincidence that the young pianists such as Fats Waller and Duke Ellington chose to cut their musical teeth on James P. Johnson's 'Carolina Shout', the most forward looking of his compositions with its thrusting rhythmic momentum and capacity for improvised extension.

This circumstance must surely be taken into account and added to all the varied explanations which have been put forward to explain Fats Waller's personal and artistic shortcomings. The dichotomy between his training in the sternly disciplined school of Harlem stride and the new romanticism that was sweeping through jazz must have mirrored the tension in his childhood, between his strictly religious family background and the creative opportunities offered by Harlem's uninhibited and 'sinful' night-life. Had his career ended in 1929, none of the theorizing nor the myth-making that now accumulates around his memory would have come about. Knowledge of his drinking habits and convivial nature, already fully developed, would have been confined to his close accociates, and nothing in his recorded output up to that time would have prompted anyone to investigate or analyse them. We would know him today as the composer of two of Louis Armstrong's greatest hits who popped up with some exhilarating solos of records by Fletcher Henderson and the little-known Tom Morris Hot Babies, and whose solo piano recordings constituted a fine and final flourish to the parlour piano era.

But it didn't end there. Surviving—nay, rampaging—into the Thirties, with the vogue for all-black Harlem revues on the wane, Fats needed to discover a new role for himself, a task to which he applied himself with characteristic insouciance, carousing his way from one impromptu recording session to another and, at one stage, prising himself away from his beloved Harlem long enough to make what, for jazzmen of that period, seems to have been an obligatory pilgrimage to Paris. Then fate took a hand. His success as a broadcaster, a role in which he played, sang and gave rein to ribald and often risqué off-the-cuff humour, suggested to his manager that the time was ripe for him to be equipped with a band for stage, ballroom and recording work. When it finally took shape, the band known as Fats Waller and his Rhythm proved ideally suited to Fats's impromptu style of presentation. In reed-men Gene Sedric or Rudy Powell, guitarist Al Casey, and trumpeter Herman Autrey, he had three regular soloists of distinctive style, the latter capable of explosive, if often erratic, ride-out trumpet in the Armstrong manner in response to Fats's verbal encouragement. Fortunately for our peace of mind, none of these sidemen were outstanding enough to arouse in us resentment at the constant stentorian interruptions from the piano stool that often obliterated their work.

Verbal participation played quite a prominent part in the presentation of stride piano. Both Willie the Lion and Eubie Blake have been known to punctuate both recorded and stage performances with running commentary, and in the atmosphere of a rent-party cutting contest, badinage between rivals and crosstalk from player to audience and back no doubt added to the excitement. One theory is that when he started broadcasting, Fats compensated for the absence of a visible audience by indulging in backchat with the station's master of ceremonies as he played. Whatever its origins, Fats Waller's capacity for maintaining a stream of chatter throughout the proceedings became an instant feature of his band recordings. The interruptions, which range from exhortations to the musicians to lengthy dialogue with some imaginary female presence, are not just laboured attempts to whip up 'atmosphere'. Some of them seem to be taking place within a private hallucinatory world in which voices are answered, insults are returned, manic laughter is induced and strange surrealist notions are pursued. Sometimes this stream of consciousness is inspired by the title or the content of the song, sometimes by the playing, or even the name of a musician taking part. When he recorded with a British group in 1938, a tenor solo by one Ian Shepherd initiated a line of thought. 'Yeah! What? Shepherd of the flock? Blow, my lamb, blow! He's up in the mountain!'

It was the success of the recordings by Fats and his Rhythm, sparked off in 1935 by a best-selling version of a previously unsuccessful new ditty called 'I'm Gonna Sit Right Down and Write Myself a Letter', which led to the orgy of critical heartsearching that has centred upon Fats Waller's role in jazz history. Could a man whose major contribution to the art form between 1934 and his death in 1943 consisted of churning out unrehearsed versions of generally trashy popular songs, mocking the lyrics and burying the tune in ribald commentary, really be counted among the giants?

Before we venture any sort of answer, we must counter some of the myths that have been erected to explain away the phenomenon. Most dubious of these is the theory that commercial pressure forced Fats to play the clown against his own inclinations. Other musicians, notably Louis Armstrong, Billie Holiday and Teddy Wilson, operated under the same kind of recording contract, playing inferior songs forced upon them by the studio managers and aimed at the same market. There is no evidence that they were expected to lay on the comedy—and plenty of evidence that Fats's managers were, indeed, begged from time to time to restrain their artiste's audible conviviality. Nor does the theory that the newly acquired mass audience created a demand for frivolity cut much ice. Fats's most successful hits were such songs as 'I'm Gonna Sit Right Down and Write Myself a Letter', 'When Somebody Thinks You're Wonderful', 'My Very Good Friend the Milkman' and 'Until the Real Thing Comes Along' in which the music has a danceable lilt and there is a minimum of horse-play. Further to this, there is nothing of the ingratiating, Uncle Tom crowd-pleasing in Fats Waller's humour. In his few film appearances he made a firm stand against having to utter the stock, 'Yassuh, boss' lines of the stage Negro, and the familiar Wallerisms—'One never knows, do one', 'I wonder what the poor people are doin' tonight' and the valedictory 'Well, a-a-a-ll right, then' came from his own personal vernacular and often had a derisive cutting edge.

A variation on the above theme suggests that the fearful grievous bodily harm that Fats inflicted on the lyrics of much of his material expressed his anger and disgust at the trash that he was called on to perform. Certainly, he had lethal ways of dealing with sentimentality—in 'It's a Sin to Tell a Lie' the line 'If you break my heart I'll die' becomes 'If you break my heart I'll break your leg and then I'll die'—and other sugary or melodramatic sentiments are delivered in a childish falsetto or a quivering operatic bass. Any notion that this often extremely funny lampooning of the songs was a one-man demo against the fatuities of Tin Pan Alley will not long survive the fact that, while some truly dreadful lyrics escape unscathed, Fats's own songs, with the relatively sharp and clever lyrics by Andy Razaf, came in for the treatment. In an early version of his 'Crazy 'bout my Baby', the repetition of the word 'baby' strikes him as funny—or, perhaps, embarrassing—so he milks it for laughs by singing 'Crazy 'bout my . . . *bebby, bebby's* crazy 'bout me'. In another version, the title line acquires, at the end, a spurious dignity by being translated into 'I'm exasperated about the offspring, the offspring's exasperated about me'!

Dick Wellstood, one of the post-war generation of stride men and an objective admirer of Fats, wrote in the magazine *Jazz Review* in 1960, 'It's so hard to tell what Fats could do because he was always trying to entertain, and so made his playing entertaining at the damndest times . . . the trouble with a lot of the guys of that age is that they really in a sense are ashamed of jazz.' If we take 'to entertain' in this context as meaning 'to make people laugh', then the judgement is in keeping with the early picture we have of young Fats rolling his eyes and wiggling his eyebrows for the amusement of his schoolfriends. This, and the available aural evidence, contradicts another of the Waller myths—that he was a deeply serious musician who was frustrated and angered by the refusal of the public to appreciate or even listen to the more sober and considered aspects of his work. It may be true—we have no reason to doubt the stories—that closeted with friends behind closed doors he would enthral his listeners with deeply reflective improvisations and performances of his favourite classics. It is not a side of him which makes much impression on record, though he had the opportunity to reveal it. A large number of the tunes which he recorded were ballads—i.e., relatively slow popular songs of the kind which inspired thoughtful and often noble interpretations in his contemporaries. That he could play in this vein is hinted at in several of his solo pieces, which show him indulging in the sort of harmonic exploration and melodic paraphrasing which can turn a modest Tin Pan Alley theme into fine jazz. But for his ballads he chose instead a more obvious, fulsome style, rich in decorative embellishment, full of heavy, organ-like chords and ready to pounce on any turn of phrase that invited some eyebrow-wiggling fun. There are a few recorded examples of him playing themes from the classics, in the established stride tradition, but they hardly nourish the image of the misunderstood artist. When he played the Quartet from *Lucia di Lammermoor*, for instance, he reduced the melody to triviality by rendering it in a series of right-hand trills for which the eyebrows must have been providing some hyperactive visual accompaniment.

The search for another Fats Waller, a Thomas Waller, perhaps, who will offer himself as a more seemly candidate for the jazz hall of fame, has led some commentators to lean heavily on the piano solos, of which 'Handful of Keys' was just one. Is it as a composer of piano rags in the stride idiom that we should salute him? Yes—and no. Yes, because recordings such as 'Valentine Stomp', 'Smashing Thirds' and 'African Ripples' provide exhilarating collections of the formidable weapons in Fats's stride armoury. No, because if we listen to them carefully, we soon detect that they are not carefully considered compositions at all, but demonstrations of Fats's ability to sit down and rattle off a convincing and catchy melody at will, sometimes using second-hand spare parts when originality failed. The facts speak for themselves. The opening theme of 'Valentine Stomp' is based on what I have described as the 'curlicue' triplet device used in the second middle-eight of 'Handful of Keys'. The second theme in 'Valentine Stomp' bears a strong family likeness to the second theme of 'Handful of Keys' sharing, in fact, its final sixteen bars. The third section of 'Valentine Stomp', a minor-key variant of the opening theme, turned up again in 1939 as the 'Piccadilly' section of the London Suite, which Fats is said to have 'composed' at miraculous speed at the keyboard. The first strain of 'Gladyse' in 1929 performed the same duty in 'African Ripples' in 1934. And the phrases on which most of these pieces are based occur, everywhere, in the solos in Fats's band recordings.

Fats Waller employed a similar technique of instant production in the writing of his show tunes. It in no way lessens the great virtues of such songs as 'I've Got a Feeling I'm Falling', 'I'm Crazy 'bout my Baby', 'Keepin' out of Mischief Now', 'Ain't Misbehavin' ' and 'Black and Blue' to say that many of the tunes which he polished off in the legendary ten or twenty minutes sounded like potboilers. Maurice Waller's biography lists three hundred and twenty-five Waller compositions, published and un-published, of which a mere handful live on in the public con-sciousness—hardly enough to set him among the Jerome Kerns and George Gershwins. The flaw in Fats's composing method shows up strongly in 'Honeysuckle Rose', a tune based on phrases that flow effortlessly from a stride pianist's hands. The melody is awkward to play on a blowing instrument, almost impossible to sing unless reduced to a manageable tempo, and sounds best when played on the piano by Count Basie, Earl Hines or Fats himself.

The object of the foregoing paragraphs is not to debunk Fats Waller as a man of many talents. It is simply to point out that those talents were not concentrated in any major body of work but were distributed, with profligacy and abandon, in handfuls of small fragments. To dismiss the Fats and His Rhythm output and search for 'the real Fats Waller' elsewhere is to court disappoint-ment or self-deception—and to miss a lot of fine jazz. His achieve-ments as they stand are not inconsiderable. He wrote a handful of memorable songs and played a barrelful of excellent piano solos, on his own or with the band. His harmonic and rhythmic innova-tions, rarely assembled in one piece but scattered all over his recorded work, influenced Art Tatum to the extent that he told an interview, 'Fats, that's where I come from—and it's quite a place to come from.' Most of his contemporaries and many musicians of a subsequent generation have paid tribute to him, either in words or in musical dedications. In an era when most informal jazz led an underground, after-hours existence, he stormed the best-selling charts with a band that swung and stomped like a sort of institutionalized jam session. It was not in his line to ennoble the popular songs of Tin Pan Alley by musical trans-formation, as Louis Armstrong and Billie Holiday did. Instead, he brought them down, with a relentless barrage of good-natured chaffing, from the sentimental, sickly sweet, escapist clouds to the world of merry-making, woman-chasing, wife-deceiving, in-nocence-pleading, trouble-fleeing and payment-dodging that he inhabited himself. As an entertainer in the broad sense—and almost all jazz musicians prior to 1945 performed that role in one way or another—he was extremely funny in a way that made no concessions to popularity and yet reached a vast audience outside those who would profess to be jazz enthusiasts. Several of these activities appear on paper to be conflicting and yet he reconciled them.

To choose one record from the three hundred or so that Fats made with his Rhythm between 1934 and 1942 is like trying to pick the juiciest from a barrel of apples. There are few out-and-out duds—the band had a formula for coping with the most intractable material, and throughout the years of almost permanent carousing, Fats's piano playing was remarkably consistent in its swing and buoyancy. Some of the slower songs nudge the borderline between jazz and superior dance music, especially when Fats plays rippling decorative figures around Gene Sedric's crooning sub-tone clarinet in a manner that clearly influenced the strict tempo music of Victor Sylvester. But lower the stylus at random on to any of the Waller Rhythm collections and the odds are good that you will hear a hot, driving jazz performance graced by some superlative stride piano and infused with an unforced party spirit.

The very first recording which the group made was wholly characteristic. Called 'I Wish I were Twins', it lacked the benefit of Sedric's distinctive and versatile playing (he didn't settle permanently with the band until late in 1935) but had an adequate substitute in Ben Whittet's dry-toned clarinet. Herman Autrey is in fine stabbing form, and the two front-line men share the opening chorus. The song, with such lyrical highspots as 'you great big babykins', gets gentle treatment from Fats, who was perhaps not yet into his full destructive stride. It enables us to hear that, with a voice with less tonal warmth and consistency than Louis Armstrong's, Fats nevertheless knew how to phrase a song in the jazz manner, and even the spoken or bellowed interjections have a certain rhythmic relevance. After the vocal there is the leader's piano solo in which, as is often the case, he converts the popular song into an exercise in stride piano, following the harmonies of the tune but substituting a whole procession of figures, arabesques and percussive chords for the melody. Then the horn men return for a chorus of jamming in which Herman Autrey generates a fervid head of steam with a succession of Louis-esque sustained notes, some with a downward glissando at the end, some shaken ferociously and some literally blurted out as if they could be contained no longer.

The above synopsis, varied sometimes to the extent that Fats's solo often opened the proceedings, could apply to almost every one of the Rhythm's up-tempo recordings. The one I have chosen as among the very best is a version of Euday Bowman's 'Twelfth Street Rag' recorded in 1935. On this occasion Rudy Powell played clarinet, but his style was so similar to Sedric's that the substitution makes no difference to the band's approach. The choice of material seems an odd one. 'Twelfth Street Rag' was first published in 1914, and subsequently hung about for four decades until Pee Wee Hunt gave it the *coup de grâce* in the Fifties. For a tune which is virtually unplayable in its pristine form except as a joke, it has had some distinguished interpretations. Louis Armstrong's Hot Five raised it far above its station in life with a stately, impassioned performance in the mid-Twenties, and it has been played by such distinguished leaders as Duke Ellington, Count Basie, Lionel Hampton and Sidney Bechet.

Fats gets around the problem of making musical sense out of the silly tune by ignoring it. After a crashing introduction that sounds as if the Harmful Little Armful had momentarily hopped kitten-like on to the keys, he takes off with steady momentum into a stride chorus based solely on the tune's harmonies. While the left hand follows the correct changes, the right hand plays a repetitive pattern of alternating adjacent thirds—those favoured 'smashing thirds' again—which seem to mock the sterile nature of the original tune without actually duplicating it. In the second half of the chorus, the figure is varied rhythmically with more percussive effect. If one probes beneath the surface impression that Fats Waller's solos were spontaneous firework displays of assorted stride effects, a sound sense of construction reveals itself, often expressed in the sandwiching of solid, strongly rhythmic passages in between the bravura playing. In this instance, lightness returns at the end of the chorus in the form of the triplet curlicues that made their early appearance in 'Valentine Stomp'.

At some stage in the life of 'Twelfth Street Rag', someone by the name of Sumner provided a lyric. Typical of the 'hot' numbers of the first jazz age, the words divide their allotted space between

instructions on how to dance to the number ('first you slide . . .
then you glide') and exclamations as to what irresistible fun it all
is ('I can't get enough of this . . . play it over 'gain'). Apart from a
cry of 'Here she comes—look out for that funny feelin' now!'
half-way through, Fats uses the words as written but distributes
them in a rhythmic pattern against shifting guitar figures to produce
what, for all the sense which the words impart, could be described
as an effective scat chorus.

What happens between the end of the vocal and the record's
explosive conclusion can best be described in terms of two con-
current strands of activity. In one, Rudy Powell and Herman
Autrey deliver characteristic solos. In this period, Powell played
clarinet with a persistently rasping tone, not very attractive in
itself, but geared, like his restless, angular phrasing, to generating
heat. Herman Autry was capable of fine playing in a style pitched
somewhere between Louis Armstrong and Henry 'Red' Allen,
and this is one of his best solos. The entrance, a note sustained
over two bars in which Fats establishes a heightened, two-handed
beat, gives masterly notice that a frontal assault on the senses is
about to begin. An obvious rapport existed between Fats and his
trumpeter arising, no doubt, from the latter's lack of inhibition
in responding to his leader's musical and verbal call to frenetic
action. Sometimes the result is erratic to the point of incoherence,
but in 'Twelfth Street Rag' Autrey successfully builds up the
tension with terse phrases pitched on and across the beat, reminiscent of Henry Allen's 'impressionistic' manner.

The second strand of activity involves Fats himself. I have
noted earlier the surrealistic, hallucinatory quality of much of his
verbal interruption. Close study of the band recordings, including
some alternative takes, reveals Fats actually devoted some thought
to the shape and style of the seemingly *ad lib* comments. Often
related to the sentiments of the song, they create a scenario that
hangs together—of Fats in altercation with a landlady or pursuing
an unsuccessful courtship or, as in this instance, in the throes of a
hectic party. Most of the noises behind Rudy Powell's solo
suggest someone engaged in an ecstatic dance, at one point regaling
his partner with 'Look what you can get for nothing, baby!' The
trumpet solo seems to arouse an appetite. 'Waiter get some hot

dogs ready. Get some chitlins, too. Or hot potato salad,' are the cries which intersperse the action here. It is worth noting that while some of the utterances are quite independent of the music— uncannily so when one considers that the perpetrator is simul- taneously pounding out on-the-beat piano—others play a rhythmic part in the proceedings. Obvious examples are the exclamations of 'My, my!' and 'Ah, mercy!' which act as riffs behind the soloist. But it is interesting, too, that, for example, the words 'Waiter, get some hot dogs ready' match, in the rhythm of their syllables, the one-note trumpet figures that Herman Autrey is playing.

The notion of Fats Waller's voice as a third member of the front line, and not simply extraneous buffoonery in the back- ground, strengthens when, in response to Fats's persistent injunc- tion to 'Turn it loose!', the band roars into the final chorus. Now the two strands of activity come together. Herman Autrey assumes his favourite role, that of blasting out crackling single notes at judicious intervals while the clarinet frisks around his ankles. On this occasion, Fats answers his declamatory notes with shouts of 'Yeah!' which must have dislodged plaster from the studio ceiling. And all the time the piano is pumping away in support, celebrating the turn of the chorus with a glissando that rips from one end of the keyboard to the other. I know few other performances which demonstrate so unashamedly the sheer joy of taking part in spontaneous jazz creation when total rapport and momentum have been reached. That Fats presided over scores of such performances in sessions designed for the commercial market is all the more wondrous.

The end of 'Twelfth Street Rag' brings joy to its culmination. Fats overruns the ensemble with portentous descending octaves culminating in crashing Chopinesque chords, Herman Autrey blows a derisive 'that's all' phrase on trumpet and then Fats unleashes a final ear-splitting shout of 'YEAH!!!'

I can think of no better way of summing up Fats Waller's contribution to life. Since his early death from aggravated pneu- monia, in 1943, the huge gap which he left has been filled by frequent reissues of all his recordings. It takes nothing away from James P. Johnson and the other great stride men to say that, in the public mind, the rich, roundly satisfying piano style that emanated from Harlem in the Twenties is known as 'Fats Waller piano'. Other musicians played jazz, offering a body of work for the sober and austere judgement of posterity. Fats Waller *lived* jazz, radiating music which one must either take or leave, because it was indivisible from his personality. At the end of it all, there is only one thing to be said.

YEAH!!!!

Coleman Hawkins

NOTHING SUMS UP the development of jazz in the 1930s better than the career of Coleman Hawkins. He appeared in the first volume of this series as a founder-member of what I described as 'the first jazz big band in the modern sense'. Fletcher Henderson's Orchestra in the early Twenties was strong on musicianship—most of its members, including the teenage Hawkins, had studied music formally—but manifestly weak on jazz. The influences that converted it from a stiff and jerky dance band into a convincing jazz unit were undoubtedly more varied than the history books of old tended to suggest. There is a good excuse for giving all the credit to Louis Armstrong. Most of Henderson's musicians acknowledged at one time or another the vitalizing influence which Louis had on the band when he joined it for a year or so in 1924. It was Armstrong's advanced rhythmic ideas, his ability to 'swing', which brushed off on Henderson's men. But the thrusting, forward-moving rhythm that was the foundation of Armstrong's style could be found, before his arrival, in the music of the Harlem stride pianists, and I do not believe that it was a coincidence that Henderson's first convincing recording in jazz terms —'The Stampede'—was written for the band by Fats Waller.

'The Stampede' marked the emergence of Coleman Hawkins on record as a jazz soloist of giant stature. His achievement was not simply to acquire a mature and integrated style of his own. He had also to provide a convincing jazz voice for the tenor saxophone. The clarity, vibrancy and eagerness of response which made instruments like the trumpet, clarinet and trombone so ideal for azz expression are not qualities indigenous to the saxophone. I shall say more about this when we come to discuss the impact that Lester Young made upon jazz in the mid-Thirties; it is enough to say here that Hawkins overcame the problem in such an emphatic way that he dominated the field for a decade and was still challenging all-comers for several years beyond that.

In a sphere of human endeavour that resounds with stentorian claims to priority and originality, it is refreshing to find that Coleman Hawkins invariably brushed aside suggestions that he 'invented' the tenor saxophone as a jazz instrument. Interviewed by jazz encyclopedist, Leonard Feather, for the 1957 publication *The Jazz Makers*, he said, 'Why, I heard saxophones on record when I was just a little kid. There was one trio with a tenor sax that was about the earliest music that I can remember. There was a whole lot of ofays [white musicians] playing tenor, even when I was just beginning; and before I'd really started making records and everything, there was Happy Caldwell in Chicago and Stomp Evans out of Kansas City, and Prince Robinson . . . no, I certainly wasn't the first.' The nearest he came to acknowledging the legend was to say, 'Well, yes, I suppose you *could* say I was responsible for the making of the tenor.'

From a man whose life revealed an atavistic urge to achieve and retain tribal leadership and domination, this modesty and generosity towards rivals may seem unconvincing. But to Hawkins—and indeed to the general discussion of his place in jazz—the basic question was irrelevant. The making of music is not a definitive achievement, like climbing Everest or running the four-minute mile. If, within the next year or two, someone succeeds for the first time in producing a series of convincing jazz solos on the bassoon, the event will be of negligible significance unless that musician goes on to reveal himself to be a jazz improviser of consistently high talent. If and when that happens, the fact that he brought a recalcitrant instrument into the jazz fold will be added to his laurels. Stomp Evans—or 'Stump', as he was alternatively, and probably more aptly, nicknamed—died young in 1930, but nothing that he left on record in the Twenties suggests a promising jazz musician. Both Prince Robinson and Happy Caldwell were active throughout the Thirties and beyond, but contributed no more than a handful of pleasant, unambitious solos. It matters little if they were the first. Coleman Hawkins was the best by a street—and he knew it.

The development of the jazz style of Coleman Hawkins can be charted by a succession of key recordings. One of them, 'The Stampede', was discussed in *The Best of Jazz* Volume One. Here the saxophone was wielded in the manner of a trumpet, stabbing out phrases based on crotchets or half-notes played ahead of or all around the beat and beginning to 'swing' lustily in the Armstrong manner. This was clearly a starting-point. Encrusted like a well used candle with keys, pads and connecting rods, the saxophone was designed for more nimble work than the echoing of a trumpet's voice. By the time we reach the next landmark, Hawkins had expanded his conception to make fuller use of the instrument.

'Hello Lola' and 'One Hour' look, in the discographies, unlikely material for classic recordings. The session was organized by entrepreneur, singer and comb-and-paper specialist, Red McKenzie, the man who had a few months earlier negotiated the recording début of Eddie Condon and his Chicagoan associates under the heading of the McKenzie-Condon Chicagoans. McKenzie had for some years led a novelty, kazoo-based group called the Mound City Blue Blowers. When his talent as a hustler gained him access to the recording studios, he seized the opportunity of augmenting the Blue Blowers with contemporary jazz stars, while at the same time keeping a firm grasp on his comb and paper. The results were not as bizarre as one might imagine, for McKenzie had a good understanding of jazz phrasing (his voice was considerably tastier strained through paper than *au naturel*) and, by limiting the routines to a string of solos sandwiched between cursory introductions and codas, he avoided drawing attention to the incompatibility of the instruments.

The first M.C.B.B. session with Hawkins in November 1929 quickly established itself as a milestone in the tenor saxophonist's career. It was the first time that he had been heard on record in informal, small-group, jam session surroundings. And the choice of material—an up-tempo piece borrowing the surging, hold-on-to-your-hat rhythms of the then sensational Luis Russell Band, and a popular James P. Johnson ditty taken at dreamy tempo—

brought his playing into sharp focus. In the fast piece, his solo shows why he was the scourge of every other tenor-saxophone player within reach. Letting off a series of rhythmic toots to warn of its approach, it is suddenly upon us in top gear, like an express train coming round the side of a mountain. The suggestion of steam locomotion is heightened by Hawk's use at that time of a heavily-tongued attack by which the notes were ejected forcefully from the instrument like explosive puffs of steam. For all their overwhelming vigour and bursting confidence, the 'Hello Lola' choruses still reveal innumerable signs of immaturity. The style of improvisation, with its rooty-tooty articulation and skipping arpeggios, bears more than a fleeting resemblance to the flamboyant 'speciality' pieces through which non-jazz exponents of the saxophone achieved fashionable distinction in the Twenties. As if to counteract this, Hawkins invests each chuntering fusillade of eighth-notes with a sense of passion and urgency against which the instrument often seems to rebel. High notes intended to crackle fiercely in trumpet style succeed only in whinnying desperately. The uncontrolled application of vibrato to short notes gives some of the fast phrases a wobbly feeling that weakens their rhythmic effect. And every now and then, a passionate outcry seems to get stuck in the instrument's gullet with choked results. It is an amazing, awe-inspiring solo in conception, but one is left with the feeling that player and instrument were not, at that stage, fully agreed on how it should come out!

Turn to the slow number, a charming eighteen-bar love song by James P. Johnson called, in full, 'If I Could be with You one Hour Tonight' and behold a different musician altogether. There are few, if any, suggestions in the previously recorded solos of Coleman Hawkins with Fletcher Henderson of the slow tempo tenor-saxophone style which Hawkins presented, fully fledged, in 'One Hour'. Gone are the indiscipline, the haphazard phrasing, the staccato attack and the feeling of rather breathless over-excitement of the up-tempo work. Instead, the huge tone is richly controlled, the vibrato is steady and expressive, the phrases ride serenely over, under and across the beat. Where before we had a careering express train, here is a stately ship at sea, all sails to the wind.

A 'rhapsode' is defined in the dictionary as an ancient Greek minstrel or reciter of epic poems. A 'rhapsody' originally meant the poem or part of a poem thus declaimed. And presumably through the emotionally exaggerated style of that declamation, the word acquired the secondary meaning of an 'enthusiastic, extravagant, high-flown utterance or composition' and an 'emotional, irregular piece of music'. In the light of these definitions, I suppose it was inevitable, and indeed reasonable, that writers in the early days of jazz criticism would apply the word 'rhapsodic' to the manner in which Coleman Hawkins played slow and middle-tempo tunes. Enthusiasm it certainly had, and extravagance, too, which often carried emotion dangerously close to the brink of sentimentality. In 'One Hour' the phrases, airborne on great gusts of tone, soar and billow in fine declamatory style, paying as little attention to the beat to which they are anchored as a high-flying kite does to the insignificant figure holding the string far below.

Since this chapter is moving towards the apotheosis of the rhapsodic Hawkins style, we should pause here to speculate on its origins. We know enough about jazz evolution to suspect that it didn't spring unprompted from the imagination of Coleman Hawkins. Since we have already established that there were no jazz tenor saxophonists of significance before Hawkins, we must look elsewhere. The 'ofay' saxophonists whom Hawk had heard in his early days need not detain us. There is no evidence in primeval dance-band recordings that the tenor saxophone was ever used in such a lush, extravagant way. If it had been, its influence on his style would surely not have been so long delayed. Was there any other jazz instrumentalist of the period whose music had a 'rhapsodic' feeling?

There were, in fact, two. Asked once about the musicians who impressed him on the Chicago scene in the Twenties, Coleman Hawkins cited Louis Armstrong, Earl Hines and Jimmy Noone. The clarinet playing of Jimmy Noone had three distinct facets. In fast numbers he played rapid runs and figurations with a machine-gun articulation, tongueing each quaver or eighth-note sharply. Without labouring the point, I submit the notion that if the Hawkins solo on 'Hello Lola' were transcribed meticulously

Louis Armstrong *(his manager Joe Glaser is on the left)*

Fats Waller at the organ

for the clarinet, it would remind the listener strongly of Jimmy Noone. In his slower-tempo blues playing, Noone often used slurs and flourishes that, in vocal terms, came nearer to the singer of sentimental songs than to the shouter of down-to-earth blues. And when he actually tackled a sentimental song, all restraint went out of the window and a treacly sentimentality ruled the day. It was this area of Noone's playing, full of oily smears and fulsome *portamento*, to which the Hawkins rhapsodic style came perilously close in its more extravagant moments.

My second candidate may well seem a perverse choice. When Louis Armstrong left Coleman Hawkins and the other Henderson men late in 1925 to return to Chicago, his influence on their music did not cease. The steady stream of recordings which he made with the Hot Five and its various permutations over the next three or four years set a standard of virtuosity which challenged musicians everywhere. These records showed a rapid expansion of his own style, usually summed up in the history books by the cliché that he 'burst the New Orleans format at the seams'. That style did not develop in a vacuum. Chicago in the second half of the Twenties was a burgeoning entertainment centre, rivalling— and in terms of jazz talent, surpassing—New York itself. For three years, Louis undertook a range of work which in addition to playing for dancing, called for solo performance and accompaniment in theatrical surroundings. Aimed as they were at the so-called 'race' market, the Hot Five recordings were largely confined to the sort of stompy, blues and vaudeville-influenced material which that market demanded. In *The Best of Jazz* Volume One, I quoted Bud Freeman's first-hand account of a typical night at the Sunset Café, where Louis played for dancing, accompanied vocal and dancing acts and undertook several solo spots himself which would draw on the popular show tunes of the day. From his earliest playing days in the honky-tonks of New Orleans, when the prostitutes used to scream for the blues, and right on through the King Oliver and Fletcher Henderson experiences, the music Louis played was influenced by popular taste. Throughout his life, every utterance of his on the subject of his profession revealed that the notion of himself as a jazz 'artist' committed to ignoring or converting the public was totally incomprehensible to him. It follows that changes in musical fashion were readily reflected in his own playing style.

By 1927, the frenzy of Scott Fitzgerald's 'Jazz Age' was beginning to wane, despite the desperate efforts of successive generations of 'bright young things' to sustain it. The dance craze of the immediate post-war period had developed from a fever into a steady social habit. Popular music had lost much of the obsession with frenetic physical activity of which the composer, Constant Lambert, complained somewhat belatedly in his book *Music Ho!* in 1934: 'The most irritating quality about the Vo-dodeo-vo, poo-poop-a-doop school of jazz song is its hysterical emphasis on the fact that the singer is a jazz baby going crazy about jazz rhythms. If jazz were really so gay one feels that there would not be so much need to mention the fact in every bar of the piece. Folk songs do not inform us that it's great to be singing in six-eight time, or that you won't get your dairy-maid until you have mastered the Dorian mode . . . What should we think of a concert aria which kept harping on the fact that the singer's mouth was open and that her vocal chords were in prime condition?'

It takes nothing away from this splendid stuff that the pieces Lambert had in mind—'I'm going to Charleston back to Charleston', 'Crazy Feet, I've got those Crazy Feet', 'Rhythm is the Thing' etc.—were not intrinsically jazz pieces. We know what he meant, and it did jazz no harm when the epidemic of St Vitus Dance which his examples suggest began to subside.

Most cursory summaries of the history of popular music attribute the decline of 'hot' music to the trauma of the Wall Street crash in 1929 and the subsequent depression. But closer investigation reveals that the shift to songs sweet and sentimental had begun some time before that. If we want to pinpoint one particular cause, it would be simpler to pick on the fact that, with the foundation in America of the Columbia Broadcasting System in 1927 in competition with the existing National Broadcasting Company, radio established itself as the prime entertainment medium. To a degree which made the previous recording boom seem like a minority cult, music became as readily available in the home as water or electricity. One need not strain the imagination to grasp the effect which this had upon the material broadcast. Bawdy vaudeville songs, rich in *double entendre*, were hardly the stuff for domestic family listening, and at the same time it was no longer always necessary for writers of popular songs to harness them to the needs of a dancing public insatiable for excitement.

Louis Armstrong, a devotee of pretty music in all its forms, responded to these gradual and subtle changes with the acuteness of a sophisticated barometer. The first sign of an extension of his style in the direction of what, to avoid pejorative overtones, we may call the romantic side of popular music, occurs without warning in a 1927 recording of 'Savoy Blues'. I say 'without warning' because, at the outset, the piece sounds as if it is to be just another in the series of powerful, declamatory blues in which the Hot Five excelled. But instead of ripping into impassioned blues phrases in his customary manner, Armstrong's trumpet croons a couple of gentle, reflective choruses, phrased soothingly across the beat and completely devoid of the flattened third and seventh 'blue notes' that one would expect. It's an extraordinary departure. Six months later, in the next Hot Five session with a different personnel, the new mood reappears in an equally un-expected place.

While joining in the universal acknowledgement of 'West End Blues' as a supreme Louis Armstrong classic, some latter-day analysts have criticized the contribution of Earl Hines for in-troducing a foreign element of romanticism into what they consider to be a classic exposition of the blues. Whatever one thinks of this view, the charge is unjust to Hines. For in the preceding chorus, swapping vocal phrases with Jimmy Strong's clarinet, Louis himself lapses into the withdrawn, soliloquizing mood anticipated in 'Savoy Blues' and, as in that performance, totally at odds with contemporary blues practice. I used the word 'croons' advisedly in relation to the 'Savoy Blues' solo because this style, brought into heightened focus in the vocal section of 'West End Blues', has a close family likeness to the kind of lazy, off-the-beat phrasing that characterized Bing Crosby's popular singing style several years later. In the context of Armstrong's own development, 'West End Blues' is curiously isolated. The voice that he uses is a dramatic change from the extrovert bawling and scatting that had gone before. And, although there are suggestions of it in subsequent vocals such as 'Squeeze Me' and 'Save it Pretty Mama', it doesn't really re-emerge until the period, well on into the Thirties, when Louis seemed to realize his potential as a popular singer. It is customary to see the influence of Bing Crosby in the smoothed-out style of those later years. In the light of the above, should it not be the other way round?

If we seem to have strayed from the subject of Coleman Hawkins, let me return to it abruptly with another question. What else are the 'Savoy Blues' solo and the vocal in 'West End Blues' but 'rhapsodizing' in the Hawkins sense? One must always move with extreme caution when stalking artistic influences. Louis Armstrong was not the only jazz musician to be aware of, and affected by, trends in popular music. The earnest jazz buff shocked by the revelation of Louis's allegiance to Guy Lombardo must brace himself to receive the news that, a few years later, jazz saxophonists of the calibre of Johnny Hodges and Chu Berry were extolling the virtues of Freddy Martin, in whose smooth and sentimental tenor-saxophone playing no vestige of jazz could ever be traced. There is no contradiction here. Musicians are usually more concerned with craftsmanship than with artistic judgements, and the clear boundaries which now exist in our minds between the jazz and the popular entertainment music of past eras have been traced in retrospect. At the time, they were blurred to the point of invisibility.

It is possible that, without any prompting from Louis Armstrong, Coleman Hawkins arrived, by way of the same or similar influences, at an almost identical 'rhapsodic' approach. Possible, but not probable. He and his New York associates would have kept up with the trail-blazing recordings by Louis, especially after he was joined by the equally awe-inspiring Earl Hines. Red McKenzie, for example, reveals in 'One Hour' that he is well acquainted with the vocal obbligato in 'West End Blues', since he performs a grotesque comb-and-paper parody of it. His solo, followed by that of Hawkins, could fairly be described as a demonstration of the wrong and right way to do it!

The rather lop-sided nature of Coleman Hawkins's development persisted into the Thirties. The rhapsodic slow-tempo style

altered little, so well rounded and mature was it in its first manifestation in 'One Hour'. If we jump forward four years—a big
jump in the headlong career of jazz history—to the much admired
recording with Fletcher Henderson of 'It's the Talk of the Town'
in November 1933, we find that the tone has shed some of its
booming volume, the vibrato is more intense, and the rhapsodizing
—full of phrases that swell and burst, scattering a shower of
decorative notes—is even more extravagant and operatic. But the
style itself has needed no refurbishing or modernizing.

Fast tempos, on the other hand, continued to present a problem.
It was not a matter of technique. On the contrary, a flag-waving
Henderson version of 'Chinatown, My Chinatown', recorded in
1930, finds him flashing around at breakneck tempo with the
agility of a clarinettist. The trouble is that the solo *belongs* to the
clarinet, built as it is on a procession of the sort of finger-fluttering
runs that Jimmy Noone bequeathed to disciples as diverse as
Albert Nicholas, Jimmy Dorsey and Benny Goodman. We could
sense, even if the slow-tempo performances had not already
revealed it, that Coleman Hawkins had altogether grander ideas
for the tenor saxophone than simply producing clarinet-type runs
in a lower register. They began to emerge, spasmodically and
explosively, in the Henderson recordings of the early Thirties.
In 'My Gal Sal' there are two sensational saxophone breaks that
rival Louis Armstrong in reckless daring. In the same year, 1931,
an updated arrangement of King Oliver's 'Sugarfoot Stomp' (*né*
'Dippermouth Blues') produced from Hawkins an electrifying
solo. Disdaining to dabble cautiously with the familiar phrases of
the original, as his colleagues have done in succession, he launches
his solo with a thundering pedal note that continues to boom like
an irregularly chiming bell throughout the twelve-bar chorus
while linking higher-register phrases leap excitedly around it.
The way in which Hawkins places those notes on or around
different beats in the bar echoes the rather careful and contrived
orchestral stop-chords that punctuate previous solos. It is as if
Hawkins were saying, 'Right, if we're going to play rhythmic
games, let's *do* it!' Continuing into a second chorus, he follows
this daunting precedent in the best way that he knows, by moving
full steam ahead into the old express train delivery in which some

of the chuffing eighth-notes are attacked so violently that they seem on the point of letting out a shriek of protest. It's a solo which, for all its imperfect form, jumps out of its surroundings as vividly as did Louis Armstrong's solos with Henderson six years earlier.

In 'Sugarfoot Stomp', the polarization of the Hawkins tenor style at that time is emphasized. At one extreme is a rhythmically free, around-the-beat extension of his rhapsodic style into faster tempos. At the other, there's the 'Hello Lola' express train, slightly more streamlined, making up in sheer irresistible energy and excitement what it lacked in rhythmic flexibility. The formula through which Hawkins generated this instant head of steam remained the basis of his up-tempo style until the end of his life, through a whole series of stylistic modifications. It consisted of building a solo out of phrases, or blocks, of two or four bars in length, with each beat of the bar given two notes. This may seem to be saying that he simply rattled off a machine-gun burst of quavers, or eighth-notes, but it didn't quite work like that. The second of each pair of notes falling on the beat was weaker than the first, sometimes imperceptibly, and sometimes so markedly that it almost disappeared from earshot altogether. One way of simulating this rhythmic pattern is to sing two and four-bar phrases to the syllables 'DOOdle, DOOdle DOOdle'—though it has to be said here that the way Hawkins attacked those syllables was the very antithesis of doodling! A better and more significant way is to beat out the eighth-notes hand to hand on a table top, starting with the right hand (or left if you are left-handed). In the nature of things, you will find that the left-hand beats tend to be weaker, and it is quite easy to soften them even more. It may be argued—and probably will be before we're through—that the whole rhythmic development of jazz from its beginnings right up to the a-rhythmic departures of modern times has reflected the efforts of improvising musicians to overcome the 'right-handed' tendency to stress the first and third notes in any combination of four.

If Hawk's own musical development was impeded by these early rhythmic limitations, his standing as the Tenor Saxophone Champion of the World was certainly not. To hear how he could overwhelm the most promising of challengers, we have only to listen to the all-star band which the British musician, composer and critic, Spike Hughes, assembled for some New York recordings in 1933. In that band was Chu Berry, six years Hawk's junior and regarded by many musicians and critics as his first serious rival. In a piece called 'Firefly' the two saxophonists solo side by side. Chu Berry, with his softer attack, is rhythmically less hidebound than Hawkins at the medium-fast tempo, but his efforts to match the older man's wilder flights of fancy lead to a disorganized rush of ideas and some technical faltering. In the first half of his chorus, Hawkins gives a lesson in how to rhapsodize with poise, and then he's off down the track in familiar blunt-nosed fashion, swinging purposefully enough to shove Berry brusquely into a siding.

Despite Hawk's obvious supremacy at this stage, the contest is close enough to indicate the sort of pressure under which he was working in the early Thirties. Chu Berry was not the only rival. Over the years, more than one musician has told of an epic battle between Coleman Hawkins and some of the Kansas City tenor men during this period. The pianist, Mary Lou Williams, recalls it as an outright defeat for Hawkins. 'The date must have been early 1934, because Prohibition had been lifted and whisky was freely on sale . . . The word went around that Hawkins was in the Cherry Blossom, and within about half an hour there was Lester Young, Ben Webster, Herschel Evans, Herman Walder and one or two unknown tenors piling in the club to blow. Bean didn't know the Kaycee tenor men were so terrific and he couldn't get himself together though he played all morning.' The story ends with the beleaguered Hawkins overshooting the departure-time for the next Fletcher Henderson engagement in St Louis and burning out his new Cadillac in the effort to make it.

The drummer, Jo Jones, saw the same episode less in the light of an internecine struggle. 'That was the first night Hawkins was really challenged. But when I say "challenged" I mean it was a respectful challenge . . . most of the time at sessions guys would just be trying to show Hawkins how they had improved since he had last heard them.' Several contemporary musicians have suggested that such animosity as existed between the rival tenorists

Lester Young and Herschel Evans in Count Basie's Orchestra,
arose from the fact that, in challenging Hawkins with a quite
different style of tenor-saxophone playing, Lester was showing
disrespect for the master.

I was given, in recent years, an insight into this curious am-
bivalent relationship between Hawkins and his erstwhile rivals.
He was appearing towards the end of his life at Ronnie Scott's
Club in London and I went to hear him. Inside I found Ben
Webster, who had, of course, made many appearances at the club
as a jazz star in his own right. Ben had sat himself in a prominent
position by the entrance and was waiting for Coleman Hawkins to
arrive. He kept saying to me, 'Bean's really gonna play tonight . . .
when he sees me here, he's really gonna play.' Ben knew, as did
most other followers of jazz, that 'Bean's' playing had become
sporadic, sometimes rousing itself into action with some of the
old fire, but often ambling through the motions with little show of
interest or energy. In due course, Hawkins arrived and greeted
Ben warmly. Alas for Ben's expectations, it was not to be one of
the good nights. Whether through flagging energies or the strange,
secretive cussedness with which colleagues, journalists and others
had become acquainted over the years, Coleman Hawkins lit no
fires during that last set. Ben, himself an elderly and far from fit
man, showed little compassion for a fellow-performer on his last
legs. Indeed, his reaction was one of mounting indignation.
Eventually, he heaved himself up from his seat next to me, grabbed
an empty chair and ostentatiously marched with it towards the
stand, sitting himself down right in front of Hawkins. When I
left some minutes later, he was still there, glaring fixedly at the
unresponding figure on stage as if to will him into greater activity.
It was as though his mind had gone back to those Kansas City
days when he and the other young contenders had turned out to
show Hawkins what they could do, and he expected Hawk to
repay the compliment.

The story does give some hint at the enormous pressure which
was upon Coleman Hawkins in the early Thirties. Like 'the
fastest gun in the West' he had established a nationwide reputation
and, whether he liked it or not, he was called on by friend and foe
alike to justify it on all occasions. In the interview with Leonard

Feather quoted earlier, he seemed to suggest that this constant challenge contributed to his abrupt decision, in 1934, to leave Henderson and travel to England. Articles in the London *Melody Maker* by, among others, Spike Hughes under the pseudonym 'Mike', were read by musicians in the States and indicated clearly that he was a celebrity over there. 'I didn't know until then that they knew me over there. I was too busy around here just striving to stay in front of some of the boys that were coming up—Herschel and Chu and everybody—trying to cut me all the time.'

The idea of spending some time as a celebrity in a foreign land, free of serious challengers, no doubt had a strong appeal. There may have been other reasons, too. The Max Jones-John Chilton biography of Louis Armstrong makes it clear that Louis's departure for Britain two years earlier was prompted by quite different pressures. Prohibition had forged a strong link between entertainment and the underworld. As hot properties, star jazzmen resembled the top football players of today—but their transfer fees tended to come, by express delivery, in the form of small pieces of lead. Whatever the reason, Hawk's decision was precipitate. He was talking vaguely about a European trip to a fellow-musician, who suggested that he should get in touch with Jack Hylton, then leader of the leading dance-cum-show-band in Britain. He got straight into his car, drove to the nearest Western Union office and dispatched a telegram addressed to 'Jack Hylton, London, England' which read: 'I am interested in coming to London. Sgd Coleman Hawkins'. In true fairy-tale fashion an invitation arrived the following day and, within a week, Hawkins was off on a trip that was to keep him away from the American arena for four years.

Financially, the gamble was a safe one. In terms of jazz journalism, Europe was far ahead of the United States in the mid-Thirties. The man-in-the-street in Wilhelmshaven or Watford was far more likely to be aware of the style and stature of Coleman Hawkins than his counterpart in Wisconsin. In England, and subsequently in France and Holland, leading bands and musicians fell over themselves in the scramble to appear and record with the Great Man. Artistically, Hawkins was on less sure ground. There is an intriguing parallel between his sudden departure from the centre of the action and Sidney Bechet's similar defection from the New York scene almost a decade earlier. To be sure, the vastly improved media of communication saw to it that Hawkins did not disappear from view as completely as did Bechet in the late Twenties. Furthermore, Hawkins was not isolated—a steady stream of his compatriots made their way to Europe during the same period, some on short visits, others to stay. Nevertheless, there were dangers inherent in the sudden switch from a highly competitive and demanding environment to one in which unquestioning adulation took the place of rivalry. It took a musician of high personal standards and an iron discipline to resist the temptation to tread water lazily—and indefinitely—in European hero-worship.

Happily, Coleman Hawkins was just such a musician. The many recordings which he made during his European sojourn reveal that the already rounded and mature rhapsodic style continued to blossom. 'Lost in a Fog', 'Lullaby', 'Stardust', 'Meditation' and numerous other ballads were extensions of the 'One Hour' conception, enriched by ever more searching harmonies. Even more impressive was the development of his up-tempo style. A record made in Paris in March 1935 with Michel Warlop's Orchestra finds him playing to the formula which he had tended to adopt since the 'Sugarfoot Stomp' days. The tune is 'Avalon' taken at a brisk tempo. In his first chorus, Hawkins plays as if the piece were a slow number stretched over half the number of bars. This allows him to rhapsodize independently of the beat, with broad, sweeping phrases. Once into the second chorus it is brakes off and full steam ahead, as we have come to expect. But there is a difference. The notes are no longer attacked with such violence that they quiver under the impact.

There are two ways of articulating a note on a single-reed instrument. One is to apply the tongue to the underside of the reed sharply as if pronouncing the letter 't'. Utter a string of rapid eighth-notes in this way and you get the staccato 'tooty, tooty, tooty' effect of the Hawkins 'Hello Lola' period. At the other extreme, there is the technique of 'slurring' notes which, to the confusion of the layman, has nothing to do with slithery up-and-down movements from one note to another. Notes that are slurred simply move from one to the other without separate 'tongueing' or articulation. It is even possible, on both reed and brass instruments, to 'slur' the first note of a phrase, by keeping the tongue *hors de combat* and passing a strong enough column of air over the lips or the reed to start a vibration. The technique was elevated to an endearing mannerism by the late Ben Webster, whose opening note in a solo was often wafted in, with a gentle 'phooooh' sound, on the crest of a stiff breeze.

Coleman Hawkins had a natural predilection for 'tongueing', born perhaps of the necessity in his far-off apprenticeship days to keep up with all the tricks of the trade. In those days, 'slap tongueing'—that is, producing a freakish, hollow tone by slapping the reed against the mouthpiece rather than vibrating it—was a fashionable gimmick and, according to Rex Stewart, who saw him with Mamie Smith's band in 1919, the fifteen-year-old Hawkins was a master of it. Few of the tenor saxists who followed in the wake of Hawkins in the early Thirties gave the reed such a drubbing as he did, and comparison with Chu Berry's work on the Spike Hughes sessions shows the master still using rapid tongueing at fast tempos while the disciple eschewed the habit.

Some time around 1934–5, Coleman Hawkins seems to have ironed this heavy attack out of his playing. That he did so more from an urge to try something new than under compulsion to keep up to date with new methods is indicated by the fact that, in the Fifties, he reverted to the heavy attack, telling one interviewer, 'I got fed up with all that slurring . . .' The effect on his up-tempo playing of the smoother progress from note to note was pronounced. The basic formula of four pairs of notes to the bar in quaver, dotted-quaver conjunctions remained, but it received more varied treatment. If we revert to the hand-to-hand rhythms on the table top, we can simulate the new Hawkins approach by striking each strong, right-hand beat at a different strength, ranging from gentle to explosive. Played in this manner, Hawk's solos became impassioned and rhythmic orations in which the voice rose and fell dramatically, and constantly shifting emphasis gave added meaning to notes and phrases. Freed from the rather rigid patterns which the 'tooty-tooty' articulation suggested, the improvisations pursued a much freer course. More often now, a phrase would come to its natural conclusion somewhere in between the obvious two-or four-bar resting-points, and with a hurried snatch of breath that was often picked up by the microphone, Hawkins would be off in pursuit of a new idea. And instead of being kept apart in different areas of the solo, emotive legato phrases and rapid-fire passages were freely intermingled.

The masterpiece in this particular genre was recorded in Paris in 1937. Having made a number of records with the rather ponderous backing of big continental dance bands, Coleman Hawkins was in congenial surroundings on that day. His erstwhile Fletcher Henderson colleague, Benny Carter, having crossed the Atlantic in 1935, was available on alto saxophone and trumpet. Two top French musicians, André Ekyan and Alix Combelle, joined them on alto and tenor respectively, the latter doubling for one number on clarinet. Stephane Grappelly (as he was then spelt) was as ham fisted at the piano as he was fleet fingered on violin but, fortunately, he did no more than provide a discreet oom-chah in the background. His two colleagues from the Quintet du Hot Club de France, Django Reinhardt on guitar and Eugene d'Hellemes on bass, provided all that was needed in terms of chugging rhythm, and the drummer was another expatriate American, Tommy Benford, who had played with the bands of Elmer Snowden and Jelly Roll Morton in the Twenties.

For the version of 'Crazy Rhythm', Benny Carter, a fine arranger with a particular talent for extracting deep-piled sounds out of a four-piece saxophone section, scored the opening chorus. Then the four saxophones went through their paces in turn, with Hawkins taking two choruses as befitted the nominal leader of the group. On the record, the informality of a jam session is simulated when someone, probably Benny Carter, urges Coleman Hawkins on into a second chorus with the words 'Go on, Bean, go on!' As a youthful jazz fan I was mightily impressed by this evidence of spontaneity in the studio, though subsequent listening made it plain that at no stage did Hawkins harbour the faintest intention of stopping.

By European standards at that time, both the French musicians were good players with a fair idea of jazz improvisation derived, manifestly, from listening to a lot of Coleman Hawkins on record and in the flesh. Their solos on 'Crazy Rhythm' reveal the credit and the debit side of the worldwide Hawkins influence. They play in a confident, forthright, 'hot' manner which compares favourably in terms of swing with some of the tentative sounds emanating from European bands. But the effort of maintaining the impetus, of keeping the ball up in the air, leads to some rather tense and jagged phrasing. In the third and fourth bar of his alto chorus, André Ekyan runs awkwardly up and down a gratuitous diminished chord in a way that contrasts most strongly with the effortless, smooth way in which Hawkins altered and negotiated the harmonies. Combelle, an unashamed Hawkins devotee, starts off purposefully but, again, can only sustain the Hawkins-like flow for short bursts at a time. Benny Carter's solo is discussed further elsewhere: after the over-eagerness of the Frenchmen, it is an object lesson in poise and elegant construction, riding on the beat rather than trying to push it along.

At the end of Carter's solo, there are a few off-stage notes from Coleman Hawkins indicating that, as in 'Hello Lola', he is straining at the leash. His opening phrases constitute one of the most thrilling 'Look out, here's me!' entrances in all of jazz. The riff with which he opens his solo had, by the end of the decade, become a Swing Era cliché. By an uncanny coincidence, its crucial opening bar appeared almost simultaneously (just over two months later, which is 'almost simultaneously' in recording terms) as one of the climactic riffs in Count Basie's 'One O'Clock Jump'. Riffing—the playing of short, rhythmic phrases repeated over and over to build up tension—has audible connections with the preacher-and-congregation 'call and response' pattern of American Negro church music, and first made a prominent appearance in jazz in Luis Russell's supercharged band in the late Twenties. Fletcher Henderson's band made use of the device in such early-Thirties arrangements as 'Hot and Anxious' (where the familiar 'In the Mood' riff made an early appearance), 'Comin' and Goin' ' and 'Yeah Man'. In Count Basie's early band, hot from Kansas City, the riff was a fundamental *modus operandi*, with many of the first Basie compositions consisting simply of three sets of riffs, by trumpets, trombones and saxophones respectively, superimposed on each other. Small groups took up the idea which, used to excess, eventually helped to give the Swing Era a bad name. Coleman Hawkins was one of the very first musicians to make use of the riff in solo performance. Indeed, in the early Forties, he recorded a couple of solos in the context of poll-winners' all-star conventions, in which, for some perverse and possibly malevolent reason, he did little more than repeat one single phrase with minor variations. The amateur sleuths who abound among jazz enthusiasts would find limitless food for conjecture and research in the apparent fact that Hawkins anticipated a stylistic trend when he was thousands of miles from the centre of fashion in the relatively 'olde-worlde' surroundings of European jazz. That the riff which so effectively launches his solo in 'Crazy Rhythm' was no inspirational flash in the pan is shown by the appearance of the very same riff, used slightly differently but with the same rhythmic purpose, on two separate occasions in his solo in 'Honeysuckle Rose' recorded at the same session.

The effect of Hawk's entrance in 'Crazy Rhythm' is to increase at once the whole momentum of the performance. It is as if those opening phrases, uttered with such force that the last note is literally hurled away, are a warning to the listener to hold on to his hat and prepare for a rough but exhilarating ride. A player with less idea where he was going—Alix Combelle, dare one say it without offence—might come to the end of the riffs after four bars or so and go off on a different tack, leaving them in the air. Hawkins, on the other hand, hangs on to them tenaciously, like a dog attacking and worrying a bundle of rags. He chews over the two-bar phrase three times, seizes the last two notes and flings them around on to different beats in the bar, makes as if to go careering off in the ninth bar and then returns to give them a final shake in bar ten, completing a perfect rhythmic pattern. It is a fine example of how a great jazzman can 'compose' at breakneck speed.

Nor does it end there. I have put the word 'compose' in cautionary inverted commas because it can mislead. This sort of improvised solo, which in the unrestricted location of a club would probably last ten times longer, can best be likened to the flow of words of an orator speaking without notes. A great speaker, carried along by the passion of the moment, will develop his theme in an inspirational way, choosing his words and balancing his sentences intuitively, sometimes excitedly pursuing a new idea, sometimes subconsciously echoing an earlier phrase, always building his argument with a combination of taut logic and emotional power. Looked at in this light, the two Hawkins choruses in 'Crazy Rhythm' amount to a masterly oration, a miracle of sustained, concentrated invention. You can search them in vain for the faltering phrase, the uncertain pause, the insertion of those nondescript, space-filling notes that are the musical equivalent of the 'ums' and 'ers' of human discourse. Gone, too, are the melo-dramatic, almost gushing outbursts which often brought earlier Hawkins solos to the very brink of absurdity. Passion is now expressed in the sustained ebb and flow of the melody line, the controlled fervour of tone and vibrato and the irresistible rhythmic impulse generated by constantly shifting accents.

Reverting to our earlier analogy, there is a point midway through the second chorus when it seems as if the express train must surely crash headlong into the buffers erected by Benny Carter's snatch of arranged coda and disappear in a stream of wreckage down the hole in the middle of the record. But Hawk's mature sense of construction applies the brakes, and the solo comes to rest in the most satisfying way with a couple of fleeting references to the opening riff.

'Crazy Rhythm' comes as near as the old three-minute 78 could to the competitive tournament atmosphere of the jam session through which jazz giants tested the mettle of their rivals in the Thirties. It shows beyond doubt that the absence of Coleman Hawkins from the New York arena had in no way impaired his ring fitness. Indeed, it gave warning, to all who cared to hear, of the fighting form of the man who, after luxuriating in the adulatory atmosphere of Europe for a further two years, returned to America in the autumn of 1939.

The story of that return, recounted with relish by more than one eyewitness, has something of the epic quality of the poems that kept the Ancient Greek 'rhapsodes' in business. The bassist Milt Hinton recalls with a certain degree of poetic licence, 'The night Hawk came back from Europe, all the fellows came to play for him. He was sitting at a front table. They wanted him to see how they had improved.' Note once again the suggestion of filial respect, sustained no doubt during Hawk's absence by the fact, recalled by Hinton, that, 'We'd listen to a lot of Hawk's records. He was making some in Europe that we'd get.' In his book *Jazz Masters of the Thirties*, Rex Stewart draws a far more dramatic picture: 'But then the word spread like wildfire: Bean was back! Hawk started falling into the joint every night, immaculate, sophisticated and saxophoneless. The tension continued to build— is this the night he will play? Coleman just sat there sipping, with a smirk on his face, as they all paraded their talents before him.'

Rex's account of the eventual dénouement is quoted in my chapter on Lester Young. His picture of the freshly repatriated Coleman Hawkins biding his time was confirmed by Hawkins himself in a long interview in 1956 which was issued by Riverside records in a double album called *Coleman Hawkins: A Documentary*. Unfortunately, printed quotations cannot reproduce the rich chuckles, pregnant pauses and other manifestations of barely-suppressed glee with which Hawk's reminiscences are punctuated. The events described took place at an after-hours spot called Puss Johnson's at 130th and St Nicholas, where musicians would go to play when their regular work was over. On his return from Europe, Hawkins gravitated to it without prompting. 'Wherever there's good musicians, you'll always find me!' There is something strongly reminiscent of the Hollywood western in the picture of Hawkins riding back into town and heading straight for the saloon where he knew his rivals were gathered. Hawkins relished the drama of this scenario when he looked back on it seventeen years later. 'You know, when I came back, they were layin' for me. I could tell they figured I'd been in Europe so long, now this was the real chance to catch me. Because I tell you, they been wantin' to catch me ever since I been a kid. I don't know why, they never did leave me alone. They got to cut *me*, if possible, and all that, you know? Well, boy, they was waitin'!'

As Rex Stewart recalled, Hawkins took his time to sum up his opponents. The smirk on his face no doubt derived from the growing belief that all they had with which to combat his gleaming and scrupulously-maintained six-shooter was a musical armoury that was rusty and out-dated. 'So I used to go around and I'd say to myself, they ain't gonna cut me playin' *that*—not what I just

got through listenin' to. I mean, there must be somethin' they're
holding back . . . if that's the best they're gonna play, not like
that, they won't.'

At this point it is necessary to break off and say something about
the nature of the jazz musician. He is an amalgam, in varying
proportions, of artist, craftsman and scientist. Unlike, say, the
painter or the composer of 'serious' music, the jazzmen of the
generation under discussion tended to push the first-named
persona into the background, holding the view that if technique
and musical research were taken care of, the 'art' would look after
itself. We have to remember that, in the musical climate of the
times, what they were primarily called upon to communicate, in
common with bands that had no pretensions to jazz creativity,
was entertainment and a solid rhythm for dancing. It was the jazz
musician's preoccupation with the technical side of his work
which very often threw him out of step with a lay audience that
tended to judge the music in terms of such abstractions as
'sincerity', 'excitement', 'soul' and so on. It explains such apparent
aberrations as the appearance of Guy Lombardo, Freddy Martin,
Rudy Vallee, Tommy Dorsey and even Mantovani in the list of
great jazz musicians' favourites.

But absorption in the nuts and bolts of composition and execution could also interfere with a musician's judgement of his
fellows. The role of musician as scientific researcher is one which
is rarely taken into account by the outsider. A man like Coleman
Hawkins would spend a large part of his waking hours analysing
the structure of the music that he played and experimenting with
theories that emerged from it. The fact that he would refer to the
process unromantically as 'practising' or 'woodshedding' should
not detract from its seriousness. It is not fanciful to think of the
sort of after-hours jam session that took place at Puss Johnson's
as a *conversazione* in which musicians aired their findings and
presented progress reports on their researches. The danger in
this otherwise valuable and stimulating activity lies in the scientist's
quite natural belief that he and his particular line of research are
at the very hub of the universe, and that those pursuing other
exploratory routes or, indeed, still examining previous concepts
are *hors de combat.*

In the light of this, we can understand Hawk's harsh judgement
on the New York scene to which he returned in 1939: 'There
wasn't any soloists around who interested me—they didn't seem
to be playing anything. They didn't make the changes good—the
changes were kinda sad.' Changes—that is to say, the harmonic
progressions used in improvisation—were Hawk's speciality. A
piece called 'Queer Notions' which he wrote for Fletcher Henderson's band in 1933 showed that he had a knowledge of the
harmonic and scalar developments of modern European music
which few jazz musicians outside of Bix Beiderbecke and some of
his associates had boasted before. His method of improvising
was to explore the harmonic possibilities underlying a tune with
a sort of running commentary which moved smoothly and
logically from one chord to another—'running changes' is how
some musicians described it. While a rhythm guitarist's or a
pianist's left hand will state a series of chords vertically, in a
simultaneous cluster of notes, a melody instrument will outline
them horizontally, contriving a series of notes, a melodic line,
which will make use of significant notes in each successive chord.
In a striking instance of art concealing art, the good improviser
will construct a melody that is so strong, coherent and attractive
that the listener is not made aware of the ingenuity underlying it.
As a craftsman, what Hawkins complained of was the *lack* of
ingenuity in this field. 'I was surprised, you know, 'cos I been
over there for so long and I thought by the time I came back, the
musicians here would be much more advanced. But they was just
like when I left . . .' That his strictures took in the work of Lester
Young, then at his peak, demonstrates how absorption in one
aspect or theory of music can deafen a musician to experiments
going on in other fields.

All this drama and speculation took place in those highly
esoteric conclaves of musicians and hangers-on to which the
general public is seldom privy. When that public was given the
opportunity to make its views felt, they were startling. On his
return from Europe, Coleman Hawkins got a nine-piece band
together to work in a New York club called Kelly's Stables. In
November, 1939, he undertook a recording session for Bluebird,
a subsidiary of RCA-Victor that had its studios at Camden New

Jersey. In preliminary discussions on the session, the company's
A & R man suggested that Hawkins should record 'Body and
Soul', the seductive ballad number which Hawk used as a 'get
off' encore at Kelly's. The idea took Hawkins by surprise—the
other numbers for the session were two up-tempo swing arrangements designed to conform to current big-band trends, and a
commercially orientated version of 'She's Funny That Way' with
vocal by Thelma Carpenter. As for 'Body and Soul', 'that's
nothin'—who wants to hear that?' was Hawk's reaction. Leonard
Joy, the man from Victor, told him that some of the 'boys from
Camden' had heard him do the piece at Kelly's and were raving
about it, 'so I think you should do it for them'.

The story thenceforward has all the familiar, fairy-tale elements
that have surrounded so many hit recordings. Still protesting that
he had no arrangement for it, Hawkins was persuaded to record
a cut-down, three-minute version of the treatment which he gave
to 'Body and Soul' at Kelly's Stables, where he would play several
choruses accompanied by rhythm section only, and then a final
chorus with some makeshift chords from the band. Recording
time allowed for just two choruses, and in the interests of con-
densation, Hawkins limited his statement of the tune to eight
richly ornamented bars before setting out on an improvised exploration of the piece's harmonic structure. Article Number One
in the producer's creed, ever since that obtrusive middle-man
appeared on the recording scene, has always been that the public
will not accept any piece of music unless its basic message, the
tune, is stated and reiterated continuously in recognizable form.
In the light of this, 'Body and Soul' as played by Coleman
Hawkins should have been a recipe for oblivion. A few weeks
after he recorded it—'I didn't even bother to listen to it, just
packed up my horn and walked out'—he was sitting in a bar
called Fat Man's when he heard the record being played in the
influential Martin Block radio show. It was the first intimation he
had that 'Body and Soul' was a hit.

Looking back on the event in his Riverside interview, Coleman
Hawkins was still almost speechless with surprise. The reason
goes beyond the creative artist's natural scepticism about popular
taste. From the moment that he first walked into Puss Johnson's

club to hear what the New York musicians had been up to in his absence, Hawkins realized that, in his grasp of harmony, he was ahead of them. 'Body and Soul' epitomized this gap in musical development.

'A lot of them used to say I was playin' wrong notes ... when the record first came out, everybody, including Chu Berry and everybody, said I was playin' wrong notes in it.' That sentence could quite easily lead us into a lengthy treatise on harmonic developments in jazz. In these essays I have tried to avoid the sort of complex musical discussion which might make the lay enthusiast put the book down with an uncomprehending shake of the head. So let me just focus on one particular point, one which Coleman Hawkins himself cited as an example. The simplest and most familiar final cadence in music involves the mi-ray-doh, 'Three Blind Mice' sequence of notes, accompanied, in the key of C, by the chord sequence C, G seventh, C. The G seventh chord involves dissonance in the juxtaposition of the notes G and F at its upper end. As anyone knows who has ever hammered out the treble part of the elementary piano duet 'Chopsticks', the two notes on their own are a discomfort to the ear until the dissonance is resolved by the F note moving down to E. Incorporated with the rest of the notes in the G seventh chord, the two notes do not strike us as being discordant. Indeed, the inclusion of the F is necessary to give the chord the richness we expect. The history of the various fundamental changes in harmonic fashion over the centuries shows that the human ear will become accustomed, given sufficient exposure to it, to almost any combination of notes. Progress towards the acceptance of new sounds in this context has been impeded, not only by the ear's slowness, but also by the fact that that slowness has, so to speak, been institutionalized in a series of rules which it has been the advanced musical thinker's role to defy.

Jazz harmony, derived in the very earliest days from the harmonies of European hymns and marches, made very faltering steps in the Twenties towards catching up with modern European 'classical' music. The predominant reason for this is that the musicians themselves were, with a few exceptions, not particularly concerned with broadening the harmonic basis of their music. The collectively improvised ensemble, with its several contrapuntal lines moving independently, provided all the richness of texture that was required. And the great soloists, from Louis Armstrong down, were largely intuitive musicians who achieved their effect by expanding and enriching the melody of a tune while paying no more attention to its harmonies than was necessary for musical accuracy.

Pianists were the exception, of course, playing an instrument that demanded not just a melody line but instant 'orchestration' from the soloist. It is significant that in discussing the influences on his music, Coleman Hawkins was scornful of the notion that it was only other 'horn' men that he studied. 'I don't listen to any particular instrument to get an idea from. I mean, I'd just as soon listen to piano players. I can get just as much from a piano player, especially if it's the right one. I hear a lot of things that they play that I like, and I try to make that on my horn.' Rex Stewart attributes the development of Hawk's style in the late Twenties to the influence of Art Tatum who, among other things, was an advanced and accomplished harmonist.

On his return from Europe what disappointed the musician in Coleman Hawkins (while at the same time reassuring the gladiator) was that, though musicians had acquired the speed of execution with which to follow his method of harmonic exploration, the actual harmonies which they employed in their improvisations were still fairly simple extensions of the familiar diatonic harmonies. Like many jazzmen before and since, he was vague in his actual definition of the 'new' harmonies of which he made use. 'At that time, you make some kind of a D change goin' into D flat—that was wrong. At that time you had to make an A flat seventh goin' into D flat, *strictly* A flat seventh—they don't know that's a relative chord to D anyway, but I mean, they just didn't know these things and they couldn't see it that way. If they heard that D, it had to be ooh, that's terrible! It's nothing but a flattened fifth form and things like that . . . but they couldn't hear it. That's *extremely* common now, but it certainly wasn't common before I made "Body and Soul", I can tell you that now!'

'Body and Soul' is in the key of D flat. What Coleman Hawkins did, in carefully selected places, was to arrive home at that D flat

key note, not by way of the 'Three Blind Mice' route of F, E flat
D flat, but in shorter, semitone or 'chromatic' steps: E flat, D, D
flat. There is a choice of harmonies with which that D note may
be accompanied: by making a full-blooded chromatic progression
from D seventh to D flat; or by using the normal A flat seventh
dominant chord but flattening its fifth note from E flat to D. The
'flattened fifth' became something of a bogey in the Modern Jazz
era of 1945 onwards. Aspiring 'modernists' seized on it as a
passport to the realms of bebop, while adherents to the more conventional jazz forms interpreted it as the symbol of everything
that was freakish and 'far out' in the new music. Its appearance as
part of Hawk's harmonic armoury in 'Body and Soul' in 1939
may have been the reason for Thelonious Monk's apparent
bewilderment in later years at the record's success. Monk, who
as a young musician was employed by Hawkins in the mid-Forties,
said to Hawk more than once, 'You never did tell me how did
these people, these old folks and everybody *go* for your record of
"Body and Soul".'

Hawkins himself was equally bewildered, though his wonder-
ment was based on the belief that the general record-buying
public wanted to hear the melody all the time. 'Where is the
melody? There ain't no real melody in the whole piece!' He
meant by this of course that, apart from the cursory reference to
it in the first eight bars, he never actually states Johnny Green's
original tune at all. The truth is that he took considerable liberties
with its harmonies, too. Despite his assertion that the chord
progressions that he used were indigenous to the tune—'The
changes that I made in "Body and Soul"? That's the only changes
to make in "Body and Soul"—what I mean is, that *is* "Body and
Soul" '—the original piece has no such refinements as chromatic
progressions or flattened fifths. Written in 1930, the tune was
daring for its time, with the unusual excursion into three different
keys in the space of its thirty-two bars. But reference to the
original songsheet or to early recordings (viz. Louis Armstrong's
successful version recorded in the year of the song's publication)
shows no sign of the sophisticated harmonies that Hawk used. To
take two clear instances, the conventional chord for the end of the
second bar, right after the words 'sad and lonely', and for the

second half of the seventh bar, behind the words 'yours, body and soul', is an A flat seventh. Indeed, a singer who tried to sing Johnny Green's melody as written over the Coleman Hawkins chords would find several notes clashing dreadfully with the accompaniment.

This doesn't mean that Coleman Hawkins was wrong in saying that his chords *were* 'Body and Soul'. When a popular song is adopted by jazz musicians, it is as if it were leased to them indefinitely for the purpose of improvisation. They are under no obligation to stick to the composer's original conception—they would be pretty poor improvisers if they did. It is a truth which I hope songwriters themselves would admit that a performance by a great jazzman—Louis Armstrong, Art Tatum, Coleman Hawkins —has often shown an insight into the character of a melody that the composer, with his limited aspirations towards producing a singable popular song in the shortest possible time, has missed. You may take it from me that many well-known songs, including 'On the Sunny Side of the Street', 'I Can't Get Started' and 'Moonlight in Vermont', would sound wrong today if played from the original songsheet. Coleman Hawkins may fairly be said to have completed 'Body and Soul' as a finely crafted piece of music and, had not the song already a superfluity of composers in Messrs Green, Heyman, Eyton and Sour (the last three required to produce the very ordinary lyric), I would suggest that his name should be added.

In bringing modern and sophisticated refinements to a popular song, Coleman Hawkins was clearly unprepared to find his own contribution popular in the same sense, especially when other musicians were finding it full of 'wrong notes'. But in dismissing the whole 'Body and Soul' episode as a freakish aberration on the part of the public, Hawk did them and himself an injustice. (By coincidence, Jerome Kern made a very similar misjudgement in the same year, including 'All the Things You Are' in a show with the strong reservation that, with its 'advanced' harmonies, the song was 'too hard' for the public.) Music of quality and distinction may be rare in the Hit Parade, but it is not completely unknown. What record salesmen know as 'the public' is not one huge, amorphous mass with a single response. While a lot of people were no doubt going about their business in 1939 whistling and humming such nonsense as 'The Hut Sut Song', 'Three Little Fishes' and 'Scatterbrain', there were enough who preferred the more sophisticated 'Deep Purple', 'I Get Along Without You Very Well' and the reincarnation of Victor Herbert's 'Indian Summer' to establish them as 'standards' that would survive until the present. As Coleman Hawkins so often said, the people who bought 'Body and Soul' in such quantities knew nothing about music. The man in the street would not know a flattened fifth if it jumped out from behind a lamp-post and flattened *him*. What he responds to are such abstractions as a romantic feeling, a good beat, a pretty tune. 'Body and Soul' fulfilled the first of these requirements in such generous abundance that it didn't matter if the other two were not over-stressed.

And here's a paradox that is not unusual in jazz. Unlike Louis Armstrong with his insistence on pleasing the people, Coleman Hawkins was no philanthropist. In his attitude to audiences he came closer to the dismissive, take-it-or-leave-it line of the post-1945 modernists than to the jazzmen-entertainers who were his contemporaries. In person relationships, he appears to have taken a malicious, Mephistophelean glee in the discomfiture of others. The Riverside interview from which I have quoted opens with him blandly informing his questioner that he was born at sea. The inflections of the disembodied voice alone suggest to us that it is a blatant invention which eventually degenerates into a sort of deadpan crosstalk act.

'How did that happen? Were your folks travelling to Europe?'
'They were comin' back.'

On the one occasion when I had the perilous task of interviewing him backstage before a concert, he responded to my enquiry as to whether he remembered various friends from the London visits in the Thirties with a flat 'No', nad then stared at me unwaveringly as if to savour my confusion. Buck Clayton once told me of an epic row between trumpeters Roy Eldridge and Henry Allen which was entirely engineered by Hawkins, who conveyed to each of them in turn fictitious slanders allegedly uttered by one against the other. And there is something not altogether kindly about the story, which Hawkins himself was fond of telling, of how, in the Fletcher Henderson days, he worked the trombonist Charlie Green, up into a fever of jealousy by loudly holding forth in his hearing about the fickleness of musicians' wives.

Despite all this, the initial impact of 'Body and Soul' is of a great heartwarming blast of human warmth and loving kindness. This is heightened rather than otherwise by a much greater discipline in the rhapsodizing than of yore. Gone are the earlier extravagances, the tendency towards histrionics, the quavering descents from the upper register that came so dangerously close to sentimentality. The tone is now full, firm and virile in every register, and the two choruses unfold with an inexorable logic and feeling for dramatic construction that is more powerfully moving than the more impassioned exhortations of the earlier style. Poor old, much maligned Joe Public showed himself in some respects to be more advanced than those musicians who chided Hawkins for playing wrong notes. To him, the arrival at the D flat keynote by way of 'some kind of a D change', which happens in the second bar of the first chorus, was no jarring musical solecism or aggressively 'modern' innovation, but a device that prompted a warm and caressing turn of phrase. Furthermore, in accepting Hawk's variations and departures from the basic melody without complaining 'Where's the tune?', he showed himself capable of 'hearing' the unstated melody which, after eight years and innumerable interpretations, must have been quite familiar to him.

There are three more signposts that I would like to erect before leaving the reader to explore for himself all the ramifications of this rich performance. One of the most effective devices which Coleman Hawkins had perfected by this time is the one known as 'doubling up'. This simply means treating one bar as if it were two, playing four sixteenth-notes or semiquavers to each beat instead of two eighth-notes. This improvisational ploy has two advantages. It enables a soloist who is, like Hawkins, eager to pursue all the harmonic twists and turns inherent in a tune to give attention to transient chords that more widely-spaced notes would overlook. And, by suggesting a tempo twice as fast as the original, 'doubling up' endows a slow ballad with some of the drive and swing usually associated with more lively pieces. For examples of this, listen to the serpentine movement through changing chords with which Hawkins modulates into the key of D between bars fifteen and eighteen of the first chorus, and to the way in which he is able to respond to the heightened tension introduced by ensemble chords in the second chorus by bringing into play some of the elbowing aggression of his up-tempo style.

The two remaining pointers can be summed up briefly. I have given some attention to the fresh devices which Hawkins brought into play with 'Body and Soul'. The performance would not have attained the status of a masterpiece had not these innovations been used with the utmost discretion and taste. Many a jazz solo has been ruined or impaired through a musician's eagerness to show off some newly discovered trick. The chromatic movement of which I have written at length is not used by Hawkins to the exclusion of more conventional harmonic progression. For instance, his treatment each time of the D major passage in the first half of the middle-eight makes use of the relatively naïve, diatonic harmonies of the original songsheet. The effect, no doubt intuitive rather than studied, is of opening a window and letting sunshine in on a cloudy and brooding atmosphere.

Similar restraint is used in the deployment of emotional resources. We have Hawk's testimony that the recording of 'Body and Soul' was a condensed version of the nine or ten choruses which he often lavished on the number at Kelly's Stables. The mouth waters at the thought of them, but it is hardly conceivable that they attained greater emotional impact than that which Hawk achieved, with a great actor's control and timing, in three short minutes. In common with another miracle, Louis Armstrong's 'West End Blues', this performance leaves one with the impression that one has been carried high aloft and lowered to earth again on a vast wave of passion. And yet the moment of climax is masterfully delayed until eight bars from the end of the piece and then restricted to four bars in which Coleman Hawkins makes a series of chromatic leaps into the upper register, choosing deliberately unseductive intervals and implying chords far more complex and dissonant than any that have been suggested before. It's a startling and dramatic moment, a sudden explosion of fury that dissipates as quickly as it came as the piece subsides towards a coda which brilliantly, and this time with ineffable gentleness, reiterates the chromatic idea. It stimulates one's optimism about human nature wonderfully to reflect that one of the most success-ful jazz recordings was, in its own way, also one of the best.

Jack Teagarden

IN ITS TERMINOLOGY, the story of Jack Teagarden's arrival in New York tends to sound like the scenario for a corny western. Accounts by musicians who were on the spot are curiously vague as to the exact date and circumstances, but the consensus is that Jack arrived in town in the autumn of 1927. Jimmy McPartland recalled that he, Bud Freeman and Pee Wee Russell were sitting in a speakeasy on 51st Street when Pee Wee, who had been enthusing about the trombonist as 'the greatest thing I ever heard in my life', went off to round him up so that they could judge for themselves. Bud Freeman's recollection is that Pee Wee Russell called him in the middle of the night to say that Jack Teagarden, the best trombonist in the world, just 'blew in' from Oklahoma City and was in action at a speakeasy on 53rd Street. According to Eddie Condon, it was Bud Freeman who called *him* in the middle of the night, long-distance, and got Teagarden to play some blues over the telephone. Condon, who was in New York, said, 'Put a brand on his stomach and bring him in.'

The probability is that Pee Wee Russell made the introductions, since Jack Teagarden was no stranger to him. Both men had played, in the mid-Twenties, for the Texan pianist and bandleader, Peck Kelley. (Conforming to the theme, the band's name, Peck's Bad Boys, sounds like one of those gangs of marauding horsemen around which cowboy epics are built!) It is not hard to understand Russell's enthusiasm for his old colleague, nor the feeling of excitement that Jack Teagarden's playing spread among the New York musicians. Eddie Condon and his associates had themselves only lately arrived in New York from Chicago, where the trombone was respected for its supportive role as exemplified by the great Kid Ory, but not admired, as were the trumpet, clarinet or piano, as a vehicle for solo virtuosity. The evidence of gramophone records, with their spurious selectivity that favours those who were in the right place at the right time, is notoriously unreliable, and one must exercise extreme caution in using terms like 'the first' or 'the best' in respect of the jazz pioneers. For example, records reissued in comparatively recent years have shown that, in Texas during the late Twenties, the locally re-nowned Alphonse Trent Orchestra boasted, in 'Snub' Mosley, a trombonist who, in terms of sheer speed of execution, was a front-runner, if not way ahead of the field. In the book, *Jazz Masters of the Thirties*, Rex Stewart lists several influential players in New York at the same time, some of whom—Jake Green, Jake Frazier, Teroy Williams, Billy Kato, Herb Gregory—we must take on trust. But those with whose work we are familiar on record, such as Charlie Green, Charlie Irvis and Joe 'Tricky Sam' Nanton, show themselves strongest in the broad, sweeping measures of the blues. At brisker tempos, they were no match for the other horns.

The player most consistently credited with the feat of liberating the trombone from its restricted supporting role was a studious-looking New Yorker called Milfred 'Miff' Mole. The Original Memphis Five, with whom Mole made his recording début in the early Twenties, was the most successful of the bands which rode into fashion on the crest of the wave of jazz mania created by the Original Dixieland Band. With superb instrumental control that involved a wide range of dynamics, he devised a style which grafted the melodic agility and unpredictability of Bix Beiderbecke on to the staccato rhythmic manner of the ODJB's Eddie Edwards. His solos throughout the Twenties—and there are hundreds of them on record—are undoubtedly the most interesting trombone improvisations of the period. Full of daring intervals and un-expected turns of phrase, they offer melodic ingenuity and grace from an instrument more accustomed to supplying emotive bursts of raw passion. Indeed, it is on the emotional level that Miff Mole's work falls short of the best of jazz. Unlike Bix Beiderbecke, with whom he shared a strong sense of musical discipline and construction, Mole seems to have been impervious to the raw spirit of black American music. Consequently one waits in vain for his solos to flair into fervent life in the way that Bix's so often do.

By the late Twenties, Miff Mole, in loose partnership with the cornetist Red Nichols, had virtually cornered the market in what were then termed 'hot style' recordings in New York. Together and separately, with groups that recorded under a wide variety of names, they set a fashion for elegant, sophisticated jazz, giving plenty of room for 'hot' solos while keeping firm control of the temperature. Rhythmically, their music leaned heavily on the first and third beat of the bar, with the phrasing couched in the even quaver, one-and-two-and-three-and-four style descending from ragtime. By the late Twenties, this style was beginning to give way, albeit reluctantly, to something new. In the first volume of *The Best of Jazz*, I pursued the notion that the really significant changes in jazz history have been rhythmic. For many years, until chordal harmony itself came to be rejected by the *avant-garde*, 'modernism' was always interpreted in terms of harmonic discovery and innovation. Much is made in the history books of Charlie Parker's improvisatory excursions into extended chords such as elevenths and thirteenths, and indeed it was his use of the upper intervals of those chords in the first 'modern jazz' recordings of the mid-Forties that startled so many listeners. But new harmonic practice can soon be assimilated, as witness the veritable spate of clichés based on the flattened fifth and descending minor seventh chords that came in turn to hamstring jazz in the post-Parker period. It was his comparative rhythmic freedom that distinguished Charlie Parker from his predecessors and, during the Bebop years, it was the ability to handle that freedom that separated the men from the boys.

Likewise, in the late Twenties, 'modernism' was in the air. With his recordings from 1926 onwards, Louis Armstrong had opened wide the door on a hitherto unimagined vista of jazz possibilities. At its centre was a rhythmic conception which I have described in detail in earlier chapters. It was not simply that Louis, ahead of all his contemporaries, abandoned the rather square, even-quavered, one-and-two-and-three-and-four rhythmic base in favour of the looser, one-and-a-two-and-a-three-and-a-four rhythm of twelve-eight time. It was the totally free and uncontrived way in which he moved on, across, through and behind the regular, four-to-a-bar pulse which gave to his playing the sustained momentum which came to be known as 'swing'. It took some time for his example to be followed. I made the point in the earlier volume that almost all the 'classic' recordings which I discussed in that book showed some degree of rhythmic schizophrenia. But by the end of the Twenties, Louis Armstrong's influence had permeated the whole range of jazz instruments and had inspired a new generation of musicians who wanted to 'swing' as he did.

In *Jazz Masters of the Thirties* Rex Stewart gave his essay on Jimmy Harrison the heading 'Father of Swing Trombone'. After describing Harrison's impact on the New York scene in the mid-Twenties, he concluded that 'History, inadvertently and unwittingly, bypassed Jimmy Harrison'. To give history its due, it has done its best with rather flimsy evidence. At the time when he was alleged to have exerted his greatest influence, around 1927–8, he could be heard on record only in fragmentary solos with the bands of Charlie Johnson and Fletcher Henderson—and some of the Henderson solos have been reassessed in recent years as the work of another young 'modernist', Benny Morton. Indeed, in one respect history may be accused of bending the truth in Jimmy Harrison's favour. Jazz historians have always had a tendency to outline the development of jazz in terms of Old Testament lineage—Buddy Bolden begat King Oliver, King Oliver begat Louis Armstrong and so on. Add to this the risky assumption that, because an overwhelming majority of jazz innovators have been black, the flow of influence will always be from black to white, and it is not surprising that many jazz histories settle for the simple view that Jimmy Harrison begat Jack Teagarden.

The historical facts certainly do not rule out this possibility. In his recorded interview for Riverside Records, Coleman Hawkins describes the occasion at the Roseland Ballroom in New York when the musicians in Fletcher Henderson's band first heard

Jack Teagarden. Hawkins, ever alert to what was going on in musical circles, had hung around to listen to the band that was alternating with Henderson—in all likelihood it was Billy Lustig's Scranton Sirens, with whom Teagarden played at the Roseland in February 1928. Having heard a solo or two from the young trombonist in the band, Hawkins hurried down to the bandroom, his genuine enthusiasm sharpened by the opportunity for a little mischief-making. One has to hear the story in his own words to savour the malicious glee with which he sought out Jimmy Harrison 'to start kiddin' about it, you know'. Having announced to the room in general that 'there's a boy upstairs that plays an awful lot of trombone', he casually asked Jimmy Harrison if he knew him. Harrison's reply was not only predictable from a man accustomed to the Hawkins style of comradely baiting, it also throws light on the way that trombonists were responding to the Armstrong influence.

'Oh no, how am I goin' to know him. I don't know anybody—what's he play? He's a trombone player, ain't he? He can play like the rest of the trombones, that's all. I don't see no trombones. Trombone's a brass instrument, it should have a sound just like a trumpet. I don't want to hear no trombones sound like trombones. I can't see it.'

'But Jimmy,' said Hawkins, 'he don't sound like those trombones, he plays up high. He sounds a whole lot like trumpets to me.'

The upshot clearly satisfied Hawk's sense of theatre. 'I'll never forget it, Jimmy and Jack became the tightest of friends.'

The tight friendship that developed between Jimmy Harrison and Jack Teagarden during the latter's first year in New York clearly provided a historic basis for the assumption that the established star of the famous Henderson Orchestra influenced and gave formative guidance to the newcomer. But it happens that there are recordings by both musicians in that period which tell a different story. Confusion over the identity of trombone soloists with Henderson make one wary of laying down the law. But two recordings over which there seems little doubt—the version of 'King Porter Stomp' recorded in February 1928 and 'Come on Baby' from December of that year—give us a good idea of his

Billie Holiday

Lester Young

Roy Eldridge

style at the time of the Teagarden friendship. In 'King Porter Stomp', he starts in the upper register, playing three anticipated crotchets in the typical Armstrong manner. But the timing is slightly wrong. The notes do not hang in the air as Armstrong's would, and the two notes leading into the first full bar of the chorus are rushed, with a jerky effect. Later on, at the half-way mark in the solo, there is a phrase of five notes played in a sharply tongued, even-quaver manner that could have come straight from a Miff Mole solo. These and other solos from the period of 1928–9 show a certain indecision in style and rhythmic sense which hardly conforms to the legendary image of a grand master ahead of his time. The musician and musicologist, Gunther Schuller, has pointed out, in his book, *Early Jazz*, that in this period both Benny Morton and Claude Jones, temporary colleagues of Harrison's in the Henderson band, recorded solos which were, in his view, superior to Harrison's. And in Luis Russell's recordings made early in 1928, J. C. Higginbotham was demonstrating a formidably agile style, full of lip-trills and ascents into the upper register, which compares well with contemporary examples of Harrison's work.

But we must not dismiss out of hand the testimony of those musicians on the spot who have, like Rex Stewart, asserted that Jimmy Harrison held regal sway in New York while other trombonists stood back to listen and learn. When Don Redman, who had supplied the bulk of Fletcher Henderson's arrangements, left the organization late in 1927, the band moved into what would nowadays be described as a crisis of identity. In the Riverside interview, Coleman Hawkins recalled how Henderson started exchanging arrangements with other bands, to the extent that his own orchestra began to sound like them. Retrospectively, Hawkins disapproved of this—he thought that the band should have carried on 'stomping' as it did under Redman's guidance. Certainly, there is on record plenty of evidence of a passing infatuation with the cool, harmonically contrived music of the white New Yorkers— Nichols and Mole, Frank Trumbauer and, of course, Paul Whiteman—which may have inhibited Harrison's playing. But we must also remember that Jimmy Harrison had been around in New York since 1923 and so had Rex Stewart. It may well be that the period of Jimmy Harrison's pre-eminence should be pre-dated to around 1924–5 when he and trumpeter June Clark, freshly arrived in New York, constituted what Rex Stewart described as a 'red-hot team'. A couple of titles recorded by their band in 1925 —'Santa Claus Blues' and 'Keep Your Temper', made under the name of the Gulf Coast Seven—are enormously impressive. June Clark (in much later life to become road manager and court minstrel for boxer Sugar Ray Robinson) had grasped many of Louis Armstrong's precepts, and Harrison, though rhythmically somewhat stilted, played long solo passages with a drive, range and agility that was, to say the least, unusual for that time. If he seems to have been less far ahead of the field three years later, it would not be the first or last instance in jazz history of an instrumental pioneer being overtaken by ertswhile 'pupils'.

But how does Jack Teagarden's early performance stand in all this? The earliest readily available recording on which Teagarden was extensively featured is a piece called 'Makin' Friends', recorded by Eddie Condon and his Feetwarmers in October 1928 In this, Teagarden has an opening verse in a minor key which he plays with open trombone. The first thing that one notices, apart from the tone with its burnished matt surface, is the ease with which he handles every rhythmic problem. Coincidentally, the solo begins with the same launching phrase based on anticipated crotchets or quarter notes over which Jimmy Harrison had tripped in his 'King Porter Stomp' solo a few months earlier. Jack Teagarden's timing is perfect, as is the way he balances notes played on and across the beat in the bluesy phrase that follows. Stretching across the ninth, tenth and eleventh bars is a legato phrase made up of six minims or half-notes which would have thrown quite a few players of that period off balance, especially if they had any leaning towards the old style of eight-to-a-bar phrasing. Teagarden plays it with great assurance, placing the second note well ahead of the beat, the fourth slightly less so, and prefacing the tied fifth and sixth notes with a 'turn' comprising a couple of anticipatory grace-notes (a Teagarden trade-mark) which serves to avoid dull symmetry. There's a typical Teagarden vocal in which the lazy relaxation of his trombone style is reflected in a Texan drawl in which the harder consonants are replaced by their softer alternatives—f becoming v, t becoming d and s melting into an over-ripe z. The second chorus is a wordless one in which, once again, Jack shows complete rhythmic assurance. In the ensuing trombone choruses, he uses a technique which was, and remains to this day, his exclusive speciality. By removing the bell section of the trombone and covering the exposed piping with an ordinary glass tumbler, he produces a nasal, muted sound with a melancholy quality heightened by the fact that, with the limited range of notes that can be played in tune by this method, it works most effectively in a minor key. Some years later, in the film, *Birth of the Blues*, Jack Teagarden introduced the technique as a novelty effect in the song, 'The Waiter and the Porter and the Upstairs Maid', which he sang with Mary Martin and Bing Crosby. But in pieces such as 'Makin' Friends', 'Tailspin Blues' (with the Mound City Blue Blowers) and the riveting 'St James Infirmary' with Louis Armstrong's first All Star band in 1947, the music which he produced in this unorthodox way was anything but novelty stuff.

Indeed, the final choruses in 'Makin' Friends' combine with other solos of the period played in the normal way to build a formidable case for asserting that, in the significant area of rhythmic fluency and freedom, Jack Teagarden was ahead of all other trombonists, Jimmy Harrison included. In September 1929, he played two choruses on a tune called 'Never had a Reason to Believe in You' with the Mound City Blue Blowers which reveal a man whose style, at the age of twenty-two, was completely matured. In his hands, the trombone was no longer the rather clumsy heavyweight in the jazz instrumental family, but a sensitive and articulate voice capable of the subtlest nuances. The secret of his fluency was an astonishing lip control which established him from the first recordings as a trombone virtuoso, quite apart from his creative talent. The impression, especially in his high-register playing, that the trombone slide had become redundant gave rise to a legend that as a small boy he had devised alternative slide positions near to his face because his arms were too short to push the slide into the lower positions. Like most legends, it contains no more than a grain of truth. There are no alternative positions which will obtain the lower notes in the trombone register, so he would have had to stretch for them or devise some way of extending his reach. Up among the high notes, it is possible to minimize the movement of the slide with alternative positions. But having once stood alongside Jack Teagarden on a bandstand (at the Nice Jazz Festival in 1948) and marvelled at the leisurely way in which his huge, square right hand seemed to wave languidly an inch or two in front of his face while the notes tumbled out, I fancy that it was the finely controlled 'lipping' of additional ornamental grace-notes and turns that made it appear that he was getting by with the minimum of mechanical assistance. The proof of his technical virtuosity lies in the fact that, whereas it is the trombone, with its large mouthpiece, which is on paper the more cumbersome instrument, it was some fifteen years or so before modern trumpet players became adept at using the sort of fast triplet 'lipped' ornamentation which abounds in Teagarden's early solos.

It is difficult to understand the reluctance, in some areas of jazz commentary, to give Teagarden full credit for lugging the trombone into the field of untrammelled rhythmic freedom which came to be called 'swing'. Much early writing on jazz had an understandable (and in most instances justified) bias towards black performers as the true originators, leading to an assumption that Teagarden's style must have derived from Jimmy Harrison simply because of the colour of his skin. There is no excuse for us today to make such easy assumptions. We know that, in his youth, Jack Teagarden had plenty of opportunity to listen to the blues in its basic, rural form and also to the 'gospel' music of black Holy Roller meetings where the preacher would incite the singers to fervour in a manner strongly reminiscent of Teagarden's early blues style. And though the legend that he used to carry a favourite Louis Armstrong record around in his trombone case may test our credulity (I speak as one who had difficulty in keeping his old 78s intact in their *shelves*), there is no doubt that he eagerly absorbed the recordings by Louis and also by Bessie Smith during the Twenties. There is no reason to doubt that he arrived in New York with a style strongly influenced by these and other black artists and sounding, to Coleman Hawkins, 'a whole lot like trumpets'.

A more serious reason for equivocation about Jack Teagarden's role in jazz history may be that his subsequent career, for all the elegant and delightful music that it produced, did not fulfil the early promise. It can be summed up in a few sentences. After the first few years in New York, during which he recorded for practically every bandleader and session organizer who could get his hands on him, he graduated, via the bands of Ben Pollack and Mal Hallett, to the exalted ranks of the Paul Whiteman Orchestra. While under tight contract to Whiteman, he had to turn down the offer to lead a team of fine jazz players stranded by the break-up of Ben Pollack's Band. The job went to Bing Crosby's younger brother Bob who, though little more than a moderate singer himself, succeeded in attracting commercial success to a band with a strong jazz policy. Teagarden's own efforts to enter the big-band field after his stint with Whiteman led to a series of financial disasters. He lacked both the business sense and the strong auto-cratic streak which brought success to erstwhile colleagues such as Benny Goodman and Tommy Dorsey. Between 1947 and 1951, he restored and burnished his international reputation as a member of Louis Armstrong's All Stars, before returning to lead his own small groups with a predominantly Dixieland style and repertoire. He was on tour with his band in 1964, when he died suddenly, at the age of fifty-nine.

Taking recorded samples from this fluctuating career, one is reminded of one of Duke Ellington's sage remarks *apropos* the cornetist, Ray Nance, of whom someone had said that he played within a relatively narrow technical and expressive range. Duke's reply was (and I quote from memory): 'In all the years that he has been in our band, there has never been a night on which Ray did not play *something* of exquisite beauty.' Likewise, it is hard to find a single Teagarden record which he did not enhance with his beautiful, curiously blunted tone, his marvellously fluent and controlled articulation, his perfect rhythmic poise and the sheer elegance of his musical thought. There was a phase, in the mid-Thirties, when he reacted so far from the passionate and vibrant manner of his first recordings that his sound, especially with the much favoured straight mute, acquired a rather flat and distant quality, as though he were performing inside a cardboard box.

But it was a passing phase and may have been to some extent attributable to studio acoustics.

What one does find missing, after the first exciting year or two, is the spirit of adventure. The mutual admiration between Jack Teagarden and Jimmy Harrison had, by the end of 1930, produced some curious results. In his finest recordings, made with a studio band called the Chocolate Dandies in December, 1930, Jimmy Harrison sounds, in the piece 'Dee Blues' especially, much nearer to Jack Teagarden than before. The phrasing is less four-square and symmetrical, sweeping phrases are played across the beat and the phrase endings have the sort of rapid, fluttering vibrato that gave Teagarden's early playing such heat and intensity. Important differences remain, largely in the rhythmic area. Though the earlier awkwardness had been ironed out, Jimmy Harrison still tended to play dotted quaver and semiquaver combinations in a somewhat jerky manner, inherited from the 'vo-de-o-do' syncopations of earlier dance music and bequeathed, in turn, to fellow-trombonists Jimmy Archey and Vic Dickenson, in whose styles it remained an idiosyncracy for four or more decades. But in the common adherence to Louis Armstrong's influence (almost every recorded solo by Harrison, and not a few by Teagarden, start with the three ahead-of-the-beat crotchets or quarter notes that had been an Armstrong trade-mark since the mid-Twenties), both Harrison and Teagarden were briefly in the same stylistic stable.

But at the very time that Jimmy Harrison appeared to have absorbed much of Teagarden's rhythmic assurance into his playing, Jack Teagarden himself had already begun to round off the rough edges of his style and settle for a more placid approach, a process that was to continue throughout the Thirties. The symptoms went beyond the smoothing out of the tone referred to earlier. Stock phrases began to appear over some of the more familiar cadences of the blues and popular song. Blues choruses, if not repeated verbatim, took on a repetitive shape, often consisting of minor variations on a familiar structure. There is nothing disreputable about this. Few of the very greatest jazzmen have survived a lifetime of persistent improvisation without accruing a vocabulary of personal clichés with which to peg out, so to speak, the line of invention. Nor is it every jazzman of distinction who has been temperamentally disposed to keep pushing his style outwards in the direction of unexplored areas. If one feels some slight disappointment that Jack Teagarden appeared to draw in his musical horns so early in his recording career, it is because the very first records, revealing jazz trombone as it had never been heard before, aroused such high expectations—and still do when one listens to them again within their historical context.

Perhaps those expectations are in themselves misplaced. One of the choruses over which I am about to enthuse, the opening twelve bars of 'Knockin' a Jug', recurs in Jack Teagarden's contribution to a Red Nichols version of 'Basin Street Blues' made just ten weeks later. We must face the fact that a solo that can be played on record twice within three months might well have been conceived five years earlier on a gig with Peck Kelley's Bad Boys and trotted out a hundred times in the intervening years, and that Jack Teagarden was never, at any stage, the kind of jazz musician who will lay his reputation on the line with continuous creative progress. This gives us all the more reason for supposing that, in the encounter between Jack Teagarden and Jimmy Harrison, it was the former who wrought changes in the style of the latter and not the other way about.

Those who attach overriding importance to the role of improvisation in jazz may feel that, in the past few paragraphs, I have systematically destroyed Jack Teagarden's right to be included in this book at all! But the creation of jazz is a more mysterious process than the mere pouring out of spontaneous ideas. The requirements of 'improvisation' can be satisfied, in jazz terms, if an identical sequence of notes is played with the subtlest alteration in rhythmic emphasis, the slightest change in the use of dynamics or vibrato, the almost imperceptible raising or lowering of the emotional temperature. Likewise, 'originality' in jazz lies not only in the pattern of notes that is produced, but also in the instrumental tone or 'voice' in which it is uttered.

I know no better confirmation of this than in the comparison between the opening twelve bars of 'Knockin' a Jug' and the 'Basin Street Blues' solo with Red Nichols. The notes are identical for six of the twelve bars and the ensuing bars are very similar in shape. And yet 'Basin Street Blues' is merely a good solo, 'Knockin' a Jug' a great one. There is some mystery surrounding the circumstances of the recording. In his book, *We Called it Music*, Eddie Condon describes how he persuaded Tommy Rockwell of Okeh records to record a mixed group of black and white musicians featuring both Louis Armstrong and Jack Teagarden. Such politically daring sessions were not unknown—Jelly Roll Morton had recorded with the New Orleans Rhythm Kings as early as 1923, and Condon himself had just recorded a similar group for Victor records. But they were rare enough for Rockwell to have reservations. However, Eddie Condon's powers of persuasion are among the most solidly based of jazz legends. According to him, 'Louis Armstrong came on from Chicago that spring for a one-night stand at the Savoy Ballroom in Harlem with Luis Russell's Orchestra. Afterwards an impromptu banquet was staged in his honour. I looked around the table and shook my head; I had never seen so many good musicians, white and coloured, in one place at the same time. "You ought to make a record while Louis is here," I said to Tommy Rockwell, Armstrong's adviser at the time.' The upshot of this conversation was that Rockwell put back until the afternoon a session booked for Armstrong with the Luis Russell band, and 'the group made "Knockin' a Jug" and "I'm Gonna Stomp Mr Henry Lee" '.

At this point, doubts arise. For one thing, no trace has ever been found of the second title. For another, the actual recording of 'Knockin' a Jug' falls well below the Okeh company's standards at that time. The piano, played by Joe Sullivan, is distant and lacking in presence, and Kaiser Marshall's drums, using both wire brushes and sticks on the snare drum rim, dominate the proceedings. All in all, the recording sounds like something taken down during rehearsal or at a party. In a section on Louis Armstrong's recordings in the Max Jones-John Chilton biography, *Louis*, John Chilton confidently puts forward an account that differs significantly from Condon's. After referring to the scheduled session with Luis Russell, he goes on, 'All the previous night was spent celebrating with welcoming musicians, black and white. Louis, with his fellow revellers still in tow, arrived at the studio early. The party's warm-up on the impromptu blues, "Knockin' a Jug", was mercifully recorded for posterity by the enterprising studio engineer.'

The results favour Chilton's account, yet Eddie Condon was not a man given to boastful invention. It is probable that the truth lies between the two, and that the musicians arrived too late, or having 'knocked the jug' too enthusastically, for the arranged session to be completed.

Whatever the circumstances, we must be thankful that the one title emerged to mark the first meeting in a recording studio of Jack Teagarden and Louis Armstrong, and that their contributions were satisfactorily recorded. To say that between them, they dominated the performance is not to belittle the other solos. Eddie Lang had already shown himself in recorded duets with the New Orleans guitarist, Lonnie Johnson, to be well versed in the blues, and his twelve-bar chorus here is economical and convincing. Happy Caldwell had come to New York from Chicago some years earlier and established a reputation which is not satisfactorily explained by the few recordings which he made. His tenor solo, phrased in the manner of a trumpet, is attractive but seems to make rather heavy weather of the technical handling of the instrument. As I have already observed, Joe Sullivan's chunky barrel-house piano is almost obliterated by the elephantine soft-shoe shuffle of Kaiser Marshall's over-recorded brushes. But it is redolent with 'atmosphere' and contributes to the tastiness of the filling in a sandwich in which the strongest musical nourishment lies in the bread.

The opening phrases of Jack Teagarden's introductory solo would be enough to prove, had he never affirmed it himself, that the trombonist had listened avidly to the recordings of Bessie Smith. There is the *gravitas*, the immediate establishment of a mood that blends melancholy with commanding authority and proud dignity. The rawness of the phrases is counteracted by an immense poise and authority of execution, revealed in the perfect rhythmic timing, effortless articulation and complete tonal command. No white musicians of that period, and relatively few since, have so effectively combined a sophisticated technique with an understanding of the unorthodox characteristics of the blues. Of these, the most elusive are the so-called 'blue notes', produced when certain notes in the scale, most usually the third, fifth and seventh, are perceptibly flattened. The nearest that conventional European notation can get to these notes is to apply the 'flat' (♭) sign that lowers them by a semitone, turning E to E flat, for instance, in the key of C. But when the notes are played strictly according to such notation, the result is, at best, prim and colourless and, at worst, melodramatic or maudlin.

Much of the imposing character of Teagarden's solo derives from the masterly use of blue notes. The opening statement, for instance, starts with a positive and forthright two-bar phrase, not unfamiliar in the context of the blues, in which, after two introductory notes, the melody descends from an upper key note to the note an octave below by way of the notes of the major chord. This establishes the key of the piece in no uncertain terms. It is answered by a two-bar phrase with the reverse shape that takes the melody back to the upper key note by much the same route, using the third and the fifth as stepping-stones. As described, this is pretty naïve stuff. But reference to any one of Bessie Smith's recordings will show that the distortion of a naïve framework by the subtle bending of notes is the very stuff of the blues. In his second two-bar phrase, Teagarden comes to rest on a note (at the beginning of bar three of the chorus) which should, if it is to match the clarity of the opening phrase, be a straight fifth. Instead, the note starts a fraction below the fifth and drops downwards, giving a vaguely off-pitch effect which defies mathematical analysis but it is indescribably effective, introducing a fleeting element of doubt into the tonality established by the opening phrase.

A point that is often missed about these blue notes is that they are frequently directional, in the sense that the note seems to be straining away from its temporary tonality towards a preferred destination. In the fifth bar of the chorus, Teagarden plays an ascending phrase, from the third to the fifth, in which this upward straining effect is noticeable. On paper the notes would be written as D, E flat, E and F (the piece is in B flat), but by pitching the D noticeably sharp, he throws all the note placings out of true, in the deliberately casual manner of a blues singer. The 'vocalized' effect is enormously expressive, especially in the context of meticulously pitched playing.

One other striking use of instinctively off-pitch playing occurs at the beginning of the second chorus. In contrast to the measured steps with which the first chorus entered, this one is more impassioned and seemingly less articulate, with irregular phrases and long pauses. I say 'seemingly' because in fact the passage is superbly constructed for maximum emotional effect. Here is the urgent exhortation of the preacher leading the choir at the open-air church meetings to which Jack Teagarden used to listen as a boy back home in Texas. It is possible, too, that the notes which stutter so impatiently across the beat were influenced by Bubber Miley's similarly rhetorical muted cornet solo in Duke Ellington's 'Black and Tan Fantasy'. Two notes are involved in the first six bars of the second chorus, the B flat key note and a note of indeterminate pitch that hovers somewhere around the C and D flat. In other words it is neither a perfect second nor a minor third but a tone that approximates one or the other whenever it occurs. The way in which Teagarden builds strongly contrasting phrases out of these two notes underlines his rhythmic mastery. First, a whip-up to the upper note initiates a long phrase over two bars in which he plays crotchet triplets across the basic four beats in the bar on the B flat key note. One expects another whip-up at the end of the phrase, but it comes two bars later, tagged on the end of two further B flats which pick up, after a pause of almost a full bar, where the others left off. Two beats later the two notes alternate briefly, there is a further pause and back they come again at the junction of bars five and six, this time with more rapid and urgent alternation, to lead into a descending phrase which breaks the impasse. It is a fine example of the building up of tension with the simplest of basic materials. Essential to it is the use of the blue notes with all their subtle grades of pitching, giving the effect of a vital message striving for expression. Once the pattern is broken, there is an air of almost jaunty relief surrounding the remainder of the chorus, involving much skipping across the beat and a casually 'lipped' upward glissando—involving lip pressure rather than the crude use of the slide—that was a Teagarden trade-mark.

Since this chapter concerns Jack Teagarden, it is not the place to dwell on Louis Armstrong's solo that ends the piece. But it is beyond my will-power to deny myself the opportunity of pointing to two of its main features. One is the dramatic element which Louis introduced into instrumental jazz and which Duke Ellington, with his great sense of 'theatre' was among the earliest to exploit. The opening of the trumpet solo in the low register, heightened by a temporary cessation of the drumming as Kaiser Marshall juggles with brushes and sticks, is one of the most gripping theatrical entrances in all of jazz, combining an overwhelming presence, a feeling of high expectation and a certain dark foreboding that transcends the customary emotional range of the blues. This would be so much huff and puff without the second element, which is Louis Armstrong's capacity to conceive a solo as one developing unit rather than a succession of 'choruses'. Jack Teagarden's two twelve-bar choruses complement each other splendidly, but each is a self-contained unit capable of standing alone if the other were removed. Armstrong's solo, on the other hand, is indivisible. The veiled menace of the first twelve bars in the low register demands some kind of resolution, the impassioned leap into the upper register for the second twelve bars would sound ludicrously abrupt and melodramatic without the emotional build-up. It is an astonishing *tour de force*.

Jack Teagarden was never to rival Louis Armstrong as a dramatic performer in the grand manner. I have already noted that much of his standing as a great jazz master rests on innumerable exquisite cameos—brief choruses of matchless form and eloquence dropped into the middle of big band or Dixieland performances. Slow ballads apart, it is rare to find a Teagarden record in which he takes the lion's share of the limelight. My second Teagarden masterpiece is a rare exception and I have chosen it for that reason without prejudice to all the other fine examples of his work. It is also another blues, giving us the opportunity to compare it directly with his youthful work on 'Knockin' a Jug'.

'Jack Hits the Road' was recorded in 1940 during a session under the leadership of Bud Freeman. It says something about the pervasive myth of 'Chicago-style' jazz that, of Bud Freeman's

Famous Chicagoans, only Freeman and Dave Tough were actually born in that city. The remainder of the principals came from areas as far flung as Boston, Missouri, Buffalo and Texas. Most of what is generally considered a classic session was devoted to the sort of loosely knit, free-swinging, all-pile-in-together music that matured in New York rather than Chicago and inherited its genes from such diverse sources as the Original Dixieland Jazz Band, King Oliver and Louis Armstrong, the New Orleans Rhythm Kings and a heavy injection of Bix Beiderbecke. Jack Teagarden, with his preference for fluent, upper-register playing as against the trombone's limited harmonic role in the formal New Orleans ensemble, was ideally suited to these faintly anarchic surroundings, and titles such as 'Muskrat Ramble', 'Prince of Wails' and 'Shimme Sha Wabble' contain superb trombone solos.

The blues piece earned its title from a lyric which Jack put together for the occasion. 'I started up to see Bud Freeman, but I lost my way—and I thought for a minute I was on the road for MCA' made oblique reference to his current troubles with his big band and the booking agency that handled it. Apart from a chorus each from Pee Wee Russell and Bud Freeman, the whole track is devoted to the Teagarden trombone and voice. Since the work and place in jazz of Freeman and Russell will be considered more fully in the third volume of this series, when I shall discuss both big bands and small groups, I shall confine my comments here to the three trombone choruses by Jack that are spread through the record.

There are two things which one notices at once, coming to this record after listening to 'Knockin' a Jug'. One is that after Dave Bowman's chunky piano introduction, Jack Teagarden makes a similarly imperious entrance, ascending for his take-off to the same upper B flat key note. It was his favourite opening gambit in the blues, and he always attacked it with gusto. The second remarkable thing is the complete disappearance of the rapid 'shake' which intensified his sustained notes in his early recordings. I have remarked earlier that this characteristic, which he shared with most of the black trombonists of the late Twenties, disappeared quite early from his playing when he seemed to settle for a more placid approach. In his best work, its departure was compensated for by an even greater fullness and control of tone, as exemplified in the wonderfully sustained singing quality of that first high B flat.

We hear in this later performance that Jack Teagarden's conception of the blues had changed very little over the years, in contrast to Louis Armstrong's, whose blues work from the mid-Thirties onwards underwent drastic simplification. Jack's blues choruses were from the start built on a spare, economical framework in which Bessie Smith's influence was always to the fore. Here, in the first chorus, we have the twelve bars divided into broad, sweeping four-bar phrases, with a characteristic intensification of fast, decorative flourishes around the ninth and tenth bars. It is always dangerous to make pronouncements about tone on the strength of recordings, but it always strikes me that on this session, and in this number in particular, his playing regained in full and with interest the warmth and generosity of tone which it had sometimes lacked in the intervening years.

On careful listening, one discovers that the rhythmic modernity and assurance which marked Teagarden's earliest work had blossomed even more fully by 1940. The evidence is in the way in which his solo is draped, so to speak, over the regular four beats in the bar without ever adhering closely to them for support. In 'Knockin' a Jug', the high B flat that virtually launches the opening chorus is played firmly on the first beat of the bar, and we find that in the subsequent phrases, despite frequent across-the-beat excursions, the important notes similarly land on the beat. In 'Jack Hits the Road', the short climb up to B flat reaches it ahead of the beat, giving notice of an independence which is sustained throughout the chorus. Indeed, if some electronic device existed to remove all accompaniment from the record, the result would sound like an out-of-tempo trombone cadenza. The fact that we don't notice the absence of a strict toe-tapping tempo is further evidence of total jazz mastery.

The second chorus is particularly intriguing. Whereas in 'Knockin' a Jug', Teagarden raised the intensity of the second chorus by the impassioned use of blue notes, here he does the opposite, deliberately 'unblueing' the normally flattened seventh note of the scale and playing three repeated phrases based on the arpeggio of a major seventh. Here again, the timing is not what it seems. Each time that seventh is reached, it falls further behind the beat, successively defusing the threat of rhythmic squareness inherent in the notes themselves. In bars five and six there is a prime example of Teagarden's natural instinct for 'elegant variation', an ascending one-bar phrase that is then rearranged rhythmically in the most blithe way. In bar eight the 'blue' flattened seventh receives due recompense for having been shunned earlier on, emerging with a roar to initiate a final four-bar section that is pure, down-home blues.

Of Jack Teagarden's blues singing, opinions have over the years ranged from eulogy—'the only white man who could sing the blues authentically'—to dismissal from the blues purists. My own view is that, as a *jazz* singer, he showed all the qualities of rhythmic assurance, warmth of sound and effortless swing that belonged to his trombone playing, and they were consistently apparent whether he was singing a ballad, a breezy Dixieland standard or one of his stock blues variations. These latter tended to be stereotyped ditties on the 'Mama, Mama, Mama, why do you treat me so?' lines and, as such, neither deserved nor expected to be rated as profound blues singing. But taken in the context of other excursions into the twelve-bar blues idiom by jazz singers —Louis Armstrong, Mildred Bailey, Wingie Manone, Henry Allen, Ella Fitzgerald and others—they come out near the top of the pile. The single chorus here has the added attraction of some probing and sensitive backing from Pee Wee Russell's clarinet.

And finally to the last chorus, which follows the solos by Russell and Bud Freeman. It may be that Louis Armstrong's dramatic entrance in the low register on 'Knockin' a Jug' had lodged in Jack Teagarden's subconscious, for he adopts a very similar ploy for his re-entry. A more obvious precedent is the famous chorus in the New Orleans Rhythm Kings recording of 'Tin Roof Blues' which, since George Brunies recorded it in the early Twenties, has taken its place alongside the Alphonse Picou clarinet chorus in 'High Society' and King Oliver's 'Dippermouth Blues' solo on muted cornet as an instrumental set-piece. But somehow Teagarden invests the first low B flat, approached from the depths by a gruff upward glissando, with a much darker sense of foreboding, threatening, as did Armstrong's entry, more impassioned and explosive things to come. Compressed into a single chorus, Teagarden's dénouement comes sooner. After four bars of intensely sad soliloquy in the bottom register, he makes an unheralded leap of two octaves to unleash, over bars five and six, a great cry of anguish of such uncharacteristic volume that it causes a perceptible tremor of distortion in the recording. What follows is even more startling. Connoisseurs of Teagarden's work over the years are familiar with the decorative flurries, full of rapid turns and triplets and the cadenza-like, across-the-beat phrasing with which it was punctuated. Here, the same outbreak of complexity is used for more than decorative purposes. Something is needed to dispel the tension which the sudden impassioned outcry in bar six has generated. Like a cascade of molten larva after an eruption, the notes tumble across the ensuing three bars in a complicated and yet logical pattern that rivals Louis Armstrong's famous introduction to 'West End Blues' for intuitive, on-the-spot composition. To say that the long phrase is totally independent from the regular four-to-the-bar pulse is to risk underrating its musical skill. Any fool can close his ears to the beat and take off on an out-of-tempo joy ride. The way in which accomplished jazz performers can float above the beat, seldom if ever actually alighting on it, and yet remain firmly and audibly in touch with it, is one of the qualities in the term 'swing' that defies verbal definition. Throughout, 'Jack Hits the Road' demonstrates the art at its highest, and never more so than in the magnificent last chorus.

Art Tatum

COUNT BASIE ONCE TOLD, in an interview, of his first encounter with Art Tatum. He recalled (and I reconstruct the quotation from memory): 'We were playing in Toledo, Ohio, and everybody's talking about this young piano player they have there, how great he is. After a while this young fellow comes up and asks if he can play a number. I moved off the piano stool, but stood nearby so that I could move back real quick if necessary. Well, I'm still standing there . . .'

Count Basie is a notoriously modest man, but his dumbstruck reaction to the youthful Tatum's playing is shared by every other contemporary musician. Fats Waller, so legend asserts, once stopped playing when he saw Art Tatum walk into the premises, announcing to the audience, 'I play piano, but God is in the house tonight!' In an autobiographical section in Stanley Dance's book, *The World of Earl Hines*, that other great pianist is more explicit. 'Art . . . didn't know anything but playing the piano, and that's all he wanted to do. He lived with the piano, day and night. Every time he saw one, he was playing. I don't think he really knew how much he could play. He was certainly one of the greatest and most individual pianists I've ever heard in my life. He could do as much with his left hand as most people could do with their right. I never did try to have a jam session with him, because I knew exactly what this man could do. There are many who are sorry that they did!'

Many indeed! Like an iceberg, Art Tatum's professional career presented only a small fraction of itself to be chronicled in terms of engagements, tours and recording sessions. Born and raised in Toledo, he was working steadily in local clubs in 1926 when he was only sixteen years old. Three years later, he procured a contract with a local radio station which lasted two years and helped to establish a reputation already being spread by the word of mouth of such as Count Basie and other travelling musicians. In the early Thirties, he went to New York, having been recommended by the pianist Joe Turner as accompanist for the singer, Adelaide Hall. In 1933, he recorded the first of the piano solos which were to occupy by far the largest space in the catalogue of his work on record. From then on until his death in 1956, he worked mostly as a club pianist—in Chicago, on the West Coast and, briefly in 1938-9, in Britain and Europe. But it was to New York, whether it be on 52nd Street in the Thirties or at Clarke Munroe's Uptown House in the Forties, that Art Tatum belonged for most of his creative life. His highest peak of commercial success came in the World War II years when the Art Tatum Trio with guitarist, Tiny Grimes, and bassist, Slam Stewart, broadcast prolifically on programmes aimed at US Forces the world over. Altogether, his was a relatively unruffled musical career, although even he, forerunner as he was of many of the innovations that Modern Jazz was to bring in the late Forties, felt a cold draught from the obsession of critics, bookers and the jazz public with the rival claims of Revivalism and Bebop. The crowning achievement of his last years was a monumental series of recordings, as soloist and with such distinguished contemporaries as Ben Webster, Benny Carter and Roy Eldridge, made at the instigation of impresario Norman Granz. The project was finished in March 1955. In November of the following year, Art Tatum died.

The cause of his death was uraemia, a kidney disease. The reason why it should have carried him off at the early age of 46 leads us straight to that submerged area of Art Tatum's career to which I referred earlier. After-hours sessions, in which clubs sporting (and paying) no more than a trio could confidently expect to be inundated with star soloists in a gladiatorial frame of mind, are nowadays largely things of the past. It is not simply that musicians, or their union representatives, became wary of the opportunity for exploitation inherent in such profligate distribution of unpaid talent. As musicians have increasingly moved towards 'doing their own thing' in musical surroundings of their own idiosyncratic choosing, the common ground of popular songs, show tunes and blues on which the older players would stage their tests of improvisational skill has been deserted. The 'Lot Vacant' signs began to go up in the early Forties when the young 'modernists', either by accident or design, devised a new musical code that effectively kept the masters of a previous generation off the stand. Before that, in every city where social conditions offered round-the-clock entertainment, epic subterranean battles raged. Whether it was Willie the Lion Smith resisting the challenge of Fats Waller, Louis Armstrong fighting off Jabbo Smith or Louis Metcalf, or Coleman Hawkins battling his way out of an ambush laid by the fierce tenor men of Kansas City, no jazz hero, however much he was revered, was immune from the gauntlet.

In this nocturnal jungle, Art Tatum was in his element. The picture we have of his progress through it, built as it necessarily is on hearsay that belongs to legend rather than verifiable history, is a fascinating one. The cornetist Rex Stewart recalled having heard him in Toledo in 1926 or '27 and being amazed that the young virtuoso was humble and insecure, expressing himself not yet ready to 'make it in the big city'. A few years later, with innumerable encounters such as that with Count Basie behind him, the attitude was different. He is alleged to have told bandleader, Don Redman, 'Tell them New York cats to look out. Here comes Tatum! And I mean every living "tub" with the exception of Fats Waller and Willie the Lion.'

Much of the background to Tatum's nocturnal career in New York comes from an interview which pianist, Billy Taylor, gave to jazz writer, Orin Keepnews, printed in the book *The Jazz Makers*. Taylor recalls that Art Tatum 'would usually sit around for quite a while before he'd feel ready to play'—a situation which satisfied club owners who had enticed in other pianists worth hearing and didn't wish to have them put to flight before time. So it might have been seven or eight in the morning before Tatum started. As his fame increased, his procedure became more and more lofty and Olympian. He would visit the clubs with a protégé in tow, like some medieval monarch with a trusted knight at his elbow. In Los Angeles in the mid-Forties, Billy Taylor fulfilled this lieutenant's role. Tatum would seek out the top man in the region. 'He'd know that fellow's best number,' recalls Taylor, 'and he'd ask me to play it, to sort of bait the guy. I wouldn't know what was going on, so I'd play it. Of course, if I (or any of Art's boys) were getting carved, he'd just step in and take over.'

In an appreciative sleeve-note to a posthumous album by the superb stride pianist, Don Lambert, Dick Wellstood allowed himself an anti-Lambert story which illustrates the magisterial attitude which Art Tatum acquired towards his challengers: 'One night, Lambert got all liquored-up in Jersey and headed for Harlem, looking to do battle with Tatum, who was generally acknowledged to be the king. He found Tatum and Marlowe Morris (considered second only to Tatum), sitting in the back room of some bar. Lambert flung himself at the piano, crying, "I've come for you, Tatum!" and things of that nature, and launched into some blistering stride. Tatum heard him out. When it was all over and Lambert stood up, defiant, Tatum said quietly, "Take him, Marlowe." '

There is a danger, in recounting anecdotes such as these, that the newcomer to jazz will receive the romantic notion that all jazz is created in the heady atmosphere of a tournament, a sort of world championship prize-fight set to music. The impresario, Norman Granz, who devised and presented the touring package show, *Jazz at the Philharmonic*, was once reported as summarizing his policy by saying that he provided the best possible working conditions for the great musicians who toured with him—'but when they get out on that stage, I want blood!' One has only to listen to the live recordings of his concerts to realize that some musicians thrive under such competitive, gladiatorial conditions and others do not. 'Cutting contests' have played an important role in jazz history, concentrating the minds and raising the ambitions of those whose role has been to extend the boundaries of instrumental technique. But as a means of judging a musician's creative worth, they are no substitute for considered critical assessment. In refusing to do battle with Art Tatum, Earl Hines was not admitting inferiority. He was simply declining to offer himself for judgement on those terms. One can reel off a list of fine jazz artists—Bix Beiderbecke, Johnny Dodds, Benny Carter, Jack Teagarden, Bobby Hackett, Johnny Hodges, Buck Clayton, Count Basie, Miles Davis—whose talents were not designed to prosper in the atmosphere of a jousting arena.

Having said this, one must go on to confess that 'considered critical appraisal' often did scant justice to Art Tatum during his lifetime. In the Thirties and again in the 'revivalist' Fifties, it was easy to find jazz *aficionados* who did not consider him to be a 'real' jazz performer, as witness the fact that in widely read and authoritative books on jazz by the Americans, Wilder Hobson and Winthrop Sargent, and British writers, Iain Laing and Rex Harris, his name does not even appear in the index. In the majority of commentaries by writers of wider knowledge and vision, you will find praise for his brilliance hedged with a thick outcrop of 'ifs' and 'buts'—for instance, the judgement by Whitney Balliett, jazz critic of the *New Yorker*, that 'if Tatum had played with more musicians of [Jo] Jones's strength, he might in time have pocketed some of his insuperable fireworks and got down to business.'

To understand the yawning gulf between the views of many critics and those of musicians of Art Tatum's generation and since, it is necessary to digress for a moment on the prickly subject of 'technique'. I say 'prickly' because the time is not so very distant when 'technique' was a dirty word in the terminology of jazz. We have to remember that the first generations of jazz writers consisted predominantly of enthusiasts who had little musical training, and indeed declared a bias against schooled or 'conservatoire' music. If many of their idols were self-taught musicians who defied the academic rules of music, then it seemed justifiable that they should be judged on the same terms. Thus we find that much critical writing of the Thirties, Forties and, so far as traditional jazz was concerned, Fifties was expressed in terms of abstractions such as 'feeling', 'sincerity', 'swing' and 'hotness' rather than in analysis of the actual notes or harmonies which were being played.

One must add to this the fact that much of that early criticism had strong sociological, if not political, undertones. In the pages of the now defunct British magazine *Jazz Music*, published in the late Forties, jazz was once lengthily discussed, by pundits on both sides of the Atlantic, as 'the music of the proletariat'. And, generally speaking, there was a tendency to think of jazz as the expression of an underprivileged and oppressed minority which was somehow betrayed by too great an assimilation of established and alien musical practice. In extreme instances, a patent inability to handle an instrument properly and produce the ideas which the player had in mind actually commended that musician to some listeners, who took it as a demonstration of 'sincerity'. In this climate, it is not surprising that Art Tatum, who appeared on the jazz scene with a piano technique unrivalled in all of jazz, was given a reserved reception. Musicians, on the other hand, to whom the acquisition of instrumental skill is of central importance, could have been expected to take a position at the other extreme, applauding a fellow-artist in much the same way that athletes will applaud a colleague who has far out-stripped them.

In reality, the question of technique and its application in jazz is far more complex than these two extreme positions suggest. One can best circumvent profound philosophical discussion on the role of primitivism and sophistication in art by calling in Duke Ellington, whose rare excursions into musicology were often wise and penetrating. An interviewer once asked him to comment on the discrepancy in technical prowess between two of his featured trumpeters. 'Let's be like the businessmen and talk in percentages,' said the Duke. 'Nobody plays a hundred per cent of the instrument. But some guys play ninety per cent of the instrument, and that's great. Another guy will play just ten per cent of the instrument—but on that ten per cent he'll be better than anyone else in the world.' Musicians as diverse as clarinettists Edmund Hall, Pee Wee Russell and Jimmy Guiffre, trumpeters Ray Nance, Max Kaminsky and Miles Davis, pianists Count Basie, Jess Stacy and Thelonious Monk—the reader can make up his own lists—have demonstrated that original, diverse, profound and, in some instances, highly influential jazz can be created with an instrumental technique that falls far short of virtuosity. But fit into these categories the names of Benny Goodman, Barney Bigard and Buddy de Franco, the early Louis Armstrong, Clark Terry and Dizzy Gillespie, Art Tatum, Bud Powell and Oscar

Peterson, and it becomes clear that the converse is also true. Each group has its own special pitfalls—inarticulacy, slow-footedness and poor execution in the first, garrulity, flashiness and dexterity for its own sake in the second—and both share the proneness to repetition, platitude and cliché which is the occupational hazard of every improvising jazzman.

Am I saying, then, that technique is an irrelevance, to be dismissed from our minds when judging the final product? If we are to apply strictly the refined principles of high art, I suppose the answer should be 'yes'. But in reality, for better or worse, jazz has shown itself, in the brief sixty-year span of its overt existence, to be the most human of all the arts. Despite the social elevation of jazz from the brothels and seedy nightspots to the concert platform and the recital room, jazz enthusiasts resolutely continue to refer to their idols in terms which, in matey familiarity, go far beyond the call of democracy and social equality. Europeans, brought up in a tradition which would regard the public reference to Fred Delius, Fats Handel or Hector 'Red' Berlioz as grotesque, have taken naturally and unselfconsciously to the native American habit of applying nicknames, abbreviations and descriptive tags to citizens great and small.

This is not the frivolous point which it may seem. Unlike so-called classical music, jazz is not the distillation of a composer's personality. Taking 'composer' to mean an improvising musician, jazz offers the raw spirit, impurities and all. A jazz fan need go to no biographical dictionary to learn that Ben Webster was emotional, Roy Eldridge aggressive, Pee Wee Russell shy. The personality is not only tightly woven into the music, it is essential to our response to it. It used to be said that Benny Goodman would visit Eddie Condon's club in the Forties especially to hear Pee Wee Russell extricating himself from the labyrinths into which his melodic explorations would sometimes accidentally lead him. By the same token, the listener who did not confess to relishing Art Tatum's technical magic for its own sake would be taking a more clinical attiude to the music than most.

To enjoy and admire Art Tatum as a jazz musician, it is essential not to be overawed by the elaborate genuflexions of critics and musicians alike in recent times. Fats Waller notwithstanding, Tatum was not God, neither was he Superman. As many commentators have remarked, his playing incorporated every facet of jazz piano style that preceded or was contemporary to him, and foreshadowed much that was yet to come. His essays into the boogie-woogie idiom (which he did not despise and eschew as did his idol, Fats Waller) were lightweight and superficial compared to such specialists in the idiom as Albert Ammons and Tatum's somewhat unlikely friend and sidekick, Meade Lux Lewis. His straightforward blues playing, though better than critics have acknowledged in the past, quite often subsided into luxuriant, feather-bedding harmonies that softened the firm and muscular outline of the best blues. And there were times when the thematic content of his solos almost vanished beneath the decorative runs and embellishments, like a Christmas tree groaning invisibly under an excess of tinsel and silver balls. To assert that any criticism of Tatum is *lèse - majesté* is to do injustice to the genuinely startling and astonishing flashes of inventive brilliance in which his work abounds.

The origins of Art Tatum's style—and, indeed, of his *modus vivendi*—lie in Harlem stride piano. 'Fats, man. That's where I come from,' was no casual affirmation of his. As we have seen, he eagerly assimilated the stride pianist's zest for battle, about which he must have heard from the New York musicians who passed through Toledo. He carried to extremes the stride men's propensity for flashy technical devices with which to floor an opponent. The existence in his repertoire of such clear favourites as Dvořák's *Humoresque* and Massenet's *Elegie* carried on the Harlem pianists' tradition of giving stride treatment to chosen items from the classical repertoire. And, although he greatly extended its scope, he based his left-hand work on the 'oom-chah' alternation of bass note and middle register chord cluster from which, according to the most plausible definition, the term 'stride piano' derived. Predictably, as a young modern, he moved away from the ragtime affiliations of the style, preferring to work predominantly on material taken from contemporary Tin Pan Alley. But among his relatively few compositions, there are some which suggest that he could well have contributed as rich a collection of original rags as James P. Johnson and Willie the

Lion Smith, had he been so inclined. There's one piece in particular, with the appropriately raggy title 'Gang o' Notes', that is
a dazzling up-dating of the idiom. Recorded as late as 1944, it has
all the elements of the old Harlem piano test-pieces—several
developing themes, plenty of 'fingerbusting' virtuoso passages
and constant variation on the left-hand figures. One cannot help
thinking that the corporate body of contemporary pianists must
have heaved a sigh of relief that 'Gang o' Notes' did not establish
itself as an obligatory test-piece, in the way that James P. Johnson's 'Carolina Shout' did two decades earlier!

There were several elements in Art Tatum's style which
derived specifically from Fats Waller rather than from the stride
pianists in general. As I observed in the essay on Fats, he himself
extended and, in some degree, moved away from standard stride
practice. Compare Fats's famous solo blues 'Numb Fumblin' '
with the early version of 'St Louis Blues' which Tatum recorded
in 1933, and it is not hard to recognize the inspiration for the
Tatum habit of clothing a simple melodic or harmonic line in a
rippling, billowing mantle of cascading notes. From Fats, too,
came the use of 'moving tenths' in the left hand as a variation
from the 'oom chah' bass patterns of stride. This device of playing
simultaneous notes a tenth apart with little finger and thumb of
the left hand, and moving them smoothly upwards or downwards
depending on the direction of the harmony, would have appealed
to Art Tatum with his advanced harmonic sense. Since only two
notes of the chord are specified, there are opportunities for the
player to fill out the moving tenths with all sorts of enriching
harmonies. Art Tatum took full advantage of them, sometimes
modulating out of the original key and back again within the
space of a single two-bar movement.

Before looking at specific Art Tatum performances, we should
give some attention to the ways in which he digressed from
accepted stride practice, and they were innumerable. As I have
noted, his playing incorporated, in every phase of his career, all
the contemporary piano styles. When he first emerged on record
in 1933, the two predominant keyboard models were those of
Fats Waller and Earl Hines. There are two characteristics of the
latter which can be readily discerned in Tatum. One is the dis-

tinctive 'trumpet style'—the use of octaves in the right hand to produce a single declamatory melodic line in the manner of a trumpet player. In his later years Tatum was to develop this in a characteristic way, often interpolating a short octave passage in a run of notes at breakneck speed, with startling dynamic effect. The other Hines characteristic was more extensively used by Tatum, and has been the cause over the years of much of the adverse criticism of his style. It is the practice of suspending the stated rhythm of a piece for several bars, during which a complex elaboration is played over an implied beat which often does not declare itself until the regular left-hand rhythm is resumed. Thus, in their varying ways, Hines and Tatum often seemed to be challenging themselves to depart ever further and further from the regular pulse without, on their return to earth, having missed so much as a fraction of a beat. Response to Art Tatum's regular use of this device depends largely upon the listener's demands. To those—and I am not unsympathetic to them—who relish the exhilarating, roller-coaster momentum of an up-tempo Fats Waller solo, for example, the constant interruptions in a comparable Tatum piece will sometimes prove frustrating, especially as Tatum in full, two-handed career was irresistible. Against this, of course, it can be said that the Tatum pyrotechnics offer their own exhilaration.

As one would expect from an artist acclaimed as an original, there are elements in Art Tatum's style which are entirely his own, offering the analyst no very clear precedent. Most of them spring from his astonishing keyboard technique, which enabled him to perform, with apparent ease, feats of dexterity which, were they to occur to other pianists, would be rejected as an invitation to disaster, if not suicide. The ability to career at breakneck speed over the keys led him away from the normal practice of the stride pianists, which was to break a tune up into strong rhythmic patterns, pounding out percussive phrases by the fistful. There were times when he used this conventional stride method, but his more usual practice was to weave a complex, decorative tapestry around the theme, which itself was no more than a central thread, sometimes predominant, sometimes disappearing from view, and occasionally popping up unexpectedly in the low, left-hand

register or in the middle of a great spray of right-hand embellishment. Slow ballads were no deterrent to this practice. The device
known as 'double time'—superimposing eight beats at medium
tempo over four beats to the bar at slow tempo—had previously
occurred somewhat formally in the music of Jelly Roll Morton
and more loosely, in the improvising of Louis Armstrong and his
disciples. But its use was usually restricted to bravura passages or
'breaks'. With Art Tatum, it was far more central to his improvising
technique. Such was his facility that, in all but the fastest tempos
he could as easily *quadruple* the time—that is, rattle off a fusillade
of sixteenth-notes or semiquavers so that, in effect, he was
fitting four bars at high speed into one bar of the regular tempo.

As well as digital dexterity, this sort of playing called for an
advanced and sophisticated command of harmony. The extra
notes crowded into service must have somewhere to go, and this
meant adding to the basic chords all manner of harmonic detours
and diversions.

Art Tatum's ingenuity in this respect was limitless. The use of
passages based on the whole-tone scale and extended chromatic
harmonies were not unknown to the jazz of the early Thirties.
Bix Beiderbecke's piano solo 'In a Mist', recorded in 1927,
epitomized the fascination which the 'impressionist' European
composers such as Debussy and Ravel held for the young musicians
of his generation and circle. Notwithstanding the protests of the
advocates of New Orleans-style contrapuntal improvisation, the
arrival on the jazz scene of the arranger from the mid-Twenties
onwards made the exploration of so-called 'European' harmonies
inevitable, and the orchestrations of the bands of Paul Whiteman,
Frankie Trumbauer and, ultimately, Fletcher Henderson and
McKinney's Cotton Pickers, were rife with them. What distinguished Art Tatum from other musicians who toyed with these
(for jazz) advanced harmonic notions, was the easy and unself-
conscious way in which he incorporated them into his solo
improvisations. Rex Stewart propounds the theory that it was
hearing Art Tatum in Toledo in the late Twenties that inspired
Coleman Hawkins to move away from his Louis Armstrong-
inspired, stomping saxophone style towards the more fluent
method of 'running changes' (pursuing a continuous flow of

changing chords) which I discuss more fully in another chapter. Whether it actually happened in such a sudden, revelatory way or more gradually over the years, it seems more than probable that, in the challenging and competitive atmosphere of the early Thirties, Tatum's formidable combination of harmonic sophistication and speed of execution exerted an influence beyond the boundaries of piano playing.

I have in these essays reiterated to the point of tedium that selecting individual masterpieces is a difficult and invidious task. With Art Tatum, it is manifestly absurd. Art Tatum *was* a masterpiece, compounded of several hundred consistently fine, frequently superlative performances. Many of these were recorded in the later years of his life and are readily available in LP collections for the reader to study and enjoy. I am concerned here, as I have been with the other artists under discussion, with his early impact on the jazz scene of the Thirties, and both my selected subjects come from that period.

'Tiger Rag' was one of four solos recorded on Tatum's very first recording session in March 1933. A listener taking in these pieces for the first time will be struck by their enormous variety. 'Tea for Two' has, for Art Tatum, a curiously dated air, presenting such an anthology of Fats Waller mannerisms—heavy broken tenths in the left hand, skittish punctuations in the treble and characteristic stride figures in the upper register for climactic effect. 'St Louis Blues' is approached altogether more gently, padding along on a lush carpet of moving tenths in the left hand and lavishly decorated, as I have noted earlier, with fulsome cascades of notes. As the title might suggest, Duke Ellington's 'Sophisticated Lady' prompts the most 'modern' interpretation of the four in terms of both harmonic and rhythmic adventurousness.

'Tiger Rag' clearly appealed to Art Tatum as a vehicle for a breathtaking and all-conquering display of fireworks. There is plenty of evidence in his version that he took his cue in this respect from Louis Armstrong, who had already recorded two interpretations of the tune in which tempo and arrangement were designed to support an awe-inspiring exhibition of trumpet bravura. Art Tatum offers first a slyly humorous introduction, its out-of-tempo, impressionist langour giving no hint of the fronta assault on the senses that is to come. Then suddenly we are off into the opening theme. In the earliest versions by the Original Dixieland Jazz Band, one of which was dissected in *The Best Of Jazz* Volume One, much use was made of 'breaks' in which the clarinettist, Larry Shields, filled in with the sort of virtuoso phrases which the musical press used to call 'hot licks'. When Louis Armstrong adopted the tune, the clarinet breaks were developed into a running clarinet counter-melody over band riffs —a sort of supercharged version of the clarinet's decorative role in the New Orleans ensemble. Art Tatum, setting an even more headlong tempo than Louis, focuses his version on this clarinet part, firing off a succession of eighth-note runs that hurtle over the keyboard with barely a pause for breath. The interlude in the key of F which relieves the opening B flat theme highlights Tatum's two-handed facility. While the right hand continues to scurry hither and thither, the left hand assumes the staccato melody, both hands maintaining such steady momentum that one doesn't notice that the stated four-in-a-bar rhythm has been suspended. The second main theme, in E flat, begins as in the original, with more slashing breaks, and then settles into some romping stride that develops towards the end of the section into declamatory trumpet-style octave phrases.

We have not yet reached the main, trio section of the tune, and already almost all the resources of contemporary jazz piano have been drawn upon and demonstrated with masterly ease. What happens next shows that Art Tatum's much suspected technical virtuosity was no mere luxury to be turned on or switched off at will, but essential to his keen sense of construction. Where other pianists would have taken the arrival of the principal A flat theme as the cue to go stomping off down the final straight, Tatum 'holds that tiger' in a state of suspense. In demonstrating how he played the tune long before the Original Dixieland Band got hold of it, Jelly Roll Morton played a crashing bass discord with his elbow at those explosive points in the tune later assumed by the trombone, going so far as to say that the tune acquired its title when a listener remarked, 'Why, that sounds just like a tiger roaring.' Art Tatum eschewed such crude methods, replacing the tiger's roar with a sustained growl, a rumbling bass tremolo over which the right hand stabs out the riffs of the original. Since these riffs are phrased across the beat and the bass continuo has no noticeable pulse, the listener is left, for most of the chorus, in a state of anticipation. Bigger and better fireworks are to come, we feel, but only in his own good time. The tantalizing effect of this chorus is heightened by a glorious stroke of wit. Coming to the last eight bars of the chorus—that familiar sequence which Fats Waller used, in several of his compositions, as a pretext for a joyous, untrammelled romp—Art Tatum holds out on us once again, replacing the familiar chord sequence with dreamy, impressionist, whole-tone harmonies which echo that incongruous introduction. Were it not that their adverse comments were made retrospectively some years later, one might well think that Art Tatum was deliberately thumbing his nose at those critics who poured such scorn on technique and 'alien' European harmonies.

From this point on, the solo roars off in top gear into three choruses which 'build' in the manner, if not the established style, of the classic stride piano solo. The first consists of a stream of eighth-note runs similar to the opening passages but with greater flow and continuity. For the break, Tatum plays an escalating figure that overflows into the second half of the chorus, continuing upwards almost to the limit of the keyboard and then, with a hop and a skip, turning to descend again, like Fred Astaire dancing on a staircase. Technically, the passage is dazzling, the ascending figures being played in thirds so that, if one did not hear the left hand discreetly marking time throughout, one might justifiably assume that both hands were involved in them. The chorus ends in a riotous tumble of notes that congeal into a thunderous, shuddering chord, anticipating the style of the following thirty-two bars.

As these start, the emphasis is on rhythmic, jabbing chords in the right hand punctuating a series of moving bass figures suggestive of boogie woogie. Here one is strongly reminded of Louis Armstrong's treatment of the tune, in which he would blow repetitive high-note phrases over the bustling rhythm. Once again the break prompts a return to a more pianistic approach, and, behind a few tumultuous bars of stride piano, the shades of Fats Waller and Earl Hines can be discerned, smiling appreciatively but nervously. The trumpet-style ride-out to this chorus is pure Armstrong, and seems to signal the end of the piece. But the climax has yet to come. In the traditional firework display, after the rockets and catherine wheels and squibs have soared, whirled and crackled, it is the massed waterfalls of gold and silver rain which signal the finale and draw the biggest 'ooohs' and 'aaahs' from the audience. And so it is with Art Tatum's 'Tiger Rag'. The notes that cascade down no longer come singly or in thirds but by the splashing fistfuls over a pumping left-hand rhythm. If one remarks that the repetitive nature of the first and third beat chords of this stride bass (involving a sixth note that rings out rather monotonously), reveals in this early Tatum a rare glimpse of immaturity, one might seem to demand a technical miracle. Suffice it to say that the Tatum of later years did indeed bring variety to the traditional stride left hand in a miraculous way. When, with the return of the Louis-esque ride-out figures, the performance gallops to a close, the recording seems to lack only one thing—an incredulous voice saying, 'Phew!!!'

Devotees of Art Tatum who come to these first solo recordings late in the day, having been familiar with his later work, will be struck by the brilliance, even harshness, of the piano sound. No doubt some of this can be attributed to studio acoustics and the fact that accurate tuning does not appear to have been high among record companies' priorities in those days. But it is also clear that, as he developed away from the initial Fats Waller influence, Art Tatum cultivated a touch which became progressively lighter and more muted—so much so that even his last recordings, made in the hi-fi era of the mid-Fifties, sound today strangely distant and tonally subdued.

This change is noticeable when we come to my second Tatum selection, a remake of 'Tea for Two' recorded in April 1939. Already the sound is less brash, the texture more silky. Gone is the suggestion, discernible in the first recordings, of a shy and reflective youngster of relatively slight build trying to play in the manner of a rip-roaring twenty-stone extrovert. The most valuable legacy of Fats Waller remains intact—the ability to swing with an express train momentum. But of the mannerisms, no trace remains. Along with this lighter touch has come a more considered organization of material, the result no doubt of six years' work, mainly as a soloist, in clubs of a more intimate and sophisticated atmosphere than those in which the earlier stride pianists flourished.

Comparison between the 1933 and 1939 versions of 'Tea for Two' illuminate the change dramatically. The early version has a jaunty, Wallerish introduction in tempo, leading straight into three choruses of stride piano with relatively few innovations and refinements other than the wealth of decorative runs and bursts of double tempo in the right hand. The strongest hint of things to come occurs in the twentieth bar of each chorus, when Tatum employs a trick which he was to develop markedly in the later version. This is a brief shift of key, an episode no more than a bar in length in which the melody momentarily sidesteps into an adjacent key, rather as if the piano keyboard had been moved an inch or two to the right by a mechanical device. In the otherwise conventional harmonic surroundings of the early version, this movement is quite unexpected, characteristic of many such stimulating surprises which Art Tatum was to perpetrate upon his listeners before his career was over.

If we now concentrate on the second recording of the tune, we find it furnished with an out-of-tempo introduction and opening chorus, a familiar format nowadays when jazz in a concert hall or recital room ambience is commonplace, but unusual enough in the late Thirties to bring upon Art Tatum's head a further critical accusation, that he was no more than a superior cocktail pianist. The charge, still voiced occasionally today, seems to me to ignore the *quality* of the music in favour of its manner. It can only be refuted by pointing to the spare and muscular frame that lies beneath the decorative surface of Tatum's playing. Even in superior cocktail piano one would expect to hear the lush over-statement, indulgently perfumed harmonies and romantic *kitsch* of 'mood music'. What Tatum builds on the melodically unpromising see-saw movement of the Vincent Youmans song is a sober and firmly-constructed piece of composition in which no concession is made to the flippant sentimentality of the original. The repetitive melody line, a challenge to improvisation if ever I heard one, is tossed between right and left hand, between middle and upper register, with the utmost deftness. On the sparing occasion when extended or substitute chords are used—for example, in bar twelve of the opening chorus—they offer an astringent and bracing dissonance rather than extravagant seduction of the ear. And, as if to impose and sustain a sense of discipline and gravity upon the proceedings, Art Tatum ends each out-of-tempo section —introduction, opening chorus and coda—with the same austere, almost sombre middle-register cadence.

Had the performance consisted simply of that one introduction and chorus, played out of tempo, we would look upon it today as a little gem which raised the song 'Tea for Two' far above its modest station in life. But in Tatum's scheme of things it has a purpose beyond its own excellence. That purpose is to establish a calm and reflective mood from which to launch a couple of choruses which, to use a vulgar phrase for which I can find no expressive alternative, swing like the clappers. It is a device which Erroll Garner was later to borrow and extend with exhilarating effect, and it can only be brought off effectively by a jazz pianist with that total command of time that swing demands. The style of these gloriously propulsive choruses is stride piano, decorated without any loss of momentum with the familiar cascading runs over suspended rhythms. To substantiate my claim that Art Tatum's technical prowess could in itself stir the emotions and uplift the spirit, there is a 'break' spanning bars seven and eight of the first chorus which must surely draw spontaneous applause from any listener who is not crabbed by suspicion of 'technique'. Half-way through an escalating series of eighth-note triplets upon which most improvising pianists would need to lavish their un-divided attention, Tatum nonchalantly picks up the rhythm in the left hand with walking tenths that move in the opposite direction.

The 'break' in the middle of the chorus introduces another aspect of Art Tatum's playing which has attracted adverse criticism. Quoting brief excerpts from the classics or from popular song was not a device (some would say 'vice') originated by Art Tatum, nor did it end with him. In discussing Louis Armstrong's 'Sweethearts on Parade', I pointed to a quotation from 'High Society' which Louis had previously used, in a similar context, in his recording of 'Squeeze Me'. The very same quotation (from

the first two bars of Alphonse Picou's traditional clarinet variation)
occurs more than once in the solos of Charlie Parker. The newcomer to jazz who is encouraged by my earlier references to Louis
Armstrong's version of 'Tiger Rag' to explore that recording will
find at least three obvious quotes from sources as varied as 'The
Rising of the Lark', the 'National Emblem March' and *Pagliacci*.
The latter is used in a manner no less dramatic than in the original,
establishing the point that not all such quotations are for humorous
effect. One can best justify them by pointing to the conversational
aspect of jazz improvisation and drawing a parallel with the often
enlivening use of phrases from Shakespeare, Wordsworth, Damon
Runyan or Groucho Marx in casual talk. If overdone or inapposite,
they are a bore and, I am bound to say, *apropos* Art Tatum's
injection here (and elsewhere) of 'The Campbells are coming,
hurrah, hurrah', that I would have preferred it if the Campbells
had remained where they were.

But the episode is over in a flash and one need not make too
much of it either way. Before the chorus is ended there is a further
ecstatic 'break' to put censoriousness to flight, occurring in bars
twenty-five to twenty-eight. The guitarist, Everett Barksdale,
was once reported as saying, 'Art Tatum is absolutely infallible—
with a man like that there is no such thing as a mistake.' Those
who, like myself, prefer their jazz geniuses to acknowledge some
symptoms of human fallibility, will prefer Billy Taylor's recollection that Tatum encouraged him to make deliberate mistakes 'to
see how quickly you can recover'. When, in bars twenty-five and
-six, Art Tatum plays a left-hand run of ascending triplets, the
passage differs from the right-hand runs that precede and follow
it in that it is not continuous. There is a hole in the middle of it,
suggesting that his fingers may have baulked at the preposterous
demands made upon them at a moment's notice. If so, his powers
of recovery proved equal to the occasion. Without a fraction of a
beat's hesitation the triplets are resumed in bar twenty-six. They
are still trumbling up to their conclusion when, out of the sky, a
silvery cascade of treble notes come down to meet them. It is a
dour listener indeed who does not feel the urge to throw his hat
in the air at such a display.

The chorus that follows, the last in the piece, is justly famous among connoisseurs of jazz piano. Just as the deceptively placid opening section of the piece may be said to enlarge upon the sly, impressionistic introduction to 'Tiger Rag', so the device with which Art Tatum brings his performance to a climax may be called the apotheosis of the transitory shift of key to which I drew attention in the 1933 version of 'Tea for Two'. Jazz purists, past masters in the art of having it both ways, have complained that to modulate from a parent key to one a minor third away, only to return by semitone steps to the parent key, is no more than an empty piece of technical sleight of hand. These are the same people who allege that Art Tatum strayed from the true path of jazz towards 'cocktail', 'salon' or even 'concert hall' piano, turning a deaf ear to the fact that this bit of keyboard 'business', pursued in romping two-fisted style without any drop in swing or momentum, is the very stuff of the stride piano tradition. Years later, when the younger pianist, Bud Powell, came to record the 'Tea for Two', he borrowed this device of Tatum's in the same way that Fats Waller inherited tricks of the trade from James P. Johnson. No words on paper can describe the fluent ease with which Tatum negotiates the manoeuvre, carrying the melody with the left hand while at the same time continuing the 'oom-chah' rhythm of stride against bouncing counter-rhythms from the right hand. The change from the naïve, monotonous and subservient left hand heard in the climatic chorus of 'Tiger Rag' is miraculous.

Art Tatum is consistently cited in the summaries of jazz history as one of the forerunners of the modern jazz of the mid-Forties. In this respect, there is a startling piece of clairvoyance in the second eight-bar section of 'Tea for Twos' final chorus. In contrast to the scintillating runs that have characterized most departures from the melody hitherto, Tatum fills bars eleven to sixteen with abrupt, angular and rhythmically diverse, single-note phrases that belong stylistically to the 'bebop era' that was still six or seven years away. In the context of this superb final chorus, which with one vast stretch of the fingers links the eras of James P. Johnson and Charlie Parker, the term 'stride piano' acquires a new meaning.

Johnny Hodges and Benny Carter

IN VOLUME ONE OF *The Best of Jazz*, I compressed discussion of the two New Orleans clarinettists, Johnny Dodds and Jimmy Noone, into a single chapter. My reasons were several. Neither musician had a well-documented background history nor a career that went through a succession of developing phases. Neither was the sort of 'character' around whom anecdotes cluster. But between them, they dominated jazz clarinet for roughly a decade, offering contrasting models—a heavy, mordant blues style from Dodds, a lighter, decorative style from Noone—from which subsequent clarinettists could, and did, draw at will.

To a large extent, the same reasons prompt the conjuncture of Johnny Hodges and Benny Carter in one essay. There will be some who will bridle at the exclusion of altoist Willie Smith from my reckoning. It is customary in summaries of jazz history to speak of a 'triumvirate' of Hodges, Carter and Smith having dominated jazz alto style throughout the Thirties. But Willie Smith was a comparative latecomer on the scene, making his mark with recordings by the Jimmy Lunceford Orchestra which began to emerge in 1934—by which time both Hodges and Carter had influenced a whole generation. The same considerations apply to the iconoclastic Pete Brown whose 'jump' style, influencing the rhythm 'n' blues music of later times, will be discussed in Volume Three.

In the reminiscences of Harlem musicians, Johnny Hodges makes an appearance around the middle Twenties. Duke Ellington sets the scene in *Hear me Talkin' to Ya*: 'Small's [Small's Cabaret

Club, later the Paradise] was the place to go, the one spot where everybody'd drop in. And a lot of musicians from downtown, too. Jack Teagarden used to bring along his horn, and Benny and Harry Goodman, Ray Bauduc and a gang of others. Then on Sundays, Small used to hire a guest band, the best he could get, and there'd be a regular jamboree ... all kinds of musicians worked that job, Johnny Hodges, and guys from Chick Webb's band and a lot of others. There was always plenty of whisky around those places and the music would jump and everything else besides.'

The bandleader and saxophonist, Cecil Scott, remembered another meeting-place for musicians, the Capitol Palace, a more relaxed rival to the famous Cotton Club. 'When the other clubs closed, one by one their band members and patrons would drift into our spot, and musicians from such places as the Cotton Club, Club Alabam, Roseland, Paradise Inn, used to vie for the chance to sit in with us. We usually had a waiting line holding their horns against one far wall waiting turns. Fellows like Johnny Hodges, members of Fletcher Henderson's gang, Fats Waller, Earl Hines and fellows from Charlie Johnson's band, Luis Russell's band— all these and many others ... often we would pile out of the club about dawn, shouting and too excited to go to bed. There was an iron fence which divided Lenox Avenue at 135th Street and we would line up along it; it became the regular musicians' hang-out. We would cluster as thick as thieves discussing music and gossiping about fellow-players until maybe noon. Then home for an afternoon's sleep and that evening we'd begin the same routine.'

It is significant that these and other reminiscences of the period in Harlem around 1926-7 should single out the twenty-year-old Johnny Hodges for special mention. Clearly he had even at that early stage a quality which made him particularly memorable among the finest musicians in town, amongst whom were almost certainly the young Benny Carter and probably Coleman Hawkins, too. That quality is unlikely to have embraced technical pyrotechnics. In his autobiography, *Music is my Mistress*, Duke Ellington included an appreciation of Hodges in which he wrote, 'His sultry solos were not done in an attempt to blow more notes than anyone else. He just wanted to play them in true character, reaching into his soul for them, and automatically reaching every-body else's soul. An audience's reaction to his first note was as big and deep as most applause for musicians at the end of their complete performance.' These words are applicable to the very first recordings which Johnny Hodges made, from whose gritty grooves a powerful musical 'presence' emerges.

For a clue to the origins of his charismatic style, to which Duke Ellington retrospectively applied the fashionable term 'soul', we have available the saxophonist's own reminiscences in the book, *The World of Duke Ellington*, compiled by Stanley Dance. These go back beyond those of his contemporaries, to his first meeting with Sidney Bechet. As with most musicians' recollections, there is a certain conjectural quality about the date. Hodges recalls that he was thirteen when, through his sister, he was introduced to Bechet, who was in Boston playing in Jimmy Cooper's *Black and White Show*. But John Chilton's indispensable *Who's Who in Jazz* puts Bechet's stint with Cooper around 1923–4, when Hodges was seventeen or eighteen. The relevant part of the story is that Johnny Hodges met Bechet when he was a young musician in Boston and was given encouragement by him. In 1924, he travelled to New York to play with Bechet in a place variously known as the Club Bechet or Basha. (The second variation, with the final 'a' long as in 'day', is how many musicians, including Johnny Hodges, would pronounce Bechet's name.) 'He had a second soprano, a straight one, which he gave to me, and he would teach me different things in the duet form. Then I learned all the introductions and solos, and if he was late I would take over until he got there.'

In citing the origins of his own style, Johnny Hodges said, 'I had taken a liking to his [Sidney Bechet's] playing, and to Louis Armstrong's, which I heard on the Clarence Williams Blue Five records, and I just put both of them together, and used a little of whatever I thought of new.' The fact that the Blue Five records were issued during 1925 gives some idea of the period over which the Hodges style was taking shape. During that time, his working visits to New York were sporadic, and he constantly returned home to Boston, where he clearly made his own influence felt. In the final years of the Twenties, a procession of fine alto saxophonists followed Johnny Hodges from Boston into New York—Charlie Holmes, Howard Johnson, Harry Carney (before he turned to the baritone sax)—and all of them played in the Hodges style. In the Stanley Dance book, Harry Carney recalls the period when he first took up the alto. 'Now I felt the influence of Sidney Bechet and Johnny Hodges. Johnny and I used to live a few doors apart and we'd listen to all the records together ... Charlie [Holmes] used to sound like Johnny, because that was the accepted alto style in those days and everyone was trying to borrow ideas from Johnny and get his sound.'

Everyone in Boston, that is. In New York, there was another strong influence operating from the mid-Twenties onwards, tending to draw musicians away from the passionate, 'hot', blues-saturated music which Bechet and Armstrong purveyed towards a more reflective, carefully-structured approach. This was the influence of the white musicians, most of them working in such highly respected and commercially successful bands as those of Paul Whiteman, Jean Goldkette, Frank Trumbauer, Red Nichols and Miff Mole. Evidence is all around us of the part which these men played in the formative years of jazz. We shall soon see that the alternative which Benny Carter was to provide to the Hodges style was based on an admiration for Frankie Trumbauer, to whom Lester Young also gave acknowledgement. Though we may find it hard to believe, we must accept the word of Roy Eldridge that one of his earliest idols was Red Nichols. Several musicians who were sooner or later to join Johnny Hodges in the Duke Ellington band made no secret of their indebtedness to the white New Yorkers—trombonist Lawrence Brown to Miff Mole, Harry Carney to the bass saxist, Adrian Rollini, Rex Stewart to Bix Beiderbecke.

In no reminiscence that I have been able to find did Johnny Hodges make any reference to such players as Jimmy Dorsey or Frankie Trumbauer, to whom his fellow-saxophonists were listening with such respect. In a first draft of this chapter, I made the bold assumption that the Bechet influence, so richly endowed with passion and blues feeling, was strong enough to immunize his young protégé against seduction from that quarter. But after listening to all the very early recordings which Hodges made with

Duke Ellington, I have to modify it. It would indeed be surprising, in view of the general impact which the white players had on the New York scene, if the young Bostonian, so eager to take in everything that New York had to offer, had remained totally untouched by what was a prevailing fashion. There are hints, in the 1928–9 solos, of the doodling runs and self-consciously modish and angular phrasing that characterized the work of both Dorsey and Trumbauer. But hints they remained. In the one recording—a piece by Ellington called 'The Dicty Glide'—in which he does play in a strangely stilted, on-the-beat manner strongly reminiscent of Trumbauer, he is harnessed closely to the Duke's melody, the title of which ('dicty' was the equivalent of 'posh' or 'toffee-nosed' in Harlem slang) suggests that the composer was drawing upon musical high fashion.

On the whole, I believe that my first assumption was right. With the possible exception of the shallow upward glissando which was to become such a feature of his romantic playing in later years, the jazz style of Johnny Hodges shed all traces of white influence as it developed into maturity. By the time the Thirties dawned, the Bechet influence had completely reasserted itself, its sandpapery edge and sweeping turbulence smoothed and modified to reflect the young man's more equable temperament. Duke Ellington was an unqualified admirer of Bechet, and had employed him in one of the early manifestations of the Ellington band before Bechet's maverick instincts took him off on his lone trek across Europe. When Johnny Hodges eventually gravitated into the Ellington band, after a short engagement with Chick Webb's band, there was a certain inevitability about the move. I drew attention in Volume One to the links that Ellington's early music had with New Orleans jazz—to the origins of Bubber Miley's 'jungle' growling in the style of King Oliver, and to the close resemblance of pieces such as 'Creole Love Call' and 'Black and Tan Fantasy' to certain themes that Oliver used. When the New Orleans clarinettist, Barney Bigard, joined the band in late 1927, followed within a few months by Johnny Hodges with his Bechet sound, the New Orleans connection was immeasurably strengthened. Bigard was to leave after fifteen years, but Hodges remained, except for a brief four-year 'sabbatical' with a small group of his own in the early Fifties, until the day he died, from a sudden heart attack, in May 1970.

Few musicians in jazz history have led such a settled life, and those that come to mind were mostly Ellingtonians. The sturdy, unruffled temperament that made it possible reflects itself in the music of Johnny Hodges. From the time that his style became fully matured in the mid-Thirties to the day that he died several jazz revolutions later, he saw no reason to change it. He was one of the few musicians from the Swing Era who remained totally impervious to the revolutionary changes wrought by the beboppers in the mid-Forties. Indeed, though vulgarity was no part of his musical make-up, the only external influence to impinge upon his music appears to have been the rhythm'n'blues epidemic in the early Fifties that gave rise to rock'n'roll. With his own small group, his intense but highly controlled and economical blues playing was often harnessed to a fashionable shuffle-rhythm with much rugged riffing and belabouring of the off-beat.

It was in his refusal to soften or decorate the stern simplicity of the blues that Johnny Hodges revealed most consistently the influence of Sidney Bechet. Harry Carney's reference to the 'sound' which other altoists tried to emulate draws attention to an aspect of jazz playing which is sometimes overlooked or at least downgraded in all the discussion about melodic, harmonic and rhythmic development. In his obituary remarks about Johnny Hodges, Duke Ellington wrote: 'Never the world's most animated showman or greatest stage personality, but a tone so beautiful it sometimes brought tears to the eyes—this was Johnny Hodges.'

The notion popular among the *avant-garde* in all branches of music that, to paraphrase Marshall McLuhan, 'the sound is the message' (rather than its organization into melodic lines or harmonic or rhythmic patterns), is not totally original, although they characteristically take it to extremes. In the immediate post-World War II days, when 'modernists' and 'traditionalists' in jazz were at each other's throats, Dizzy Gillespie was once subjected to a so-called 'blindfold test' in which, among others, a recording of a blues by Sidney Bechet was played to him. He identified Bechet, but showed no interest in the performance, simply asserting 'Nothing happens'. Writing about this some time later, I made the point that Dizzy's lack of enthusiasm was understandable. As a musician, he was preoccupied with a whole range of experiments and innovations in the context of which the Bechet solo was, indeed, quite devoid of incident. To the listeners, however, who rated the Bechet performance among the jazz classics, a subjective response to the *sound* of the music was more relevant than the nuts and bolts of musical organization. To them, the starkly simple phrases were given profound and powerful meaning by a range of musical effects—involving the manipulation and variation of tone, articulation and volume—just as complex and mysterious to the layman as Dizzy's theoretical explorations.

This mastery of sound was the most valuable asset that Bechet bequeathed to Johnny Hodges. Adapted to the younger man's quite different personality and temperament, it produced some of the most lordly music heard in jazz. Visitors to an Ellington concert during the touring years of the Fifties and Sixties will have etched in their minds the picture of Johnny Hodges emerging, with a routine show of reluctance, from the front rank of the orchestra to play his set of solo features, taking up a golfer's stance with legs wide apart and raking the auditorium with a huge sound the very authority and perfection of which had about it a touch of disdain. A British critic once noted how the soloist's eyes would sweep from one side of the hall to the other 'as if he were counting the exits' (the probing beam of a searchlight always came into my mind), and this combined with the voluminous swelling tone to complete the image of a man almost arrogantly sure of his command of both his music and his audience. Johnny Hodges was small and square in stature, and when he was not actually playing, his features, with the widely spaced, heavily lidded eyes, long muzzle and spacious upper lip that earned him the youthful nickname 'Rabbit', would assume the weary and detached expression of a minor diplomat enduring a tedious conference and wishing devoutly that he were elsewhere. But behind the alto saxophone he was a giant.

It is no surprise that from the outset Duke Ellington, with his keen ear for the dramatic effect, assigned special roles to Johnny Hodges. In fast numbers his solos had an exultant, strutting quality to be found in the Bechet-Armstrong collaborations which he so much admired. With his every entrance, the music positively jumped for joy. But his very first session with the Duke showed another side to his music. 'The Mooche' is an Ellington classic, bursting with that eerie atmosphere which Ellington always seemed able to evoke in a recording studio as well as on stage. Here Hodges demonstrated an ability to match the sinister 'jungle' growling of Bubber Miley and Tricky Sam Nanton with blues playing that combined the declamatory and exhortatory manner of the street-corner preacher with a quality altogether darker and more menacing. Ellington's music around the start of the Thirties was much affected by black church music, an important aspect of his beloved Harlem, and several compositions—notably 'Echoes of the Jungle' and 'Saturday Night Function'—have a distinctly 'gospel' flavour. The former is a Hodges masterpiece in which he invokes the Bechet spirit to match, and even surpass in sheer 'presence', the mood of heavy foreboding established by the muted and open trumpet of Cootie Williams and the low-register clarinet of Barney Bigard. Later on, Duke Ellington and his collaborator, Billy Strayhorn, were able to draw upon another facet of the versatile Hodges style by featuring him in compositions—'Passion Flower', 'Daydream' and so on—of a lusciously warm and romantic kind.

The reader will gather, from the way in which I linger over these examples of the Hodges mastery, that any one of them would keep me happily employed for the next ten pages or so. But the two Johnny Hodges recordings which I have chosen to bring into sharp focus come from the period at the start of the Forties, when the combination of a fully matured style and relatively advanced recording techniques enable us to appreciate to the full the talent that had set the pace for a decade and a half.

It is symptomatic of the magnetism which he could exert even from the impersonal grooves of a gramophone record that we tend to refer to Ellington's 'Never No Lament' as a Johnny Hodges feature, even though he plays for less than one chorus and shares the solo honours with Cootie Williams, Lawrence Brown and the Duke himself. The composition has an involved history. It was originally conceived as a counter-melody to the tune 'I Let a Song Go Out of My Heart', an Ellington hit of 1938. In *Music is my Mistress*, Duke Ellington recalled: 'In preparing my big song of the season for the Apollo [Theatre], I decided to do a new arrangement with rather a strong counter-melody. Opening day, I soon learned that the audience, as always, wanted to hear the version they had heard on the air. So we took out the new chart after the first show and went back to the old arrangement, and that's the way it stayed. The following year, 1939, the new arrangement was reworked and recorded as 'Never No Lament', which brings us to another later story.'

That story is now part of popular music history. 'Never No Lament' was provided with lyrics by Bob Russell and published as 'Don't Get Around Much any More'. With recordings by, among others, the popular Ink Spots, the song became a hit which surpassed the success of 'I Let a Song Go Out of My Heart'.

As was often the case with Ellington instrumentals-turned-popular-song, the original band version is greatly superior to the song. With the Duke, a three-minute recording was never presented simply as a tune dressed up with an introduction and arrangement, but as a composition of which all the components were of essential value. The piece starts with a statement by the muted brass of the familiar theme—but in a very unfamiliar form. The melody over which the lyricist draped the words 'Missed the Saturday dance' is presented in two chunky, rhythmically-symmetrical phrases, as it might be '*Missed* the Sa-*tur*-day dance', with sinuous answering phrases from the saxophones. Here again is the 'churchy' feeling that pervaded so many of Ellington's pieces. It is intensified in the second eight bars, which do not match the opening, but offer an alternative, if closely related theme, in which Ellington's piano does the haranguing and Lawrence Brown's trombone the response over congregational chords from the band. We are now only forty seconds into the piece, and already an evocative atmosphere has been established, preparing the way for a solo 'voice' in a manner that, for all its simplicity, is worthy of grand opera.

Notwithstanding the title, Johnny Hodges clearly interprets the piece as a lament, taking his cue from the closing phrase in the opening theme which, in contrast to the song version, uses the blues minor third interval (where the words 'any more' occur in the lyric) with a pervasively melancholy effect. Indeed, the Hodges solo is a blues in everything but its actual musical shape. Jazz people use the word 'wailing' to denote a certain passionate intensity and drive, but here Hodges wails in every sense of the word. The F note from which the tune's opening phrases descend (the piece is in D flat) is attacked each time from below in the manner of Bessie Smith and the classic blues singers. The first time, he holds it for its normal length, but the second time it is attacked more violently and prolonged with the characteristic Hodges 'swell', pulsating with vibrato. And from this voluminous note the tune's descending phrase is broken up and extended into a stream of agitated semiquavers or sixteenth-notes in double-time, a touch of pure Bechet. When, at the end of the first eight-bar section, he plays without variation the phrase to which the title words were eventually put, he affirms the blues affiliations of the original piece by hitting almost every note marginally off pitch, a blues subtlety which, through the ages, has been the despair of musicians trained in a classical school that acknowledges no fraction of pitch smaller than a semitone. In the second eight-bar section, the ghost of Sidney Bechet is evoked even more vividly in the opening phrase when, once again, the F provides a vehicle for a swelling wave of sound that breaks in a flurry of scattered notes.

It is neither necessary nor, indeed, possible to spend time dissecting the rest of this Hodges solo. His style of improvisation (or, more strictly, of solo-building, since he often repeated a solo once it had become set) adhered closely to the blues tradition, in which the central structure of the theme remained intact save for some minor variations, while the principal embellishment was confined to the spaces in which, in a classic blues, the accompaniment would fill in. As we shall see in a moment, this contrasts strongly with the approach of those contemporaries of Hodges who would use a theme or 'tune' as a base upon which to build what amounted to a fresh composition. Like Bessie Smith and, later, Big Joe Turner, Johnny Hodges had the power to move the listener mightily with the simplest of melodic variations. Thus, after a middle-eight in which the whole orchestra 'sings the blues' lustily, Johnny Hodges returns to the now familiar theme but, in the third and fourth bar, replaces it with an anguished, contorted phrase in which, amidst much twisting and sliding among the notes, his alto-saxophone tone is attenuated to approach that of the soprano sax. In these final eight bars, blues all the way, we can see clearly why Hodges was regarded with such awe by contemporary saxophonists whose speed of execution and complexity of thought equalled and, in some cases, surpassed his. They may have been able to dazzle and astonish by their agility and ingenuity. He could cast a spell with one note. As 'Never No Lament' continues on its stately way, with respectively fierce and mournful contributions from Cootie Williams and Lawrence Brown, it is the Hodges chorus that stays in the mind, a jewel in the superbly contrived setting.

In the later years of his life, Johnny Hodges was rarely featured by Duke Ellington in up-tempo numbers, probably because the technical advances in jazz and the extended concert-hall format called for more complex and energetic displays than he was able—or willing—to provide. But from time to time, usually in informal, small-group sessions, we would be reminded of the joyful and exhilarating side of his playing. In the late Thirties, the agent and impresario, Irving Mills, who then handled Duke Ellington's affairs, instigated a series of recording sessions in which star Ellington soloists were featured as the leaders of small groups from within the band, invariably with the Duke himself at the piano. Known nowadays as 'the Ellington small groups', these sessions, led by Barney Bigard, Rex Stewart and Johnny Hodges successively, inevitably exuded an Ellingtonian flavour, with the Duke providing both compositions and arrangements. Of them all, it was the Hodges sessions which reflected most strongly the distinctive musical taste and background of the temporary leader. Many fine blues pieces later featured in the Ellington band's repertoire—'Wanderlust', 'Jeep's Blues', 'Things Ain't What they used to Be'—had their origins in these sessions, as did the romantic pieces with which Billy Strayhorn brought out the lusher, more sophisticated side of Hodges. But in amongst the slower numbers were up-tempo pieces—'The Jeep is Jumpin'',
'Good Queen Bess', 'Squatty Roo'—which bear an unmistakable Hodges stamp ('Jeep' was another sobriquet bestowed upon

Johnny Hodges at a time when the band broke out in a rash of nicknames derived from the 'Popeye' comic strip).

'Squatty Roo', a reference to the composer's shortness of stature (originally, and still often, misspelt as 'Squaty Roo'), is a favourite of mine for several reasons. It was recorded during the short time in which the Ellington band enjoyed the services of the brilliant young bassist, Jimmy Blanton. Condensed into a mere two-and-a-half years with Ellington before he died at twenty-one of tuberculosis, Blanton's recorded work had a mighty impact upon jazz history. As I will come to in the chapter on Lester Young, the Count Basie rhythm-section of the mid-Thirties radically changed the role of piano, guitar, bass and drums in jazz accompaniment, achieving with a crafty distribution of effort and responsibility greater flexibility and swing than the previous 'all hands to the pump' approach could achieve. In the process, the fine bassist, Walter Page, was relieved of the necessity to pound up and down the arpeggios of the basic chords as his predecessors had done. Harmony and drive were provided in a more subtle way, with the bass helping to define the harmonic progress with a 'walking' movement up and down the scale rather than giving strict attention to every note in the chord. Page was a tower of strength within the Basie section, but it required a player of more precision and agility to take full advantage of the freedom which his new style offered. The man for the occasion was Jimmy Blanton, through whose virtuoso example the double-bass achieved a considerable measure of the creative capacity enjoyed by the front-line instruments. It is indicative of the numbing effect which the sudden exposure to genius can have on slumbering senses that Blanton's arrival on the Ellington scene was greeted, by the leading American music magazine, with the words: BULLISH BOWING ENDANGERS DUKE'S REPUTATION!

The bringing together of Jimmy Blanton's buoyant, thrusting bass playing and the already sparkling and ebullient Hodges alto results in three minutes of sheer joy. One beneficial result of the pragmatic approach to recording that existed in the Ellington camp was that tunes originally conceived in conventional AABA thirty-two-bar form often assumed different and more interesting shapes through parts being curtailed or lopped off to fit the three-minute format. (The original version of 'Cottontail' is a classic example of this 'made-to-measure' approach.) 'Squatty Roo' is a happy, skipping theme based, as have been innumerable compositions in every era of jazz, on the harmonies of George Gershwin's 'I Got Rhythm'. The record opens straightaway with the two opening A sections. But instead of proceeding to the B middle-eight and the final A chorus, we go straight into a full alto solo, starting again at the top. This is followed by what would in any conventional performance be the final 'out' chorus, a reprise of the theme with the alto taking the middle-eight. But since it happens prematurely, there's time for a further alto solo which, after the middle-eight, yields to a final eight bars of ensemble which is then repeated sotto voce for 'one more time'. Set out in alphabetical form, this emerges as AA/AABA (solo)/ AABA (ensemble with solo middle-eight)/AAB (solo) AA.

This choppy format, sustained in interest by Jimmy Blanton's ceaselessly inventive bass lines, suits Johnny Hodges admirably. He was never the most long-winded of jazz players, sounding most at ease when popping up for short bursts of joyful, dancing activity rather than piling chorus upon chorus. By comparison with such contemporaries as Benny Carter, Coleman Hawkins and Lester Young, his approach to improvisation may be said to be naïve. No long lines of finely wrought and elegantly balanced melody emerge, no tangled and devious harmonic routes are explored, no startlingly fresh alterations are made to the conventional rhythmic structure of the piece. And yet the whole performance springs along with an abandon which is irresistible.

Popping, dancing, springing—I find that in trying to define the virtues of 'Squatty Roo' I have without thinking used words that go straight to the heart of the matter. For the origins of this side to the Hodges musical personality we should perhaps look to Louis Armstrong of the Blue Five days rather than to Sidney Bechet. The most important lesson that the twenty-five-year-old Armstrong taught to the jazz world at large was how to endow a performance with that rhythmic momentum that came to be called swing. Even in his earliest days, when he was still striving to find a role for the alto saxophone in fast tempos that did not involve decorative doodling more appropriate to the clarinet,

Johnny Hodges swung with that particular buoyancy of Armstrong's that came from applying such seeming irrelevancies as vibrato, articulation and variation in pitch to the service of rhythmic uplift. Since, as I have explained, there are few, if any, melodic or harmonic ramifications on which to dwell here, let us pick out just some of the ingredients, whether borrowed or new, which go towards achieving this highly infectious swing.

The first thing that must be established is that Johnny Hodges in fast tempos played in a manner not dissimilar from that of Coleman Hawkins. Though he lacked the heavy attack and machine-gun delivery of Hawkins, he played his long phrases in a string of uneven quavers or eighth-notes, normally stressing the first, third, fifth and seventh quavers in a bar and sometimes articulating those in between so lightly that the effect was of 'DOOdle-DOOdle-DOOdle-DOOdle'. Rhythmic variety would then be introduced when the emphasis was applied in varied strengths, sometimes switching from the strong to the weak quavers in the way that a drummer will create a shifting rhythm.

From the outset of his first chorus in 'Squatty Roo', this drumming effect is very much in evidence, the phrases skipping along with frequent shifts of emphasis. In the seventh and eighth bars, for instance, the rhythmic pattern can be roughly described in the onomatopaeic method above as 'dooDLE-dooDLE-DOOdle-doodle-DOOdle-doo-WAH'. Of course, this is a crude exposition, there being many more shades of accent than I can put on paper. But it gives an idea of the frequent skipping changes in step which give a Hodges solo its continuous lift. He was less relentless in pursuing this rhythmic pattern than Coleman Hawkins. For instance, at the start of the second eight bars of the first solo, the flow of quavers is interrupted by a sustained, singing high note from which a long phrase full of variety descends in a series of blithe, skipping steps.

As one would expect from a player so steeped in the blues, there is in a Hodges up-tempo romp a more generous use of those slurred, distorted and otherwise maltreated tones appertaining to the blues than one finds in contemporaries such as Benny Carter or Coleman Hawkins. In bars twenty-five and twenty-six of the first solo chorus, for example, he utters a repetitive call very reminiscent of the whoo-hooing train-whistle sounds made by blues harmonica players. And in the third full chorus, when Hodges, Blanton and the discreet brushes of Sonny Greer have it all to themselves again, the first sixteen bars are pure blues. That Johnny Hodges was a master in this idiom may seem surprising and, in some cases, unsettling to those romantics who believe the blues to be the exclusive cultural property of one social and geographical area of black America.

Boston, Massachusetts, is about as far from the Deep South as one can get without crossing a border, and the environment into which Johnny Hodges was born could aptly be described as respectable middle class, with good educational opportunities especially in the field of music. Yet he embraced the blues with manifestly more enthusiasm, conviction and understanding than, say, Coleman Hawkins from Missouri, Don Redman from West Virginia and Buster Bailey from Memphis, all of whom were born and bred within earshot of the migratory route of the Southern blues. When all of these musicians, including Hodges, were finding their feet in New York, the city was enjoying a blues boom, especially in the recording studios. As members of Fletcher Henderson's Orchestra, Hawkins, Redman and Bailey were in the thick of it, providing backings for many of the so-called 'classic' blues singers including Bessie Smith. If receptiveness to the raw spirit of the blues were a matter simply of proximity to the source, one would expect them to be infected more, not less, deeply than Johnny Hodges, who was outside their circle. But when it comes to the instrumental interpretation of the blues, we are dealing with music, not sociology. Geography and environment affect a musician only to the extent that they decide whom he hears and with whom he plays and discusses music in his formative years. In one respect, environment may have had a part to play in the direction that Johnny Hodges took, in that by commuting regularly to Boston, he did not become associated with the rather standoffish and contemptuous attitude of the New Yorkers to the powerful but relatively rough music coming into the city from the West—New Orleans, Chicago and the South. While their fastidiousness led them to keep at arms' length the music of Bechet, the blues and the 'soul' or 'gutbucket' extremity of the

New York musical spectrum, Johnny Hodges devoured it all without inhibition, harnessing it to a polished and highly disciplined musicianship. There was, as I have said, a certain inevitability about his gravitation towards the Duke Ellington band. With its extraordinary blend of naïvety and sophistication, of lush saxophones and savagely growling brass, of ancient blues themes and modern concert works, of dark, brooding harmonies and joyful abandon, it was his spiritual home.

Nothing could illustrate the importance of personality and temperament in a musician's development better than the juxtaposition of Johnny Hodges and Benny Carter. A native of New York, born less than a year after Hodges, Benny Carter undoubtedly shared many of the former's youthful experiences and influences. True, he never worked alongside Sidney Bechet and, since he was away from New York for a year or two in the mid-Twenties, it is quite possible that he never heard him in the flesh at that time. That he was not deaf in his youth to the earthier aspects of New York music is shown by the fact that, when he initially chose the trumpet as his instrument, it was the growl-specialist Bubber Miley who was his inspiration. A diligent researcher into his recorded works over the years could come up with plenty of examples of impressive blues solos (the clarinet part in 'Dee Blues' by the Chocolate Dandies, mentioned in the chapter on Jack Teagarden, is particularly convincing). But the same researcher would be forced to the conclusion that, although Carter has always cited Hodges among his early influences, the blues that so permeated the Hodges style have not been an integral part of Carter's music. His ambitions—and the contribution which he made to jazz in the pursuit of them—lay in a different direction from those of Johnny Hodges.

Some light is thrown on them by the other names often mentioned by Carter as his chief sources of inspiration. Coleman Hawkins, Don Redman, Frankie Trumbauer each made an important contribution to his musical make-up. With Hawkins, a colleague on many recordings over the years, Benny Carter shared an intense musical curiosity, an eagerness to explore all that orthodox musical teaching had to offer while at the same time showing deep interest in the eccentricities of which jazz is compounded. Less aggressive than Hawkins, he nonetheless assimilated much of the tenor star's gritty drive and momentous swing, sufficient to turn aside the charges of effeteness and dandyism which his elegantly turned solos might otherwise invoke. To the strong tone inherited from Hodges he added a hard cutting edge comparable to Hawkins's tenor sound, resulting in a solo voice that could sometimes be as declamatory as that of the trumpet and an incisive ensemble sound that has been the model for lead alto players ever since.

Much of the orthodox strength in Benny Carter's playing will have derived from Don Redman, the man whose section playing and arrangements did much to give a style to the Fletcher Henderson Orchestra in the Twenties. Clearly, Redman was a powerful influence on Carter the ambitious professional, who dogged the older man's steps from the outset with almost uncanny success. Don Redman arrived in New York in 1923 with a Pittsburg band called Billy Paige's Broadway Syncopators. When he left a year later to join Fletcher Henderson, it was Benny Carter who went back to Pittsburg with Paige. A few years later, Redman left Henderson to become musical director of McKinney's Cottonpickers. Shortly afterward, the Fletcher Henderson discography begins to list Benny Carter as alto-sax soloist and arranger. At the same time, Carter assumed from Redman the leadership of the *ad hoc* studio bands which Redman had founded and which recorded under the name of the Chocolate Dandies. The pattern now so well established that it seems almost platitudinous to add that when Don Redman left McKinney's Cottonpickers, it was Benny Carter who took over the band's musical directorship, only to leave a year later to start his own band, as Redman had done before him. Just as Don Redman's trade-mark as arranger with Henderson had been the 'choir' of clarinets working as a section, so Benny Carter was later to specialize in passages written for the saxophones, drawing from the standard team of two altos and two tenors a remarkably rich texture which was then adapted to the fluent lines and bursts of double-tempo of a characteristic Benny Carter solo.

The fourth candidate among Benny Carter's influences, Frankie Trumbauer, represents the sharpest point of divergence between the Carter and the Hodges approaches. If Johnny Hodges ever flirted with Trumbauer, it was only for the briefest of periods, after which Bechet and the blues reasserted their hold. Consequently, a Hodges solo would first and foremost create a mood, an atmosphere, using the simplest of musical materials and relying on nuances of tone, pitch and volume to provide the depth. Trumbauer's stock-in-trade was phrase-making—the spinning of a melodic line that aimed for elegance, poise, balanced design and neat construction, with the occasional odd interval or convoluted phrase thrown in to startle and divert. To my ears, his solos were often glaringly contrived and always totally without the swing and buoyance that good jazz demands. But his playing in general, and his solo in 'Singin' the Blues' (cited in Volume One as a Bix Beiderbecke classic) were greatly admired by contemporary musicians of every background.

Its effect upon Benny Carter was to sharpen his already acute sense of musical construction. The writer, Rex Harris, whose book *Jazz* for Pelican Books epitomized the 'purist' approach of the early Fifties, summed up Carter's mature style in a series of apt phrases—'tremendous talent', 'powers of invention, technique, tone, all are of the highest order', 'a demonstration of beauty', 'beautiful, refined, delicate'. The fact that I have had to extract those phrases, in the manner of a theatrical publicist, from a passage that denied Benny Carter the right to be regarded as a jazz musician at all, demonstrates the deep suspicion with which overt musicianship was, and sometimes still is, regarded by the protagonists of 'pure' jazz. By the time Benny Carter's alto style had fully matured, around the mid-Thirties, a curious thing had happened. The conjuncture of the attack, incisiveness and swing that came from other sources, and the penchant for felicitous phrase-making that derived from Frankie Trumbauer had resulted in music that came much closer in style to that of Trumbauer's erstwhile colleague, Bix Beiderbecke.

In pursuit of this idea, I asked Bruce Turner, the distinguished alto saxophonist with my own band and an ardent devotee of Benny Carter, to play me the Bix Beiderbecke solos in 'Singin' the Blues' and 'Way Down Yonder in New Orleans' in the Carter style. They sounded uncannily like original Benny Carter solos.

In detail, the resemblances are striking. Both Carter and Beiderbecke showed an adherence to strict underlying rules of construction in building their solos. In this respect one could say that a player such as Coleman Hawkins, charging along whither his theme took him and piling sub-clause upon sub-clause, improvised in a 'prose' style, while Carter and Beiderbecke observed the metric rules of formal poetry, setting phrase against phrase and line against line. In discussing Bix Beiderbecke's solo in 'Singin' the Blues', I drew attention to the way in which its opening was subdivided into two phrases or 'lines' of one bar each, followed by an answering line of two bars which, in turn, is matched by a long, irregular phrase covering the next four bars. Any Benny Carter solo between 1934 and 1944 (and to a lesser extent after the arrival of bebop) can be shown to rest on a similarly formal pattern.

And there is a further likeness. Despite evidence in their solos of advanced harmonic mastery, both Beiderbecke and Carter leaned heavily upon the simple diatonic scale. In layman's language this means that, transposed into the key of C, a solo by either musician will be full of phrases that can be played entirely on the white notes of the piano keyboard, without recourse to the extraneous sharps and flats that give chromatic harmonies their particular complexity. If we think of a simple progression from dominant to tonic, or from G seventh to C, and express it by playing the cadence F, D, B, G, C (or, alternatively, D, lower G, B, D, C), we have phrases which might well occur in a Beiderbecke or Carter solo. Compared with the progression D, D flat, C that Coleman Hawkins liked to use, or with the flattened or 'bent' thirds, fifths and sevenths of the blues scale favoured by Johnny Hodges, these cadences have a fresh, open, even innocent quality that has prompted, in each instance, the response, 'Very beautiful, but is it *jazz*?' If one believes, as I do, that jazz is a many-splendor'd music that can match the Mozartian, Wagnerian, Schoenbergian and other schools of European music, then the answer will be 'yes' and we can proceed with a clear conscience to look in detail at two Benny Carter fragments.

Fragments, alas, they must be, because although Benny Carter in the Thirties made a strong contribution, as arranger, altoist, trumpeter and/or clarinettist, to all of his recordings, he produced on alto no solo performance comparable to the Hawkins 'Body and Soul' or the Hodges 'Squatty Roo'. When it came to stretching out on a ballad he seemed to prefer the trumpet, on which he was a formidable but derivative performer. Readers eager to hear his best work on trumpet should track down 'Once upon a Time' by the Chocolate Dandies in 1933, when he played very much in the majestic Armstrong vein, and 'More than you Know' by his own orchestra in 1939, by which time he had acquired a lusher style that hints, if ever so slightly, at an admiration for Harry James. On clarinet he played good solos with a strong, fruity tone, but in a manner that was much less distinctive than his alto-saxophone style. His claim to recognition as a jazz giant, as distinct from a superb all-round musician, rests on innumerable alto solos from the late Twenties onwards that bore his unmistakable stamp and established him alongside Johnny Hodges as a leading jazz voice on the instrument.

Between 1935 and 1938, Benny Carter followed the example of Coleman Hawkins, Dickie Wells and many other American jazz stars and moved to Europe, occupying for a short time the curious role of staff arranger to Henry Hall's BBC Dance Orchestra. During this time he made recordings with both British and Continental musicians, often meeting up in the studio with his old friend and colleague in the Henderson band, Coleman Hawkins. One of their collaborations, 'Crazy Rhythm', recorded in 1937 under the heading of Coleman Hawkins and his All Star Jam Band, features in these pages as a Coleman Hawkins masterpiece. It also contains a chorus by Benny Carter which is often cited by musicians and commentators as one of his best and most characteristic.

Before we consider the Carter solo, it is worth taking note of the opening ensemble chorus which has all the hallmarks—the richly textured voicing, the biting attack and the full-bodied, chesty tone—of a Benny Carter saxophone section with himself in the lead. True, this is no more than a hastily sketched out 'head' arrangement with none of the complex phrasing and bursts of double-time that are found in a full Carter saxophone outing. Nevertheless, it has the distinctive sound, almost as elusive in its composition as some of Duke Ellington's voicings, by which a Benny Carter arrangement can instantly be identified.

In the discussion of this record in my essay on Coleman Hawkins, I noted that André Ekyan, as well as Alix Combelle, shows the influence of Hawkins in his solo. There is certainly little of either Carter or Hodges in the bustling, rather untidy phrasing. It may be invidious and unfair to highlight the skill of the Americans by picking out the faults of the Europeans, but comparisons certainly do clamour for attention. The haphazard nature of Ekyan's chorus, whose jumble of ideas sound garrulous rather than fluent, highlights the supreme orderliness and lucidity of Benny Carter's solo. Jazz books—and these volumes are no exception—bristle with diverse and often complex definitions of the jazz quality known as 'swing'. There are, indeed, different ways of achieving that particular characteristic of sustained rhythmic momentum required by the term. But one essential is common to all of them, and that is perfect time. To a musician, this means placing every note, even the most transitory and insignificant, in exactly the right place in relation to the regular four beats to the bar. This does not necessarily mean 'keeping time' in the sense of neither speeding up nor slowing down. There are plenty of examples in jazz of solos and ensembles which continue to swing even though there is noticeable accelerating or slowing down of the tempo. In these instances, as the basic beat changes, the notes continue to relate to it with microscopic accuracy. A common cause of bad time and consequent lack of swing is poor execution—the failure of the fingers or tongue to articulate accurately the ideas fed to them. The solos of Ekyan and Combelle both falter occasionally in this respect, the latter especially making heavy weather of some over-ambitious flights of fancy.

There is a touch of insolence about the effortless style with which Benny Carter takes over the baton from a huffing and puffing Combelle. It is surprising that, among all the efforts that have been made by jazz historians to attribute influences to Lester Young, no one to my knowledge has mentioned the name of Benny Carter. It must be said that Lester Young himself never mentioned him either, suggesting that, from the common inspiration of Frankie Trumbauer, both musicians arrived independently at a very similar rhythmic style. In the comparisons between Young and Coleman Hawkins, much is made of the contrast between the latter's system of unevenly stressed eighth-notes— the DOOdle-DOOdle effect as I have described it—and the flatter, more flowing pattern of even eighth-notes that Lester Young employed. Exactly the same point can be made to distinguish Benny Carter from Johnny Hodges, whom I have placed in this context in the Hawkins school. If I hesitate to put Lester Young in the Carter school it is because we have no evidence of his playing prior to 1936 and therefore cannot judge who preceded whom. But it is certainly worth putting on the record the fact that the even-quaver rhythmic style with which Lester Young and the guitarist, Charlie Christian, paved the way for the rhythms of modern jazz was used by Benny Carter from his earliest days.

The opening of Benny Carter's solo, with its lead up to an isolated 'balancing' note on the first beat of the bar, is very similar to Lester Young's entrance in 'Lady Be Good'. But thereafter, the moods of the solo are different, with Carter's frank preference for explicit, finely balanced lines of melody contrasting with Lester's oblique, veiled approach. At the end of bar one, we have a characteristic Carter trade-mark, a phrase that starts with a note, usually near the bottom of the solo's range, which is leaned on heavily to give it special emphasis, a signal that it is going to play an important part in some ingenious musical pattern. Sure enough, the elegant opening phrase, looped across the beat, returns to the same note, completing a languid four-bar motif which is then balanced, in the next four bars, by one similar in shape but more intricate. A demonstration of beauty indeed, breathtakingly designed and executed. But this is only the start. A linking phrase across bars seven and eight initiates a burst of melody, uttered with that sharp-edged, trumpet-like attack that makes the heart sing. From its joyful opening notes to the more fluent phrases with which they are developed and resolved, the structure is impeccable and the poise complete.

The middle-eight produces further delights—a long, looping, continuous phrase spread over six bars, perfectly shaped, and outlining an idea which, taken up again at the end of bar seven, itself becomes the opening gambit in a further chain of pure melody that sees the solo out. In other words, the whole half-chorus, from the start of the middle-eight onwards, represents a continuous line of spontaneous composition, logically and lucidly expressed without one extraneous note. Much of the elation which the solo inspires derives from that predilection for diatonic lines which have such a Bixian flavour. Indeed, the bursts of melody in bars nine and ten and again in bars twenty-five to twenty-nine, have something of the triumphant, militant sound of Bix in full cry. The very end of Benny Carter's chorus throws new light on the premature entrance by Coleman Hawkins which I have put down to a 'straining at the leash'. Eagerness to enter the fray is certainly there, but there is also the necessity to fill up the final thirty-second bar of Carter's solo, since that meticulous man, having concluded and rounded off his whole musical scheme in bar thirty-one, disdains to fudge the design with the sort of mumbling, semi-audible soliloquy with which many soloists cover their retreat from the microphone.

A chance to hear Benny Carter in a more extended vein arises from a fine session under the revived name of the Chocolate Dandies which was recorded for the American jazz label Commodore in 1940. With limited ensemble work, no piano and only three soloists—Carter, Coleman Hawkins and Roy Eldridge—to be accommodated, each player has plenty of space in the up-tempo numbers. Benny Carter is well represented on both 'I Can't Believe that You're in Love with Me' and 'Smack' and if I choose the latter for special consideration, it is because with two opening choruses and a final middle-eight, Carter is here the principal soloist.

'Smack' (presumably a reference to the nickname of the three principals' erstwhile bandleader, Fletcher Henderson) is not really a composition at all, but a thirty-two-bar chord sequence in conventional AABA form over which the soloists improvise freely from the start. Benny Carter opens the proceedings with eight bars which may or may not have constituted a sketchy theme and which are not repeated. They are very characteristic of Carter, building a symmetrical pattern of four two-bar phrases, a regular feature of which is a descent to one of those stressed low-register notes on the second beat of the first bar. In fact, this downward leap, quite a familiar device in Carter solos of the period, is elevated here to the status of a motif that recurs throughout the solo, sometimes thrown on to another beat, sometimes interjected, with surprise effect, against the directional tide of the melody. In some ways, Benny Carter is less fluent and more daring here than in the previous example, perhaps challenged by the pushing and explosive personalities of his front-line colleagues to take risks. The result is a solo of a more devious structure than before. For instance, the phrase at the end of the first eight bars by which he emerges from the opening pattern is, for him, curiously convoluted, both rhythmically and melodically.

In the second eight bars a more typically elegant line is established, flowing into a middle-eight in which the downward-leaping motif is exploited in a sly and humorous way. The listener will notice, as this solo unfolds, that Benny Carter's style has lost some of its erstwhile innocence. Where a solo would once spin blithely along pursuing a seemingly inexorable melodic course, this one constantly turns aside to give playful chase to a melodic or rhythmic idea, often chivvying the beat in the manner of Coleman Hawkins and, in one extreme instance near the end of the solo, of his fellow-altoist, Pete Brown. There were occasions, before and after Benny Carter's exposure to the new ideas of bebop, when the phrase-making seemed to me to verge upon indulgence, a clever idea being driven to the point of self-parody. But here the balance between ingenuity and intuition sounds to me to be just right, and the ardour of his companions seems to have kindled in his playing an even greater warmth than usual. Indeed, when he bursts in at the end of the single chorus by Coleman Hawkins with a beautifully constructed middle-eight, there is no detectable drop in temperature.

Throughout this essay I have spoken of Benny Carter in the past tense, being concerned primarily with his impact on the jazz scene in the Thirties and, indeed, of its impact upon him. Happily, at the time of writing he is still alive and active, a worthy elder statesman of jazz who has, by example and by active encouragement, assisted and inspired succeeding generations of musicians. In contrast to Johnny Hodges, he took account in his playing of the work of the bebop innovators, adapting both their rhythmic and harmonic ideas to his own style. Whether or not these changes have met with the approval of his earliest devotees, they have never undermined the exquisite poise and elegance of his music without which, over more than fifty years, jazz would have been inestimably the poorer.

Dickie Wells

OF ALL THE INSTRUMENTS in the jazz fold, the trombone seems to have experienced the greatest difficulty in living down its past. Whatever crudities and indiscretions the trumpet and clarinet may have committed in the music's early days, they could point respectively to a proud tradition of leadership and a schooled Creole background as the foundation of their jazz role. The piano derived respectability not only from ragtime, with its quasi-classical aura, but also from the sombre dignity of the blues. And as for the saxophone, its past was so negligible in jazz terms that when the generation headed by Coleman Hawkins, Johnny Hodges and Benny Carter took it in hand in the late Twenties, they virtually started with a clean slate, Bechet's example excepted.

The trombone, however, had played a vital role in the earliest manifestations of jazz. In the New Orleans bands it assumed the function which it had performed in the military bands from which jazz in part derived, supplying ripe bass harmonies and a high degree of rhythmic emphasis. In the hands of a master such as Edward 'Kid' Ory, who enhanced the bands of Louis Armstrong, Jelly Roll Morton and King Oliver in the Twenties, it was in its element, compensating for its lack of agility with the versatile mixture of sustained, staccato and sliding notes which its relatively primitive construction makes possible. Except in the blues, where it could wail and moan with the best of them, the role it played was supportive. And it was open to limitless abuse in the interests of showmanship or comedy, reinforcing its image as the amiable hobbledehoy of the band, cheerfully shouldering the heavy work and ready at a moment's notice to entertain with a little crude clowning.

It is not an image likely to have commended itself to those young musicians in the mid-Twenties who, in the wake of Louis Armstrong, were beginning to think of jazz less as a band or ensemble music and more as a vehicle for individual solo expression. We have already seen how Jimmy Harrison, when a star soloist with Fletcher Henderson's Orchestra, spoke with some contempt of trombones which sounded like trombones. Just as Miff Mole had done before them, Harrison and Jack Teagarden set about stifling or distorting some of the basic characteristics of the instrument. 'Trombones should sound like trumpets' was Jimmy Harrison's dictum, and in view of the results which he and Teagarden achieved we can hardly assert that he was misguided. By the late Twenties, a rich crop of trombonists had emerged, many of whom followed Harrison and Teagarden in their Armstrong-derived style. By contrast with Kid Ory and his contemporaries, their playing was marked by crisp, clean articulation, extensive use of the high register, rapid trumpet-like vibrato at the end of notes or phrases and an aversion to using the slide to produce glissandi or sliding notes. When the trombone underwent another crisis of identity in the mid-Forties, finding itself once again left behind in the stampede towards greater speed and agility, it was on what one might call the anti-trombone tradition of Harrison and Teagarden that J. J. Johnson and his bebop followers built. In traditional jazz, which has enjoyed a revival from the Forties on, the influence of Jack Teagarden prevailed in what is loosely called the Chicagoan or Dixieland style centred around Eddie Condon, with players such as Lou McGarity and Cutty Cutshall following his path. In contrast, those who sought to revive the fundamental New Orleans-style leap-frogged back beyond the innovations of Harrison and Teagarden to the 'tailgate' model of Kid Ory and his predecessors.

Of course, we are once again in the realms of over-simplification. But allowing for the many borderline cases and the fact that some 'revivalists' used the tailgate style in ensemble and played their solos in a post-Harrison manner, it remains true to say that in the mainstream development of jazz, the practice of playing the trombone as if it were a trumpet in a lower register has prevailed from the early Thirties to the present day.

There have, however, been important exceptions. Among the young trombonists in the late Twenties who responded to the Armstrong inspiration, there were some who were not ashamed, at the same time, to exploit the trombone's own distinct characteristics. One was the splendid J. C. Higginbotham, whose brazen tone and whooping agility was one of the major attractions of Luis Russell's band in the Thirties and who deserves to share with Jack Teagarden and Jimmy Harrison the credit for promoting the trombone to a solo role in jazz. Higginbotham's influence could be heard in the Thirties in the work of Ellington's Lawrence Brown and Chick Webb's Sandy Williams, and it surfaced again during the modern jazz era of the late Forties when Bill Harris, in Woody Herman's band, went against the fashionable staccato grain and fashioned a style whose contrasting gruff low register and grieving upper reaches recalled the Higginbotham of twenty years earlier.

But the greatest, and the most idiosyncratic, of the 'independents' who combined the new thinking with a readiness on occasion to sound like a trombone, was Dickie Wells. Though born in Tennessee and educated musically in Louisville, Kentucky, where his family moved when he was two years old, Wells was established on the New York scene by 1926, when as a seventeen-year-old he started to work with first Lloyd Scott and then his brother, Cecil Scott. I have remarked in the chapter on Jack Teagarden that the mid-Twenties was probably the period when Jimmy Harrison wielded his greatest influence and in the early records which Dickie Wells made with the Scott brothers, there is plenty of evidence, notably in the use of stabbing notes in the upper register, that Wells came under his spell. But there are signs of his own independent style, too, involving, in slow blues especially, some slipping and sliding in a manner more reminiscent of Charlie Green, Harrison's predecessor in the Fletcher Henderson band. This earthiness, together with a strain of humour that sometimes seemed to parody the awkward and ungainly characteristics of the trombone, remained with him throughout his life.

After his earliest recordings with Lloyd and Cecil Scott, the next substantial collection of his work appeared in 1933 when, as a member of Benny Carter's band, he took part in some sessions under the leadership of the Irish-born bassist, composer and critic, Patrick 'Spike' Hughes. As a musician, Hughes had played in the Jack Hylton Orchestra and had also made many recordings in London with his own relatively small groups. Under the pseudonym 'Mike', he wrote regular jazz criticism for the London *Melody Maker*, the weekly paper to which John Hammond also contributed from America. Hammond had a considerable influence on Spike Hughes's viewpoint, leading him to become the first British jazz journalist to try to wean the record-buying public away from the polite sophistication of Red Nichols and Miff Mole towards then lesser known black artists. When Hughes visited New York in 1933, with the opportunity to record some of his own compositions with American musicians, it was John Hammond who took him round and made the necessary introductions. As a result, the recording session was set up with the Benny Carter band providing the basic unit, to which tenor saxists Coleman Hawkins and Chu Berry, and trumpeter Henry 'Red' Allen, were added.

With so much solo talent literally at his command, a composer would have needed unusual resources of ineptitude to avoid memorable results. Spike Hughes was at his best at the slower 'foxtrot' tempos, and romantic pieces such as 'Arabesque', 'Donegal Cradle Song' and 'Sweet Sorrow Blues', redolent with an intriguing blend of Ellingtonian and Hibernian influences, are deservedly cherished today as something more than just adequate vehicles for inspired soloists. The fast numbers suffer from the squared-off jerkiness which marked the British brand of 'hot' arrangement in the early Thirties, but even then there is little sign that the players were at all inhibited, and when classic sessions are recalled today, those by Spike Hughes and his All-American Orchestra will always find a place among them.

In one respect, the Spike Hughes sessions are underrated today. Of the fourteen pieces recorded, all except one ('Donegal Cradle Song') contain a solo by Dickie Wells. Canvass the jazz experts for their views and they will all agree that the performances are typical of Dickie Wells at his best—adventurous, swinging, full of

Coleman Hawkins, with singer Thelma Carpenter

Jack Teagarden

Art Tatum

surprise and wit. What you will find missing, if I may venture a guess founded on almost all the established jazz histories, is a due sense of astonishment (a charge to which the British writer, Raymond Horricks, and the French critic, André Hodeir, are honourable exceptions). As often in these instances, we have to perform some mental gymnastics in order to appreciate the startling newness of Dickie Wells's style. In his previous recordings with Lloyd and Cecil Scott, his playing already showed great promise but was still somewhat gawky and immature. The last of these was made in November 1929. In the three and a half years that then elapsed before the Hughes sessions, the jazz trombone enjoyed something of a heyday. From the mutually beneficial association with Jack Teagarden, Jimmy Harrison emerged as a truly modern player in the 1930 recordings by the Chocolate Dandies. In his wake came a string of fine players, of whom Benny Morton and Claude Jones were the most impressive. But with the followers of Louis Armstrong and Coleman Hawkins performing astonishing feats of daring on trumpet and saxophone, even the best of the trombonists were often overshadowed. Jack Teagarden, as I noted in a previous chapter, quite soon settled down into a lifelong style that inclined more towards poise, elegance and relaxed warmth than reckless fervour. And only the ebullient J. C. Higginbotham, short on subtlety but full of glorious vitality, approached the adventurousness of the trumpet and saxophone men.

And then, out of the blue, came the Spike Hughes sessions, with twenty-three-year-old Dickie Wells producing a string of solos which, for range of mood, bursting eagerness and impudent (and occasionally ill-fated) daring, remind one of Louis Armstrong's playing in the later years of the Hot Five sessions. With so much talent erupting all around him, it is perhaps understandable that even Spike Hughes himself seemed not to grasp fully the unprecedented brilliance of his trombonist's contribution. In the second volume of his autobiography, entitled *Second Movement*, he referred retrospectively to 'the admirable and unusual trombone player, Dickie Wells', apt words in themselves but hardly sufficient to describe the finest jazz trombone playing yet committed to wax.

In addition to the compositions by the leader himself, there were among these recordings a couple of 'standards'—'Bugle Call Rag' and 'Someone Stole Gabriel's Horn'—which Hughes arranged, and versions of 'How Come you Do me Like you Do' and 'Sweet Sue' which were played without formal arrangement in jam-session style. The Dickie Wells solo on 'Sweet Sue' is most often picked out for special mention, and it is indeed remarkable. Preceding him there has been a characteristically urgent and across-the-beat statement of the tune by Henry Allen, a hustling and bustling Coleman Hawkins solo and a chorus by Wayman Carver on flute which is more notable for its very existence in 1933 than for its content. Dickie Wells starts with one of his familiar devices—a solitary steadying note in the bar before the chorus proper—and then launches into the solo with some Armstrong-like repeated phrases in punching rhythmic style. It is at the end of the first eight-bar section that he first airs his reckless spirit of adventure with a long phrase that ascends across the beat with a staggering gait, skids upwards to grab at a top D and slide back off it, regains its balance and resumes the rhythmic riffing through the second eight-bar section. It sounds for all the world like a man in a hurry who suddenly hits an unseen patch of ice and flails around to keep upright, startling the onlookers. The next patch of ice occurs in the middle-eight, when Dickie Wells decides to attempt some daring figure-skating based on that first involuntary skid, and all but comes a cropper in the process. First he suggests the slithering phrase from B to D and back in the lower register, then repeats it an octave up but doesn't quite reach the D, a lapse in intonation which is compounded when, going for the same figure again in the low register, he finds that it will land him on the wrong note and, in making a last minute change in direction, lands on the C badly off-centre. The whole brief escapade seems to unnerve him, and the rhythmic phrase that he uses to get out of the middle-eight has a noticeable air of desperation about it.

'Sweet Sue' reveals the only sign of impulsive immaturity in the entire set. Not that the other solos are less adventurous. 'Air in D flat' is full of leaps and pirouettes, this time sure footed and elegantly constructed. In contrast, 'Sweet Sorrow Blues' evokes a deep blues lament, echoing strongly Kid Ory's stark solo on King Oliver's 'Black Snake Blues' from 1927. Here is a trombone sounding like a trombone and proud of it, using all the broad glissando effects that the slide mechanism permits. A notable aspect of the 'Sweet Sorrow' solo is that, in singing the blues so unashamedly, Dickie Wells abandoned the exaggerated vibrato which elsewhere gave his sustained notes such intensity. The French writer, André Hodeir, in a study of Dickie Wells in his book, *Jazz: Its Evolution and Essence*, described this effect as 'terminal vibrato', a phrase which, unhappily overtaken by medical jargon, brings involuntarily to mind the instruction of Miles Davis's first teacher: 'Play without any vibrato—you're gonna get old anyway and start shakin'.' In fact 'vibrato' is not a strictly accurate term to describe the effect which Dickie Wells and some of his predecessors achieved. They did not simply apply the rapid but minute variation in pitch with which vibrato endows a note with a throbbing pulse. With them, the principal note actually alternates rapidly with notes one or two intervals above, through the application of varied lip pressure. In its gentler manifestation, this effect, in modern musical parlance, is aptly described as a 'lip trill', while in its more exaggerated form it becomes a 'shake'.

Dickie Wells was not the first or only jazzman to use it. It appears often in Louis Armstrong's early playing and became ubiquitous in his later years. Jack Teagarden began by using it in moderation, as we have seen, but soon abandoned it. It can be heard, in a sort of fluttering, asthmatic variation, in Jimmy Harrison's solos with the Chocolate Dandies, and it was from the start central to Benny Morton's style. But no one used it with as much gusto as Dickie Wells. In the ferocious 'Bugle Call Rag', it becomes an essential feature of a solo that consists of little more than three sustained notes. Playing in B flat, he starts on a middle F, stretching it taut with a series of rhythmic tugs over five bars and only relieving the tension with a short, rippling shake at the end of the fifth bar. Then from bars seven to nine he unleashes a train whistle's mournful 'whooooeeeee' an octave up, descending in bar ten to the key note B flat and shaking it for two bars until its teeth rattle. It's an amazingly audacious solo—three notes spread over twelve bars of a sixteen-bar chorus and yet imparting a great feeling of heat and urgency through the judicious use of the shake.

Two more solos from the Spike Hughes sessions demand a special mention. One is in a dreamy, ruminative theme called 'Pastoral'. If the implications of the title impinged upon Dickie Wells, he decided to ignore them, going through several startling changes of mood in his short sixteen-bar solo. Following a blithe, sunny half-chorus from Benny Carter on alto, he starts with broad, upward sweeping phrases in the Louis Armstrong grand manner, but conveying a sense of increasingly un-pastoral disturbance and agitation with the intensified use of the shake. A searing 'blue note' on the flattened seventh brings him out of the middle-eight into a last eight-bar section that starts with matching two-bar phrases in a very different manner. The voice is now gruff, the notes abrupt, the phrasing terse, with the second two-bar phrase ending on the second beat of the bar, unexpectedly but extremely effectively. We are now far removed from pastoral serenity and deep in blues country, a fact driven home by the harsh and furious flurry of notes with which the chorus ends. It is hard to think of a more powerful or moving trombone passage from that (or indeed any) period, and it serves to make the rest of the piece, including the lush rhapsodizing of Coleman Hawkins, sound faintly ridiculous, as if a scene from King Lear had been interpolated in some romantic Ruritanian operetta.

Of the other noteworthy solo, Spike Hughes wrote '[Dickie Wells's] playing (John Hammond still swears) was spoilt for life by his ingenious and thoroughly musical contributions to the abstruse "Arabesque".' We are left to guess exactly what Hammond meant, but there is, in the way that Wells slithers nonchalantly over the complex background harmonies, a foreshadowing of the droll, quasi-conversational passages which were to become an overworked mannerism in later years. Here it is extremely effective, complementing the abstract nature of the composition with unusual intervals and notes deliberately indeterminate in pitch. The re-entry, after the middle-eight by the saxophone section, must have aroused pure joy in the heart of the composer, so unexpected is the direction from which it comes wafting in. Once again, the style belonged exclusively to the trombone—neither the trumpet nor the keyed instruments could achieve the same subtle gradations of pitch without a consequent loss of tone.

Had Dickie Wells made no more records after that, he would have qualified as a jazz giant, with 'Pastoral' eligible as a masterpiece. But there were greater things to come. In 1937, the trombonist was a member of Teddy Hill's band when it made a trip to France. While in Paris, some sessions were organized by the Hot Club of France, under the active leadership of Hugues Panassié, in which Dickie Wells led some small groups of French and American musicians in informal recordings. Dickie Wells's playing, in line-ups ranging from the somewhat eccentric conjunction of three trumpets and a trombone to more conventional instrumentation, is consistently superb, especially in the several blues pieces. As often when it comes to making a choice, I have gone for two particular favourites of mine, while admitting certain pangs at the necessary exclusion of the fine all-brass arrangement (by Roy Eldridge) of 'Between the Devil and the Deep Blue Sea' and the beautifully relaxed blues 'Hangin' around Boudon'.

Both the last-named were recorded at the same session, on 7 July 1937. In the trumpet section which recorded 'Between the Devil and the Deep Blue Sea', 'I Got Rhythm' and 'Bugle Call Rag' were Bill Dillard and Shad Collins, colleagues of Wells's in the Teddy Hill Band, and Bill Coleman, who was already in Paris working with Willie Lewis's Band. Bassist Dick Fulbright and drummer Bill Beason from the Hill Band were joined by the Belgian-born guitarist, Django Reinhardt, then a revered pillar of the French jazz scene. After the four-brass arrangements had been recorded, Dillard and Collins stood down, leaving Dickie Wells and Bill Coleman to polish off three more unrehearsed sides. The two musicians were no strangers to each other, their paths having crossed in the bands of both Lloyd and Cecil Scott in the late Twenties, and subsequently with Benny Carter and probably Luis Russell, too.

Bill Coleman, like every other trumpet player of his generation, came under the spell of Louis Armstrong in his formative years. It is thanks to the vast scope of Armstrong's style, with its many different facets, that his many disciples did not all sound exactly alike. The Louis Armstrong whom Bill Coleman worshipped was the fleet-footed, mercurial virtuoso of the latter-day Hot Fives, when the newly formed partnership with Earl Hines was spurring Louis into electrifying performances. One record in particular, called 'Fireworks', made a deep impression on Bill Coleman and was clearly influential in the forming of his own agile and sparkling style. For greater mobility he avoided the heavy, declamatory aspects of the trumpet sound, cultivating a light, clear tone to which a fast, rippling shake, sparsely used, gave additional sparkle. His animated and joyous playing was just the thing to bring out the swashbuckler in Dickie Wells, and it is perhaps no coincidence that the tune which produced their most exciting playing on the Paris session was 'Sweet Sue', the scene, four years earlier, of one of his most hair-raising escapades.

The first thing that one notices about this performance is that the convention that a statement of the tune should precede the improvised variations is waived. Perhaps Dickie Wells was encouraged by the scant attention that Henry 'Red' Allen gave to the detail of the original melody in the Spike Hughes version. Anyway, the listener, after a brief reminder of the opening notes, is called on to carry the rest of the original theme in his head and, by way of reward, is granted a rare insight into the jazz art of spontaneous variation. Seemingly untroubled by Django Reinhardt's rather hearty conception of rhythmic guitar playing (not his strong point), Dickie Wells sets about building a finely constructed trombone chorus upon the opening five notes of the song. His tone is now rounded and consistent, and much more sparing use is made of the shake so that some sustained notes have barely noticeable vibrato. There is also total rhythmic assurance, with that natural and unforced movement between on-the-beat and across-the-beat phrases that defies musical notation and yet is the essence of swing.

Dickie Wells makes three separate appearances during the performance, twice in full thirty-two-bar solos and once in a series of eight-bar exchanges with Bill Coleman. Apart from general observations, I will pick out just one salient point in each of these appearances. In the opening chorus, in which the song's repetitive phrases are replaced by a developing line of melody, there is a moment of inventive brilliance at the point when the tune moves into its middle-eight. In the original melody, the second eight-bar section, as the first, ends decisively, and boringly, on the words 'It's you Sweet Sue'. There is then ample space for the singer to take a breath and launch afresh into the equally repetitive middle-eight with the words 'No one else it seems Ever shares my dreams'. Altogether, it represents the sort of dreary symmetry which jazz musicians were created to transform into music. What Dickie Wells does is play, where the words 'sweet Sue' would come, a rhythmic six-note phrase in the upper register which is completed by the actual five notes that accompany 'No one else it seems'. In other words, for the first time since the opening notes of the chorus, he reverts briefly to the notes of the original song, but uses them to end a phrase of his own rather than to start the middle-eight as the composers intended. The resulting passage stretches from bar fourteen to bar eighteen of the tune, thereby straddling the 'natural break' at the end of bar sixteen at which every popular song of this hackneyed construction stops repeating itself, heaves a prolonged sigh of relief and then trots off towards the brief respite of the middle-eight.

Bill Coleman's first trumpet solo that follows is perhaps rather less tidily constructed than his partner's, nevertheless it has a fine lithe and eager shape to it, with phrases that crackle and leap like flames. When Dickie Wells returns, the tension and excitement has been raised by several notches, and he responds with a high declamatory entry in trumpet style which would have gladdened Jimmy Harrison's heart. But as so often in his solos, he seems to be overtaken by the urge to follow one passage with another contrasting one which contradicts it. Thus the opening four bars of the solo produce a clear, positive line of melody which is then followed, in the corresponding section from bars nine to twelve, by an almost derisive descending phrase in which awkward intervals, including a sudden drop of an octave, are made even harder on the ear by a deliberately casual pitching of the notes. Here again is the trombonist taking full advantage of the instrument's unique qualities, this time the capacity for self-mockery. Dignity is soon restored, but the playful mood is not so easily banished, and returns at the start of the middle-eight in an outbreak of stammering and chuckling effected by the use of rapid tongueing to punctuate a downward glissando.

Clearly Dickie Wells is now in a devilish mood which, in turn, strikes a joyful chord in Bill Coleman. Early in his solo there is a glorious moment when he soars upwards like a lark in a burst of *joie de vivre*, and the rest of the solo literally crackles with energy. This so excites his partner that he can't wait until the end of the chorus before elbowing in with his first contribution to the eight-bar exchanges. A riff is thrown at Coleman who barely has time to respond before Dickie Wells is back, interrupting him with a challenging whoop. Now it's time for Bill Coleman to cock a snook, which he does with an insolent quotation from 'The Girl I Left Behind Me'. In the middle-eight, the slippery high-register phrase that almost dropped him on his backside in the Spike Hughes version of the tune presents itself to Dickie Wells again, but this time he is confident enough to repeat it three times with a sort of 'Look at me, I'm flying!' exhilaration, the fluttering effect heightened by more rapid tongueing. After a response from Bill Coleman, the record ends, as so many spontaneous performances do, with some somewhat indecisive riffing, but by then the listener is already silently applauding one of the most scintillating conversation pieces in all of jazz.

The second Dickie Wells masterpiece from the Paris sessions was recorded five days later on 12 July, and once again sounds as if it was put down as an afterthought when the more exacting stuff was safely in the can. Here Dickie Wells plays seven choruses of the blues backed by a trio of Sam Allen on piano, Roger Chaput on guitar and Bill Beason, drums. The art of a continuous blues performance such as this is to build the successive choruses with logic and mounting intensity, one on top of the other so that in the end an impressive and awesome edifice is erected. If 'Dickie Wells Blues' is not one of the very greatest recordings in this genre it is because, to fall back on contemporary jargon, Dickie Wells 'peaks' too soon. Over five choruses his performance completes a perfect elliptical shape, rising to a high emotional climax in the third chorus and then gently subsiding to the mood of the opening. But there are two more choruses to go after that and full of good things as they are in themselves, they have no new ideas to add to the overall structure and consequently give one a slight feeling of anticlimax.

Nevertheless, the record provides one of the finest available examples of extended blues playing. The opening chorus establishes that, like Jack Teagarden, Dickie Wells was well versed in the history as well as the structural format of the blues. The chorus is based, like the chorus of any classic Bessie Smith performance, on a 'vocal' line stated in bars one to three, repeated in bars five to seven and resolved in bars nine to eleven. The only structural difference between Wells's instrumental approach and a Bessie Smith blues lies in the fact that Wells himself, rather than a separate accompanist, fills in between the principal two-bar phrases. As the choruses unfold, we find that Dickie Wells is uncommonly strict in adhering to this basic scheme of things. Thus when he plays the 'vocal' lines (those over which words would be sung in a vocal performance) he uses simple, stately phrases, adhering closely to the beat and eschewing any decorative variation. In the intervening spaces, on the other hand, we find more elaborate, rhythmically daring passages, reminding one of the way in which the youthful Louis Armstrong would literally dance attendance on the great ladies of the blues.

It is on this strong but flexible structure that the whole performance is built. But unlike a blues singer, who has the changing pattern of words to sustain interest, an instrumentalist cannot simply repeat the same basic phrases with minimal variation for chorus after chorus. Much of the strength of this Dickie Wells performance derives from the variety and quality of the successive themes ('opening gambits', one might say). To my ears, chorus one is melancholy, chorus two defiant, chorus four anguished, chorus five ineffably wistful. I have left chorus three out because it merits separate discussion, being the climax of the whole piece. As is appropriate to what is in effect the keystone of the piece, it differs in shape from the other choruses. Here, there is no alternating pattern of statement and elaboration. The impassioned opening phrase, ending on an explosive fifth in the upper register, is not self-contained but a question, if you like, which demands an equally weighty reply. In this respect, the chorus is strikingly similar to Jack Teagarden's second chorus in 'Knockin' a Jug', with the same sense of urgency. The stretching of the principal 'vocal' line over bars one to four and again over bars five to eight, and the consequent elimination of any contrasting 'fill-in' phrases, gives this climactic chorus enormous strength and power, and serves to lift 'Dickie Wells Blues' to the exalted realms of great blues performances.

After he returned to the United States from Paris, Dickie Wells joined Count Basie's Orchestra for a six-year spell which was to produce many more outstandingly inventive and varied solos. His output of distinguished work between the Spike Hughes sessions and the mid-Forties was rivalled by only a handful of the very greatest artists. But when a decline came—the combination perhaps of hard living, creative exhaustion and the disturbing effects of the advent of bebop—it was as though that great contribution had never been made. Seldom, if ever, has an artist of acknowledged stature been so scorned and derided by the critical fraternity. Seeing how the stories of others who flagged in the race—Billie Holiday, Lester Young—have been told with deep sadness and understanding, one is left with the unattractive thought that Dickie Wells's chief offence has been to remain alive and, until a few years ago, working. Listening to his work in the Fifties and Sixties with Buck Clayton and others, one is bound to regret the absence of the great creative energy and confidence that he showed in the records I have discussed, and to note with sadness how the occasional bursts of passion or drollery in the earlier years had changed to apparent cynicism and self-parody. But musicians are not, like boxers or matinée idols, customarily afforded the opportunity to announce retirement as soon as either will or muscles begin to sag. Dickie Wells played on, adding plenty of entertaining and highly personal performances to the treasury of incomparably great ones.

A 'flower of jazz' is John Hammond's verdict on him in his recently published autobiography. Let it stand.

Lester Young

IN THE MYTHOLOGY OF ART, an innovative genius is popularly supposed to be rejected by the critical establishment, mocked by fellow-artists and scorned by the public, with starvation in a garret as the preferred corollary. Indeed, one need not be a die-hard reactionary to suspect that, sometimes, new and experimental work is prematurely acknowledged as fine art solely because it fulfils the above requirements.

Jazz in its early days offered fruitful ground for revolutionary change. In Volume One of *The Best of Jazz* I was able to propose, without incurring the charge of eccentricity or iconoclasm, that Louis Armstrong overturned, almost single-handedly, the rhythmic foundations of the music, that Earl Hines demolished the accepted notions of jazz piano playing, that Fletcher Henderson with his arranger, Don Redman, introduced an entirely new way of organizing a big orchestra, and that Bix Beiderbecke defied, Canute-like, the on-coming tide of Armstrong's influence and offered the world a less spectacular but strikingly different alternative. If we add the evidence in these pages that the constant alteration and revision that Coleman Hawkins applied to his already highly original style amounted to a one-man cultural revolution, we have enough turbulent activity to have kept the first Jazz Age in a constant state of upheaval.

When we look at the stories that surround these great events in jazz history, a sense of excitement is there in plenty, but there is a notable absence of the reactionary suspicion and hostility that we would today expect such startling change to inspire. Musicians and audiences apparently embraced each innovation eagerly, and jazz criticism, still in its infancy, toddled along behind. Thus I was able to quote the musician, Tommy Brookins, as saying, 'Opposite the young Louis, who was already prodigious, [King] Oliver's style appeared to date a little and it was frequent to hear musicians talk among themselves of "the old style".' Likewise, it took just one note from Bix Beiderbecke's cornet to persuade Eddie Condon that Bix was not the 'clam digger' that he took him to be on sight. Approval for each dramatic departure seemed to be virtually instantaneous. If the British and European writers, epitomized in the late Twenties by the newly born London *Melody Maker*, were a trifle cautious about leading black musicians, it was the alleged 'crudeness' of their work rather than its musical precocity and sophistication that was the cause.

When we come to the story of Lester Young's emergence in the mid-Thirties, we move a large step closer to the stereotyped response to change that I have outlined above. Within the Count Basie band of 1936, his controversial style was matched against that of a more conventional tenorist, Herschel Evans. The rivalry between the two men, leavened by a grudging mutual respect, is part of jazz legend. Evans, a passionate admirer of Coleman Hawkins, insisted—no doubt with a certain seasoning of malice—that Lester's light, airy sound, innocent of the sand-papery overtones of Hawkins and his followers, was more appropriate to the alto saxophone. The taunt drew from Lester Young the famous response, quoted by Billie Holiday, 'There's things going on up there, man'—tapping his forehead—'Some of you guys are all belly!'

In an erudite jazz publication in London in 1946, ten years after the first Lester Young recordings appeared on the market, a critic wrote: 'Of all the elements in the Count Basie band, Lester Young's freakish and imaginatively sterile tenor saxophone style has been the most over-praised.' (Today the writer is recognized as one of the most distinguished, perceptive and eclectic jazz commentators in the world, whose reputation is well able to withstand a few disinterred indiscretions. So if I decline to name him, it is only because justice would demand a litany of similar youthful misjudgements on my own part, and they would occupy a whole chapter.) We should understand the context in which this and similar judgements were made. The flow of new recordings from America had been constipated by the exigencies of war, so that the writer was reflecting, at a seemingly late stage, a view that some American critics had already expressed several years earlier.

Furthermore, the revulsion from the commercial excesses of the Swing Era—which, even as the British critic was writing, was being reflected in the stampede of musicians towards the twin escape routes of New Orleans Revivalism and small-group Bebop —led to much valuable stuff being summarily tipped out with the bath water. Thus his assessment of the Basie band's arrival on the scene as 'the final disastrous event in the development of swing music' was in tune with an anti-Swing trend that also involved some critical denunciations of Duke Ellington's orchestra of the very early Forties, a period now widely acknowledged as an Ellingtonian golden era.

The reactions of musicians on the spot are naturally faster than those of critics removed from the centre of the action, and it was much earlier in his career that Lester Young met the stiffest opposition from other players. It was in 1934, when he was playing in Count Basie's band in Kansas City, that he received a call from Fletcher Henderson, whose star saxophonist, Coleman Hawkins, had just left for Europe. According to Lester, he had already sat in with the Henderson Orchestra—presumably during one of that band's visits to Kansas City—and, in the temporary absence of Hawkins, had been able to show that he could handle all the saxophone and clarinet parts in Hawk's book.

Any euphoric expectations which Lester Young might have entertained after that episode were rudely shattered when he arrived in Detroit to join Henderson for a trial period. In view of my earlier comments on the reaction of critics to Lester Young, it is paradoxical that the one man in Fletcher Henderson's entourage who *did* appreciate the newcomer was critic and *ex officio* musical adviser, John Hammond. 'I thought he was the greatest tenor I'd heard in my life. He was so different. There was a terrific scene. The guys in the band all wanted Chu Berry to replace Hawkins because Chu had a sound like Hawkins. They complained that Lester's sound was "like an alto". Buster Bailey, Russell Procope and John Kirby outshouted me that day.' Despite the immediate opposition, Lester stayed with Henderson for several miserable months. In addition to the hostile whisperings of the musicians, he was subjected to attempted brainwashing by Fletcher Henderson's wife, Leora. The recollection of it in an interview twenty-three years later (with François Postif, published in the book *Jazz Panorama*) aroused in him uncharacteristic aggression. 'That bitch, she was Fletcher's wife, she took me down to the basement and played one of the old wind-up record-players, and she'd say, "Lester, can't you play like this?" Coleman Hawkins records. But I mean, can't you hear this? Can't you get with that? You dig? I split! Every morning that bitch would wake me up at nine o'clock to teach me to play like Coleman Hawkins. And she played trumpet herself . . . circus trumpet! I'm gone!'

And gone he was, back by a devious route to Count Basie's Kansas City Band. Two years later, Hammond picked up a broadcast from Kansas City on his car radio in the small hours of the morning. It featured Count Basie's Orchestra with Lester in one of the two tenor-saxophone chairs. Hammond's subsequent championing of Basie's band gave him a second and more successful chance to promote the career of Lester Young.

Careful scrutiny of all the criticism of Lester Young from musicians and commentators that was expressed between 1934 and 1946 reveals in him one fundamental flaw. He was not Coleman Hawkins. And in case anyone should think that British critics were straggling behind their American counterparts by the mid-Forties, it is worth noting that an annual jazz award organized by the American *Esquire Magazine*, and judged by a panel of from sixteen to eighteen professional jazz critics, overlooked Lester Young entirely in the years 1944 and 1946, and could only find room for him in the Silver Award category in 1945. Each year, the top Golden Award went to Coleman Hawkins. At the same time, in an article in the same magazine entitled 'Jazz Greats: Musicians and Bands', one Paul Edouard Miller omitted Lester entirely from a list of no less than sixteen all-time saxophone 'greats', at the same time scraping the barrel for such comparative lightweights as Babe Russin, Joe Garland and Prince Robinson.

Creatively, Lester Young's most fruitful and consistent period spanned a mere eight years between his first recordings in 1936 and his induction into the US Army in 1944. Throughout that time, it took a tenor-saxophone player of almost perverse individuality and persistence not to be Coleman Hawkins. Of all the tenor players who had come to the fore since Hawkins lugged the instrument into the jazz fold in the mid-Twenties, only Bud Freeman comes to mind as a player offering an alternative to the heavy-toned, chesty and romantic Hawkins model. Even so, study of Bud's playing in the early Thirties reveals a hustling, rough-edged sound nearer to Hawkins than Young. The often-made assumption that Bud influenced Lester—rejected by Lester himself in the aforementioned interview with the splendidly dismissive and original expletive 'ladedehumptedorebebop!'—seems to me to have been based on the lighter sound which Bud acquired in the late Thirties, long after Lester's style had been formed. During those eight years when he was battling his way into the jazz history books against the Hawkins tide, Lester Young fought without the ego-boosting support, such as both Hawkins and Armstrong enjoyed, of a 'school' of admirers and imitators. He was not entirely isolated. Within his own coterie of Kansas City musicians, several of them colleagues in Count Basie's band, he found staunch admiration and friendship. And there was the added compensation that the audiences in the dance halls across the country latched on to his 'new' style very much more quickly than did some critics and fellow musicians. Some recordings of on-location broadcasts by the Basie band in the late Thirties enable us to hear the clamorous response which his free-wheeling solos received. Perhaps for this reason, he never shared the jaundiced and somewhat contemptuous view of the paying customer that Coleman Hawkins so often expressed. He once told a somewhat surprised interviewer that he enjoyed playing for dancers because of the rhythmic feed-back that he received from the floor.

It was from musicians outside his own circle that he felt the chilliest draught. The article which Rex Stewart wrote in *Down-beat* in 1966 (and which was reproduced in the compilation *Jazz in the Thirties*) threw light on the prevailing atmosphere in the late Thirties. In the chapter on Coleman Hawkins, I have already quoted Rex's description of the return of Hawkins to New York after his sojourn in Europe and his appearance at Pussy Johnson's 'after-hours' club. Continuing the narrative, Rex wrote: 'Hawk fell in later than usual—it was about 3 a.m.—and as luck would have it, Lady Day was singing, which rarely happened uptown those days (1939). Of course, Lester accompanied her. Bean [Coleman Hawkins] strode in, unpacked his axe and joined them, to everyone's surprise. Then, when Billie Holiday finished, she announced that it had been a pleasure to have had the world's greatest tenor saxophonist backing her up—Lester Young!' The story continues in predictable fashion with Hawkins imperiously routing Lester Young. When the article first appeared, it prompted Billie Holiday to write an angry letter to the magazine refuting it and claiming that Lester had been the victor. The outcome is irrelevant to us now. What is significant is Billie's defensive reaction on behalf of her friend and colleague, and the way in which the resentment which the devotees of Hawkins felt at the challenge from Lester Young seemed to survive the twenty-seven years between the event and Rex's published recollection of it. In more recent times, during the rapid progress of jazz through first modern and then *avant-garde* phases, we have become accustomed to the spectacle of new sounds being angrily—and, if the truth were known, fearfully—repudiated by musicians and *aficionados* of an older school. It is a measure of the total originality of Lester's whole approach to his instrument that, before him, such a thing had never happened in jazz.

If we look beyond the scope of this volume to the fourteen years between Lester Young's discharge from the army and his untimely death in 1959, we are confronted with a terrible irony. For at the very time that swarms of young musicians were homing in on Lester's style and establishing it as the basis of modern tenor-saxophone development, his own playing went into dramatic decline. Whether because of trauma inflicted on his sensitive nature during his army stint or, more simply and probably, through sheer creative exhaustion, the once smooth-flowing and effortless stream of invention became progressively clogged up with a compound of lassitude, eccentricity and technical debility. The irony is brought into sharp focus by the story, probably apocryphal, of a young disciple who, outraged by a lacklustre and uninspired performance by the master, confronted him on the bandstand with the anguished cry, 'You're not you—I'M you!'

At this point, we should pause to look into the origins—so far as we can deduce them—and the nature of Lester Young's once-controversial style. The first thing to say about it is that, unlike the styles of so many other jazz innovators which we are able to trace through their formative, exploratory years, the Lester Young sound burst upon us fully fledged with his very first recording and thenceforward changed only to modify and, eventually, deteriorate. Sound was the principal, though not the only, new ingredient. Let's think for a moment in terms of singing. As most readers may well have discovered for themselves through experiments in the bath, the difference between the tenor, the baritone and the bass voice (or, in the upper range, soprano, mezzosoprano and contralto) is one of sound production as much as range. Indeed, the actual difference in range of pitch between the tenor and bass voice is rather less than the sound suggests. The bathroom experiment to which I referred often begins with the urge to sound like the late Paul Robeson. 'Oold mahn roover,' we intone, opening the mouth wide but shaping it into closed 'oo' and 'aw' sounds to achieve the resonant, booming effect. Instantly the bath becomes the rolling Mississippi as you and me we sweat and strain, neighbours all achin' and wracked with pain. When we switch to a Mario Lanza tenor, stretching the mouth into a permanent smile with piercing 'ee' and 'ah' vowels and bringing the sound up into the throat, the scene changes miraculously to the sun-speckled waters of Venice—but because our natural tuneless drone is neither bass-baritone nor tenor, the notes are exactly the same, restricted to a very unspectacular middle range. If you doubt me, get out that favourite Paul Robeson record and sing along with it, but in Mario Lanza fashion, all thin vowels and throaty constriction. You will find the pitch is not as low as you thought.

This light-hearted excursion into bathroom opera has a direct bearing on the Lester Young-Coleman Hawkins discussion. The sound which Coleman Hawkins produced from the tenor saxophone using, according to him, a hard reed and open 'lay' (the gap between reed surface and mouthpiece) was a rich chest tone in which impurities such as the sound of breath passing over the reed and the actual buzzing of the reed as it vibrated gave added weight to the note. Further enrichment was provided by a wide and quite heavy vibrato, which saxophonists achieve by a throbbing movement of lips and jaw around the mouthpiece. The choice of this deeply expressive sound—often referred to as a 'vocal sound' because of its similarity to the rough edge and heavy vibrato of the human voice in general and black singers of African origin in particular—was not peculiar either to Coleman Hawkins or to the tenor saxophone. It came naturally to jazzmen playing music closely allied to such folk sources as the blues and black church music. The feeling of high emotional intensity which it conveys— in the trumpet playing of Louis Armstrong, the soprano saxophone of Sidney Bechet, the clarinet of Johnny Dodds and Pee Wee Russell, the trombone of Jimmy Harrison and Dickie Wells—was largely responsible for the application of the word 'hot' to the music which these men and their contemporaries and imitators produced.

To explain why Coleman Hawkins dominated the tenor-saxophone field for over a decade we must look at the character of the instrument itself. The saxophone is not, *pace* Adolphe Sax, the most successful of musical instruments in its pristine state. Despite the claim of its inventor that it would bridge the gap between brass and woodwind, it was spurned by the symphony orchestra and found only a limited role to play in military bands. Even its apparent apotheosis in the ranks of the early dance bands was less of a triumph than it seemed. For the instrument became, in the Twenties, the symbol of everything that was oily, sickly and sentimental about popular music. In the London humorous magazine, *Punch*, decadent dance music was symbolized in cartoons by a limp and languid figure with slicked, patent-leather hair and ankle-length coat-tails, exhaling superciliously into a saxophone. Within the saxophone family itself, judged by its own aspirations, the soprano and alto instruments had at the outset a certain plaintive clarity which is attractive, while there was more masculine character in the gruffness of baritone and bass. But I fancy that Adolphe Sax might himself have conceded, in an unguarded moment, that the tenor saxophone was a flop. The flabby, rubbery sounds, evoking the image of someone trying to juggle pancakes, that can be heard on dance-band recordings made before (and for sometime after) Coleman Hawkins took the instrument in hand, provide evidence of its recalcitrance. Indeed, when we listen to some of the early recordings which he himself made with Fletcher Henderson's band, we may be excused for wondering what manic urge drove him to persevere in such an unpromising task. But persevere he did, and the means by which he gave the tenor saxophone a commanding jazz voice have already been explored. After such massive effort and achievement, it is little wonder that, for years, other tenor-saxophone players were content to base their own explorations on the Hawkins method, as if no other feasible way of playing the instrument existed.

Apart from acknowledging the influence that Louis Armstrong had on all the musicians in Fletcher Henderson's band during his brief engagement with it, Coleman Hawkins never offered any suggestion as to external influences on his style. Lester Young was more obliging. To the consternation of some jazz pundits who have exaggerated the ethnic origins of jazz to the point of a sort of cultural *apartheid*, Lester always pointed to two white musicians as his chief influences. 'I had a decision to make between Frankie Trumbauer and Jimmy Dorsey [Lester was playing alto saxophone at the time], you dig, and I wasn't sure which way I wanted to go. I'd buy me all those records and I'd play one by Jimmy and one by Trumbauer, you dig? I didn't know nothing about Hawk then, and they were the only ones telling a story I liked to hear. I had both of them made ... Did you ever hear Trumbauer play "Singin' the Blues"? That tricked me right then and that's where I went.'

Significantly, Frank Trumbauer played the now obsolete C-melody saxophone on 'Singin' the Blues', an instrument pitched between the E flat alto saxophone and the B flat tenor. So when, at some undetermined point in his career, Lester Young switched to the tenor saxophone, it was easy for him to carry over the Trumbauer influence, such as it was, on to the lower instrument. I say 'such as it was' because, by the time we hear Lester on record, it is hard to find any vestige of Trumbauer except in the lightness of his sound compared with that of Coleman Hawkins. Where Trumbauer's notes are rhythmically flat and lifeless, Lester's, though comparably light on vibrato, have a springy resilience. One note of his—and we shall see that he quite often started a solo with an isolated note as if to balance himself for the flight of fancy ahead—would swing more than a whole phrase of Trumbauer's. Likewise there is no resemblance between Trumbauer's sinuous, rubber-necked and rather contrived phraseology and Lester's free-flying, effortless inventions. Some commentators have called on the paucity of stylistic links between Trumbauer and Lester Young to back the suggestion that the latter simply dredged up Trumbauer's name to satisfy an inquisitive interviewer. But it would not be the first time in artistic history that a small fragment from a predecessor's work has sown in the mind of a fellow-artist the seed of a fully-fledged style.

Referring back to the analogy of the bathroom vocalist, we can understand why Herschel Evans and the musicians in Fletcher Henderson's band thought that Lester's tone sounded like an alto. They would have been equally fair had they alleged that Hawkins made the instrument sound more like a baritone. 'Some of you guys are all belly!' was an apt riposte from Lester, too— the sound to which the Hawkins school aspired did seem to originate not far north of the pelvic region. If the contrast between Lester and the Hawkins 'establishment' rested only in the matter of tone production, then it would hardly warrant the space it occupies in the jazz history books. But from tone production, other aspects of style spring. One consequence of the light, airy sound that Lester Young adopted was that it made him more fleet of foot.

The word that recurs in critical analyses of the Coleman Hawkins style is 'heavy', and it is a word that can be taken literally. Hawk himself had the power and the imaginative resources to overcome the sheer weight of his delivery. His imitators—and through the Thirties they were legion, in Britain and Europe as well as in the United States—often gave the impression, to borrow one British musician's evocative phrase, that they were trying to tow the *Queen Mary* through a sea of Mars Bars. The dichotomy between agility and emotional weight had occurred in jazz years before Lester Young's emergence. In the late Twenties, the trumpeter, Jabbo Smith, challenged Louis Armstrong's supremacy with a style that sacrificed some of Armstrong's richness of tone and vibrato in favour of range and speed. He failed not because his style was too different from Armstrong's, but because it was too close. Encouraged, if not coerced, by a record company to try and match the popular records by Louis Armstrong's Hot Five, he missed the mark artistically (and commercially, too, though perhaps for other reasons) because in his efforts to surpass the *method* of Armstrong's playing he lost its spirit.

At no time in his career did Lester flirt with the Hawkins method. Central to the Hawkins style, especially in heated, up-tempo work, was the technique that musicians used to call 'running changes'. This means basing an improvisation on the changing harmonies that underlie a tune. Consisting of funda-mental chords and 'linking' chords—secondary chords used to pass conveniently and elegantly from one fundamental chord to another—these harmonies often present the improviser with a complex challenge. Take a simple progression—C, C diminished, G seventh—in which the C diminished is the linking chord. This might well occur in the space of two bars at breakneck speed. To 'run the changes' impressively the player will fashion a melodic line which makes explicit use of the arpeggios of the three chords, giving the impression of a terrier snapping at the heels of the harmonies as they twist and turn. Coleman Hawkins, as we have seen, was a master at this, often choosing tunes with complex progressions or using his keenly acquired knowledge of harmony to make simple progressions more challenging by adding or sub-stituting chords.

It is a mistake to think that Lester Young set out consciously to alter this approach to improvisation. Some rather facile judgements delivered in hindsight after the advent of Bebop suggested that Lester was influential in laying the theoreretical foundations of the new style. If the hindsight is focused a little more intently, the interesting fact that emerges is that Lester's most direct influence on post-1945 (still anachronistically referred to as Modern) jazz, through the countless young tenor saxo-phonists who adopted his sound and method of phrase-building, was essentially conservative. Players such as Wardell Gray, Allan Eager, Stan Getz (in his early days), Herbie Steward and Zoot Sims were notably less adventurous, harmonically and rhythmically, than the young altoists and trumpeters who followed Charlie Parker and Dizzy Gillespie.

As regards the raw materials on which he thrived, Lester Young may be said to have been more deeply committed to the tenets of the Swing Era than Coleman Hawkins. While Hawkins was constantly chasing new harmonic patterns on which to sharpen his improvisational wits, Lester appeared to be content with the simplest of harmonies. Indeed, it may have been his upbringing in the environment of Kansas City jazz, with its great emphasis on the blues and on the building of massive rhythmic skyscrapers on the simplest of themes, that, in his formative years, pushed Lester into exploring new paths of invention. There is little future in running changes if those changes resolutely refuse to budge!

So far, our analysis of Lester Young has been somewhat negative. He did not play with a huge, positive sound like Coleman Hawkins. He did not base his improvisations as closely as Hawkins did on the details of moving harmonies. Nor on the other hand did he radically change or extend conventional theory. It has to be said that Lester's own character and personality contributed to this negative impression. One of the many idiosyncratic, short-hand phrases of which his conversation was compounded was 'No eyes'—a simplified reversal of the sentiment in the song-title 'I Only have Eyes for You'. We know of a great many things for which Lester had 'no eyes', among them honking one-note tenor players, drummers who 'dropped bombs'— broke up the rhythm with explosive accents—pianists who intruded on the soloist and so on. But on the positive side, Lester was even less inclined than his predecessors and contemporaries to put his musical ideas into words.

Fortunately, there has been no shortage of commentators ready to analyse Lester's style. Sometimes there has been a tendency to commit, in reverse, the injustice inflicted upon Lester in his early years—in other words, to suggest that, by being different from Coleman Hawkins, Lester Young was *ipso facto* better than him. If our discussions about jazz performances up to now have revealed anything, it is that the intrinsic merit in a jazz musician's work lies not in the materials that he uses, but in the use he makes of them. In the first book in this series, for example, I looked at the work of three contrasting trumpet players, Louis Armstrong, Bix Beiderbecke and Henry 'Red' Allen. We saw how, in 'Potato Head Blues', Louis took the theme and virtually redesigned it, filling it out with rhythmic, harmonic and emotional dimensions that it never possessed before. In 'Singin' the Blues', Bix did something different, building on the harmonies of the tune an entirely new melody, quite different in shape from the original. And I noted that, in 'Panama' and elsewhere, Henry Allen's method was to super-impose on the theme bursts of impressionistic sound that bore the same relationship to the 'tune' as an abstract painting has to the model or still-life that inspired it. If we deduce from this that Bix tended to improvise 'melodically' while the others did not, it does not mean that their melodies were somehow imperfect, nor indeed that they performed the almost impossible task of stringing notes together in sequence without producing a coherent melodic line at all! Least of all does it mean that any one of these jazzmen pursued his own method to the exclusion of the others. It is a matter of emphasis.

In this context, the best way to distinguish between the Cole-man Hawkins method and that of Lester Young is to say that, in basing his improvisations on the harmonies of, say, a popular ballad, Hawkins in fact was creating an elaborate cadenza around a tune or melody line which was implied rather than stated. Thus a Hawkins solo is rarely, if ever, as simple in structure as the tune on which it is based. Lester Young was not given to elaboration on these lines. What he preferred to do was to create his own tune, offering in his solo an alternative, if you like, to the nominal theme. Two extreme examples of this method come to mind.

In the Count Basie recording of 'Jive at Five' made in 1938, Lester's way of improvising on the frail, sparse theme is to create another frail theme, no less sparse than the original, and develop that through the thirty-two-bar solo. And in the 1945 version with his own quartet of 'These Foolish Things', he discards Jack

Strachey's tune altogether, jumping—or, in his characteristically diffident way, sidling—in at the deep end with a spontaneously composed melody line of his own.

The beauty and the challenge of this type of solo-building is that it offers the soloist greater freedom from the restrictions of the popular song format. Leaving aside distinguished exceptions which will spring to every reader's mind, the great majority of popular songs written between the Twenties and the Fifties have come in a standard thirty-two-bar length. Some of them, such as I Can't Give you Anything but Love' or 'Pennies from Heaven', are divided into two sixteen-bar halves, sharing an opening four-bar phrase which progresses, in each half respectively, towards an imperfect cadence or half-way mark and a perfect cadence or conclusion. The significant thing about this format in our present context is that it involves repetition, the tune going back to the beginning at the start of the second half. Even more repetition is involved in the other standard formula, represented in tunes such as George Gershwin's 'I Got Rhythm', Fats Waller's 'Honeysuckle Rose' and, with slight variation, Irving Berlin's 'Easter Parade'. Here the tune is divided into four eight-bar sections in the pattern AABA, the B section being known, in a triumph of expediency over geometric accuracy, as the 'middle-eight'. (The variation in 'Easter Parade' and many similar tunes is that there is an imperfect cadence—a musical comma, if you like—between the first two A sections.)

In the 1930s, jazz musicians, increasingly absorbed more with the solo development of a theme than with the structure of the theme itself, often borrowed tunes from Tin Pan Alley or lazily superimposed a set of 'riffs' or repeated phrases on the framework of a standard popular song (Chu Berry's 'Christopher Columbus' is one of perhaps several hundred similar 'compositions' based on 'I Got Rhythm'). The short-winded repetitiveness of these themes presented a challenge to the jazz improviser, whatever his method. Louis Armstrong revealed himself a master at reshaping the tunesmith's repetitive phrases with melodic and rhythmic variation so that they grew into a magnificent edifice that dwarfed the original. Following this Armstrong line, Coleman Hawkins added his own extension of it, which was to build on the equally repetitive harmonies of the tune an inexhaustible flow of varying patterns and embellishments that seem to jostle and fall over each other in their eagerness to pursue each new notion to its conclusion.

It might be thought that in opting for the simplest harmonic framework of popular ditty and the blues ('The blues? Great big eyes!' was how he reacted to a question about the latter) and improvising his own melody over it, Lester Young had gone for the soft option. No 'tune' to enhance and ennoble in the Armstrong manner, no complex harmonic changes to follow and resolve *à la* Hawkins—what could be simpler or less fraught with responsibility, you might ask? Indeed, the Swing Era, geared at its lowest commercial level to the whipping-up of spurious excitement, abounded in solos no less empty and inane than the themes on which they were built. We've all seen those Hollywood 'shorts' featuring big bands in which, inevitably, a trumpet player jumps to his feet, shoulders hunched and brow corrugated with distended veins, to rip off a solo for which the aptest description can be found in *Macbeth*, 'A tale told by an idiot, full of sound and fury, signifying nothing'. Subsequently, the rock'n'roll experience, in which grievous harm has been inflicted by one-note tenor men and three-cliché guitarists upon the noble structure of the blues, has provided added proof that there is nothing easy about improvising on a simple framework, unless it be the production of dire music.

To focus upon Lester Young's mastery we can go straight to one of his very first recorded solos. The session, in Chicago on 9 October 1936, represented a sort of consolation prize to John Hammond for having lost the Count Basie Orchestra to a rival recording company, due to a misunderstanding on Basie's part. But what a prize! Here was a small contingent from the band comprising Lester Young on tenor, Carl 'Tatti' Smith on trumpet and the incomparable rhythm trio of Count Basie, bassist Walter Page, and drummer Jo Jones. For good measure, the rotund Jimmy Rushing (yet to achieve immortality in Tin Pan Alley as the subject of the Gene de Paul-Don Raye novelty song 'Mister Five by Five') was on hand to sing the blues. History has given John Hammond the laugh over his zealous competitor, since these four small-group recordings, originally issued for obvious reasons under the name Jones-Smith Incorporated, gave Lester Young room to stretch out more spectacularly than on the band recordings that followed. The two wholly instrumental titles, 'Lady Be Good', and 'Shoe Shine Boy' (first listed as 'Shoe Shine Swing') are classics, and my choice of the former for close analysis rests on nothing more substantial than old acquaintance.

'Lady Be Good' (pedants please note that I deliberately employ the common jazz musicians' usage, well aware that Gershwin's song is 'Oh, Lady Be Good!' from the 1924 show *Lady, Be Good*) is just the sort of simple tune, in AABA form, that attracts musicians bent upon informal improvisation. With no more than four basic chords and fewer melodic twists, it presents the improviser with what amounts to a bare canvas. The melody gives a Louis Armstrong scope on which to build and expand, the harmonies can be enriched and augmented to provide a Coleman Hawkins or an Art Tatum ample scope for 'running changes'. But, as I have already noted, Lester Young eschewed both these basic methods of improvisation, choosing to construct a line of melody the shape of which was quite independent of the original.

At this point, we must establish the point that Lester's style imposed a heavy responsibility upon the rhythm section, and we may well wonder what would have happened had not a benign Providence brought him together, early in his career, with Count Basie and his rhythm section colleagues. Whether the perfect match was made in heaven or evolved through rehearsal-room or bandstand discussion is not important. Lester Young's requirements have emerged in interviews over the years. 'The piano should play little fill-ins. Just nice little full chords behind the horn. I don't get in his way, and I let him play, and he shouldn't get in mine. Otherwise, your mind gets twisted . . . A bass should play nice, four-beat rhythm that can be heard . . . On drumming, I don't go for the bomb. I want a drummer to be straight with the section. He's messing with the rhythm when he drops those bombs.'

Pianists, bassists and drummers may well give a wry smile when reading these instructions. They are all too accustomed to being asked to respond to the quirky requirements of front-line men. But the discipline demanded by Lester Young was absolutely essential to his style. We shall soon see that his solos abound in unexpected melodic turns, the subtlest of harmonic nuances and totally unpredictable rhythmic patterns. To have a pianist and drummer dictating fanciful harmonies or rhythmic ideas of their own would have destroyed all the freedom which Lester derived from the simplicity of the thematic framework. Furthermore, it would have been an impertinence on the grandest scale, rather as if a committee of minor sculptors had appointed itself to direct Michelangelo in the carving of his Moses.

Obviously there will be more to say about the Count Basie rhythm section when I come to discuss the Count Basie Orchestra in the ensuing volume of this series. Suffice it to say that, although the great guitarist, Freddie Greene, had yet to join them when 'Lady Be Good' was recorded, Basie, Page and Jones establish from the outset that comfortably slippered, padding rhythm which for almost half a century has been a Basie trade-mark. Though twelve years had elapsed since Gene Krupa demonstrated on the McKenzie-Condon Chicagoan's version of 'Nobody's Sweetheart' that a bass drum could be recorded without damage to the equipment, the tiny studio in which this session took place was still unable to take the strain, and Jo Jones was confined to snare drum and high-hat cymbal. Walter Page, sometimes padding up and down the scale in what is known as 'walking bass' style, sometimes striding across the arpeggios as the New Orleans bassists had done before him, contrived to exude a feeling of strength and security despite his none-too-accurate pitching. As for Basie himself, it may well have been the superb team-work of Jones and Page that prompted him to pare down his once-fulsome stride piano style so as to give them more air. Be that as it may, the three of them sketch in the outline of 'Lady Be Good' with great economy and enormous swing, rolling out a sumptuous red carpet in preparation for Lester Young's entrance.

The British critic and broadcaster, Benny Green, once a tenor saxophonist himself, has told how, as an eager young musician, he learnt Lester Young's solo in 'Lady Be Good' by heart. He was playing in an unenterprising dance band at the time, and it took time and patience to persuade the leader to abandon the stock arrangements and drop an *ad lib* version of 'Lady Be Good' into the routine. When it happened, Benny rose to his feet and reeled off the famous solo note-for-note, his triumph marred only by the fact that he was one bar adrift from the rest of the band throughout. It is not hard to understand the mishap. By the late Thirties, when the Jones-Smith recordings came into wide circulation, jazz enthusiasts had become, through listening to records by Armstrong and Hawkins and Duke Ellington, well acquainted with an established jazz vernacular. As in everyday human speech, certain conventions had emerged—standard and familiar cadences, asides and turns of phrase—which were used, even by the finest players, to achieve continuity in an improvised solo. As a result, the listener came to expect and, indeed, to anticipate a soloist's moves. In Lester Young's work, from the very outset, such expectations are constantly thwarted. In the solo under discussion, there are innumerable surprises of this kind.

The first occurs within the first couple of bars. Lester starts his solo, in characteristic fashion, with a short, isolated phrase the hub of which is a note firmly placed on the first beat of bar one, followed by a long pause of three beats in which he seems to be balancing himself, like a tightrope walker, before making further progress. As a method of launching a solo, this 'balancing note' that Lester often used corresponds to the three anticipated crotchets which were a characteristic of Louis Armstrong's entrances in the Hot Five days. Of particular importance to the surprise effect of the ensuing phrase are the two introductory notes in the preceding bar, a quaver-crotchet combination that serves no purpose other than to lead up to that arresting opening note. If these subsidiary notes are to recur at all, our expectations are that it will be at the end of bar one, as a similarly insignificant lead-in to a new phrase. In the Count Basie recording of 'Jumpin' at the Woodside', there is a concluding riff in which a similar grouping of notes—in this instance three quavers or eighth-notes—lead into the main elements of the riff and occur, as we expect, at the tail-end of each bar. In Lester Young's solo, the notes *do* recur—but they are delayed until half a beat into the second bar, where they become the much more important opening notes of a long, fluent phrase. Had the phrase begun where we expected—at the end of bar one—its main emphasis would have fallen on the first, third and first beats of the ensuing bars, which are fairly conventional stopping and starting places. Lester's 'misplaced' phrase falls heavily on beats three, one and three, altering the whole balance. It may well have been this thwarting of expectations that threw the youthful Benny Green off course.

The solo is full of such departures from common practice. In the second half of the middle-eight (bars twenty-one to twenty-four of the solo) there is another striking example. The chord sequence here is common to many middle-eights. To those acquainted with the language of the harmony text books it can be described as V7 of V, V7. Translated into the 'Lady Be Good' key of G major, these symbols become A seventh, leading on to D seventh. By the time Lester Young came to record the tune, that particular sequence had been played and recorded thousands of times by jazz improvisers. And yet Lester's handling of the sequence strikes us as peculiar and temporarily unsettling. The reason is that, at the end of the first of the two phrases which cover this section, he lands firmly on a C sharp crotchet at the start of bar twenty-two. There is nothing harmonically startling about this—C sharp is the third degree of the scale of A and is therefore perfectly in place in an A seventh chord. Why, then, does the phrase leave us feeling curiously up in the air? The answer is that the C sharp is the leading note into the chord of D seventh which follows. A more commonplace phrase would have ended on A, leaving the ear complacently receptive to several alternative moves from there. But the C sharp arouses positive espectations. As the poet might have said, when C sharp comes, can D be far behind? The answer in this instance is, yes. For with characteristic perversity, Lester Young inserts a linking A minor chord before the D seventh in bar twenty-three, thereby delaying the moment when the expected D is articulated. Indeed, in the whole of the answering second phrase, the D does not appear at all. Instead, the passage is resolved *rhythmically*, with that C sharp crotchet on the first beat of bar twenty-two answered by an E crotchet on the fourth beat of bar twenty-three. The whole episode concludes with a glorious Lesterism. Having played a tantalizing trick on us, Lester produces from behind his back the long-awaited D, drumming away at it over bars twenty-five and twenty-six as if to savour the joke.

Of course, in attributing conscious designs and motives to improvising soloists, one is exercising commentator's licence. The subtle twists and turns which I have described were the intuitive by-products of Lester Young's style, which in turn owed much to the character and personality of the man himself. Likewise, the introduction of terms such as 'modality' and 'Debussian' into discussion of Lester Young's work—and it happens, friends, it happens—can only serve to spread a smokescreen between the artist and the listener. For musicological insight, I would sooner go to Lester Young's former colleague, the blues singer, Jimmy Rushing, who would often say, 'I listened to Lester a million times—and every time you expect him to go one way, he'll go the other.' Many musicians and promoters who had dealings with Lester, especially in his later years, will testify that this judgement aptly describes the personality of the man who devised a strange, monosyllabic vernacular of his own, discouraged interviewers with oblique and devious answers and, in one phase, feigned homosexual mannerisms in order to keep the world at arm's length.

In music, deviousness and unpredictability can be positive virtues when, as in all of Lester's early work and the best from later years, they stop far short of eccentricity. One rewarding outcome of Lester's reluctance to look the world in the eye was his predilection for those notes in the scale, notably the sixth and the ninth, which introduce a degree of harmonic ambiguity. The construction of a tune such as 'Lady Be Good' presents the improviser with certain problems. In its conventional AABA form, the A sections all end with perfect cadences—in other words, they return to the key or 'home' note of G. We have seen how Benny Carter, for instance, would surmount those awkwardly repetitive cadences by disguising each one in a fresh and elegantly fashioned variation, while Coleman Hawkins would charge through and over them like an express train. To less ingenious players, the key note has often seemed to exert a magnetic pull, preventing the soloist from roaming far afield. In fast tempos, this agoraphobic constraint often seemed to afflict Lester's great rival in the Count Basie band, Herschel Evans. Indeed, there are in existence transcriptions of the Basie band in 'live' action in which Evans, and not Lester Young, takes the principal part in band versions of 'Lady Be Good', and his performance is marred by a too-frequent reiteration of the keynote in predictable places.

Lester Young recoiled instinctively from this constant returning to base, in much the same way that Louis Armstrong's built-in radar would steer him away from the dull symmetry inherent in much popular song construction. Lester's characteristic way was to make heavy use of the sixth note of the scale. In the performance under discussion this note is the E in 'Lady Be Good's' key of G. Added to the G major triad of G, A and D, the E creates a G major sixth which is a legitimate, and indeed, familiar thickening of the tonic chord of G. But in its fourth inversion, starting on the E and rising through G, A and D, the chord becomes identical to the chord of E minor seventh. This ambiguity between the major key and its relative minor was clearly attractive to Lester Young, and the arpeggio appears often in his solos, introducing an extra colour—a minor tint, if you like—into a major key composition. Thus we find that instead of returning to the keynote at the end of the first sixteen bars, as Gershwin did with the words 'Oh lady, be good TO ME', Lester ascends to alight on that neutral sixth note, providing a far less conclusive end to the section.

A very similar purpose is achieved by Lester Young's leaning towards the minor chord—in this instance A minor seventh—based on the second degree of the scale, and containing, incidentally, that much favoured sixth note. I have already mentioned this chord's crucial appearance in bar twenty-three of the solo, where it is inserted to delay the resolution from A seventh to D seventh. Lester uses it also in the fifth bar of almost every A-section of the AABA construction, although Gershwin's melody, on the descending notes D, C, A, D, clearly indicate a straightforward dominant chord of D seventh. Here again, Lester seems drawn towards the minor tonality, resulting in an oblique, sidelong quality to his solos which gives the most simple and mundane harmonic sequence an air of mystery and complexity.

A further consequence of this obliqueness is that when Lester Young did decide to succumb to the obvious and, indeed, confront it head on, the effect was electrifying. In the first thirty-two-bar chorus of his solo there is, as I have pointed out, a studious reluctance to alight or linger on key note G which plays such a prominent part in Gershwin's simple tune. In the second chorus, by contrast, Lester throws circumlocution to the wind. At the end of bar thirty-two, there's a bold upper-register variation on the 'Three Blind Mice' cadence which leads firmly to the key note. Even here, Lester drops down at once to E and A, delineating the ambiguous G sixth/E minor seventh chord on which the ensuing phrase is built. However, at the start of the second eight-bar section of this chorus, he takes the key note by the scruff of the neck, as if to exorcise it once and for all. For over three bars he dances a rhythmic tarantella around it, throwing it from one beat to another and teasing it with an uncharacteristically exaggerated vibrato. This kind of rhythmic by-play, often used by Lester as a contrast to long, flowing lines, reminds us that his first professional work was as a drummer. Sometimes (but not here) he would literally drum on a note by using alternative fingering—producing a note of identical pitch but different timbre through an alternative combination of the instrument's keys.

As in the second chorus of Lester Young's 'Lady Be Good' solo, the moments when he decided to turn from melodic invention to swinging resolution on one note were always perfectly integrated into his solos, with a positive musical purpose. No doubt they produced a tangible response from the dance floor wherever the Basie band played. Certainly, a decade or so later, they were to arouse the audiences at Norman Granz's Jazz at the Philharmonic concerts to an ecstasy of frenzy. And here's a strange irony. The seeds of the honking, exhibitionistic, one-note tenor-saxophone excesses which were rampant in the frenetic rock'n'roll of the Fifties—and for which Lester Young had positively 'no eyes'—are to be found, not in the extrovert, 'hot' playing of his rivals in the Thirties, but in the style of this shy, withdrawn and allegedly 'cool' musician himself!

Before following 'Lady Be Good' to its conclusion, it might

Benny Carter

Johnny Hodges

Dickie Wells

be instructive to examine Lester Young's historic role as the inspiration for the post-war 'cool school' of jazz. No one who has listened to the performance under discussion will accept that 'cool' in this context implies an absense of warmth. The beautifully constructed lines of melody that Lester produced—and I would draw attention to the passage spanning bars thirty-three to thirty-seven of the solo for special reference—are rich in subtly seductive inflections that tug at the heart-strings. The steady building of rhythmic lift and excitement I have already mentioned. The tone which caused such dissension at the time of Lester's début was, as we have seen, less encrusted with opulent overtones and heavy vibrato than that of Coleman Hawkins and his followers, but did it really digress so dramatically from the norm? In the early Fifties, a British writer, who would no doubt prefer to remain anonymous in this context, launched his broadcasting career with a detailed analysis of a Lester Young solo that turned out to be by the Hawkins-inspired Don Byas. A few years later, the compiler of a double album of Lester Young's work with Count Basie included the title 'Rockabye Basie' which featured not Lester, but Buddy Tate, playing in the Herschel Evans style. And as late as 1971, the American writer, Ross Russell, in an otherwise fine essay on Lester in his book, *Jazz Style in Kansas City and the South West*, attributed to Lester Young a passage in the Young classic 'Taxi War Dance' that was again the work of Buddy Tate.

All of this reinforces my view, expressed in the essay on Bix Beiderbecke in *The Best Of Jazz*, Volume One that 'hot' and 'cool' elements coexist in every period of jazz and, indeed, in the style of each individual musician. I did, however, offer one interpretation of the 'hot versus cool' theory which seemed to me to be constructive. In this, I categorized as 'hot' those musicians, from Louis Armstrong to Charlie Parker, John Coltrane and beyond, who 'pushed the boundaries of jazz further and further outwards, the cumulative effect of their key recordings giving the impression of men impelled by demons'. In contrast to this, I cited examples of a contrasting creative direction 'which has led musicians of equal genius to dwell upon, explore, refine and illuminate each new extension of the idiom'. Among these musicians I nominated Bix Beiderbecke, Lester Young and Miles Davis in his early phase. What they seem to me to have in common is a lucidity that derives from the fact that their role was to simplify rather than go out in search of new complexities. While others challenged their melodic inventiveness by harnessing it to ever more complex harmonic progressions, Lester Young set himself the no less challenging task of extracting gold from the most basic harmonic soil. Rhythmically, too, he turned away from the headlong career of his contemporaries towards frenetic speed and four-in-a-bar momentum, opting instead for a conservative, almost old-fashioned, two-in-a-bar pattern from which he extracted hitherto unimagined subtleties. Listen again through 'Lady Be Good' and note how many of the important notes in Lester's phrases are firmly placed on the first and third beats of the bar. In one place, indeed, at the start of his second chorus, this inspires Walter Page to revert to the two-in-a-bar bass of a bygone age! In the light of jazz music's almost obsessive pursuit of all that is 'new' and 'progressive', it is salutary to reflect that the most modern sound to be heard in 1936 was built on a rhythmic foundation that went out of style with Bix and Frankie Trumbauer in the late Twenties.

To appreciate how Lester Young transformed that foundation, we need only pick up the 'Lady Be Good' solo where we left it. After the eight bars of rhythmic exploitation, the G key note is given further special attention in the middle-eight, this time in its capacity as the fifth note of the chord of C with which the section starts. Here again, emphasis is given to rhythmic variation. The G occurs as the leading note of three successive phrases, the first two of which start on the first beat of the bar as if establishing a riff. But the third time, the phrase is brought forward on to the fourth beat of the second bar, a move which Jo Jones anticipates and underlines with a clairvoyance which must have brought a grin to his face. The final eight bars of the solo are pure joy. A five-note phrase is spread across the first bar and into the second in a way that once again defies our expectations, simply because the notes that fall on the emphatic first beat of each bar are the sixth and ninth notes in the scale, both secondary and auxiliary notes to the C major chord on which the phrase is based. The components of the phrase are then juggled about in doodling variations for two bars, and then, in bars five and six, its first three notes are repeated, though differently distributed, to round off another superbly balanced piece of intuitive composition.

I have given this solo more detailed analysis than most because, paradoxically, its basic ingredients are so simple. That a work of genius should emerge, like a conjurer's effects, from a childishly simple tune, five chords and a conservative two-beat rhythm is a mystery that demands some probing. If I have left the reader in an investigative frame of mind, I commend the 1939 recording of 'Taxi War Dance' by Count Basie's band as fruitful ground. Charged with opening the proceedings without any preliminary statement of a theme, Lester Young constructs a solo that suggests a composition of endless ramifications, including shifts from major to minor and other diverting harmonic incidents. It is only when one investigates the backing that it transpires that the whole thirty-two-bar 'theme', excepting its middle-eight, is no more than a vamp on one basic chord. But the reader must be left to work that one out, while I return to other things.

Billie Holiday

THE MOST INTRIGUING AND, dare I say, titillating fact in the life-story of Billie Holiday has nothing to do with drug addiction, sexual proclivities, male exploitation or police harassment. These subjects have all been explored, with varying degrees of reliability, in the semi-fictionalized film-biog, *Lady Sings the Blues*, in the book of sometimes shaky reminiscences by Billie herself and William Dufty—from which the film took its title and some of its facts—and in the excellent and thoroughly researched biography, *Billie's Blues*, written by John Chilton. They will not loom large in this essay for two reasons. One is that in the period I am discussing—that of the emergence of great individual performers in the Thirties—Billie Holiday was in no sense the tortured, embattled drug-addict which the surviving legend depicts, but a plump, cheerful teenager, popular with fellow-musicians because of her robust sense of fun and with a zest for the entertainer's life that involved a steady intake of alcohol and marijuana but nothing more. The second reason is that there is a danger that, in harping on the tragic aspect of her life and death, one can come to persuade oneself that her art arose, and was indivisible, from it. Were this true, then we would have to say that the recordings she made and the performances she gave in the last decade of her life were, artistically, the most valid and successful, and that is palpably and distressingly untrue. Many writers have drawn a parallel between the careers of Billie Holiday and her erstwhile close friend and kindred spirit, Lester Young, and indeed it exists in the sense that both were at their very best in the late Thirties and

early Forties, both then showed a gradual decline through in-
consistency to virtual incapacity, and both died, within months
of each other, in 1959.

But when it comes to the reasons for her frustration and
disintegration Billie's case is probably closer to that of Bix
Beiderbecke. Bix, as I have established in earlier chapters,
suffered not because his artistry languished in the restricting
atmosphere of the huge Paul Whiteman Orchestra but, conversely,
because he felt that his inability to sight-read fluently and play
his part in the trumpet section stood between him and the musical
respectability, and popularity, inherent in being a Whiteman
'star'. Billie Holiday, a star-struck youngster dazzled by the
success and popularity of such as Louis Armstrong and revelling
in the attention of famous Hollywood film stars, never had a
best-selling record, never topped the most prestigious of jazz
popularity polls, never broke successfully into movies and never
rose, except sporadically, above the unspectacular, somewhat
clandestine, life of a club singer. Ella Fitzgerald's youthful
success with a 'hit' version of the song 'A-Tisket A-Tasket' must
have increased Billie's perplexity, removing as it did the easy
explanation that racial discrimination lay at the heart of the
matter. That it played its part is made very clear through her
experiences as featured singer with the all-white Artie Shaw
Orchestra, when even the friendship and support of the musicians
could not protect her from humiliating treatment from those on
the entrepreneurial side. But as anyone listening to the massive
output of Billie Holiday recordings from the Thirties can tell,
the problem was more deep rooted than that. In a world in which
the catchy, the amusing and the ingratiating picked up the top
prizes, her style was subtle, oblique, harsh and uncompromising.
In other words, she was too good.

To revert to my opening sentence, the biographical fact about
Billie Holiday that will arouse a *frisson* of excitement in anyone
fascinated by the evolution of jazz is that she made her first
recordings in the very same Columbia studios in which, three
days earlier, Bessie Smith made her last. Both sessions were
organized by John Hammond, the twenty-two-year-old son of a
wealthy family who used his money, flair, journalistic outlets and

connections in the, then, near-bankrupt Columbia Recording Company to pursue, as he puts it, 'two of my favourite roles—producer and catalyst'. With the discovery of such musicians as Billie Holiday, Teddy Wilson, Lionel Hampton, Count Basie's band and Charlie Christian to his credit, Hammond can claim to have had some influence on the course of jazz history. But even he cannot have realized at the time what a significant and symbolic moment it was in jazz history that he unwittingly engineered. Bessie and Billie did not meet in the studios, their appearances being separated by seventy-two hours. In fact, their paths only crossed once or twice, so far as we know, and then it seems doubtful if they exchanged any words. Yet there is, in the circumstances of those three days in November 1933, a suggestion of the handing over of keys or the passing of a baton from the old to the new.

In the cherishing of this fancy, it matters little that Billie's first records, with a studio band led by Benny Goodman, were neither the best nor the most representative of her recordings, nor that in belting out two feeble 'novelty' numbers, 'Your Mother's Son-in-Law' and 'Riffin' the Scotch', she came closer to the vaudeville and tent-show era of Bessie Smith than she ever would again. The very appearance of Billie Holiday's name succeeding Bessie's on the Columbia record-label symbolizes the dawn of a new era, the extinction of an old one. In writing about Bessie Smith in the first volume of *The Best of Jazz*, I voiced my doubts as to whether she would have survived artistically through the Thirties even if her speciality, the blues, had not fallen from popular favour in the Depression years. Just as an actor on stage must exaggerate his movements and gestures so as to convey his meaning to the furthest parts of the theatre, so the singers who, like Bessie Smith, spent most of their working life in theatres and marquees, had to develop powerful voices and a weighty delivery. This capacity for voice projection came in handy in the early days of recording, when musical and verbal messages for posterity had to be hurled into the craning 'ear' of a recording apparatus that was distinctly hard of hearing.

Times changed with the invention and perfection of the portable microphone, which could be used not only for radio and recording, but also to amplify 'live' sounds in an auditorium. In discussing Louis Armstrong's development as a singer, we have already seen what changes technology wrought upon his style, which evolved from extrovert and musically unsubtle bawling to something far more smooth and subtle. In the early Thirties, Bing Crosby likewise shed the melodramatic dynamics which were a legacy from Al Jolson and adopted a more intimate style.

It goes without saying that the changes wrought by the development of the microphone did not meet with universal approval. One need not delve very far back into the annals of popular music to recall the adverse reaction to 'crooning' among those nurtured on the tenors and baritones of the musical stage. Likewise there were those around when Billie Holiday made her début to claim that she had no voice—or, to put it more colourfully in a phrase attributed to, among others, the established star Ethel Waters— that she sang 'as if her shoes were too tight'. If one uses the word 'voice' to describe the sort of trained, cultivated sound which academies of music classify as 'singing,' then of course the critics were right. In writing in Volume One about Bessie Smith, I suggested that she should be regarded, not as the culmination of a tradition of blues singing, but as the beginning of a new tradition of jazz singing. The word 'beginning' is important. I shall return to the jazz aspect of her work in relation to Billie's in a moment. But so far as the actual voice is concerned, Bessie Smith's retained, through the self-training necessary to project it unaided across a crowded auditorium, enough of the orthodox contralto to render it a not wholly typical jazz sound.

I must explain this. I have observed before that, since jazz criticism took shape a long time after the music itself had begun, we have the luxury of making our basic definitions in retrospect. Listening to all the music described in this book, for instance, one thing becomes apparent—the great diversity of sounds which the various instruments produce in the hands of the masters. It is not enough simply to say that the musicians were 'unschooled' and therefore produced idiosyncratic sounds, as it were, by default. This would be to class players such as Coleman Hawkins, Benny Carter, Lester Young and Jack Teagarden as 'primitives', which is patently absurd. The truth is that in European music, tradition is enshrined in and, to a large extent, exclusive to, the places of learning. The academies both define and pass on orthodoxy. In American popular music in general and black music in particular —whether we choose to define it as dance music, jazz, entertainment music or whatever—this is not the case. Musicians such as Coleman Hawkins and Benny Carter might have spent some formative years in music school, but what they learned there was theory, harmony, composition and so on. The dominant musical tradition to which they applied this learning was to be found outside—in the dance halls and speakeasies, in the vaudeville theatres and cabarets, on gramophone records and over the radio. And that tradition embraced musical sounds as diverse as human speech itself.

Interviews with jazzmen abound in evidence of the study and practice which went into the production of those sounds—the experimentation with mouthpieces or reeds, the single-minded pursuit of a particular tonal nuance or effect. But the end product was not the sort of standardized, homogenized sound that might emerge from a training-class, but a natural sound compatible with the individual's technical equipment, physical make-up, formative influences and unfettered imagination. While it is unwise to make too much of it, one must also mention the African musical tradition—or, to be more accurate, combination of traditions—which the black musicians received primarily from the predominantly vocal music in black churches, and which they imparted, by example, to their white colleagues. Leaving aside the rhythmic aspects, the most important precept to filter down from African music into jazz is that, in contrast to European music, there are no such things as 'legitimate' or 'illegitimate' sounds. I expect to be told by experts in African musicology that the sundry distortions of tone that exist in African vocal music are as 'legitimate' and as much prescribed by tradition as is the 'pure' tone in European music, but that is hardly the point. The *effect* of the African connection on jazz can easily be gleaned from the many unorthodox musical terms—'growl', 'shake', 'honk', 'smear', 'rasp', 'dirty tone' and so on—that abound in jazz criticism.

The first singer to combine this exploitation of a natural,

personal sound with the other requisites of great jazz performance —swing, spontaneity, an unerring instinct for phrasing and construction, emotional honesty and richness—was Louis Armstrong. The second was Billie Holiday. If there are others with a claim to share the very top drawer with them, they do not spring readily to mind. Billie Holiday gave the best, and most succinct insight into the origins of her style in an interview quoted in the Chilton biography. 'I wanted Louis Armstrong's feeling, and I wanted the big volume that Bessie Smith got. But I found it didn't work with me because I didn't have a big voice . . . so anyway, between the two of them, I sort of got Billie Holiday.'

The Billie Holiday that she got, after the first uncharacteristic records with Benny Goodman ('Well, I get a big bang out of "Your Mother's Son-in-Law". It sounds like I'm doing comedy. My voice sounded so high and funny.'), owed her existence to the microphone. Bessie Smith's voice was projected in conventional, if self-taught fashion, from the depths of the diaphragm, swelling in power as it made its untrammelled ascent. Billie's, on the other hand, resembled Louis Armstrong's in the way that it seemed to emerge, somewhat the worse for wear, after battling its way through a jungle of tangled obstruction in the area of the throat. Playing a Billie Holiday record at slow speed reveals a striking similarity to Armstrong, especially in the attractive 'frogginess' in the low register and in the way that notes in the upper range tend occasionally to split into separate strands, like a fraying rope. Recalling my comments regarding the jazz musician's asssiduousness in acquiring his own individual sound, the reader might well ask, with some scepticism, if I am really suggesting that these vocal aberrations, in conventional singing terms, which Louis and Billie shared were actually cultivated by her. The answer is no—but neither, after the first Benny Goodman recordings, were they suppressed. That voice, as rich in subtle and evocative nuances of tone and timbre as it was weak in range and volume, was her natural instrument, and she let it speak for itself.

Lady Sings the Blues, the title of her autobiography and of the film loosely based on it, was thought up by a publisher more concerned with the form of words than with musical accuracy. It is one of the oddest things about Billie Holiday's career that, not only in the befogged regions of publishing houses, Hollywood and the mass media but in some otherwise informed jazz commentaries, she has been frequently classified as a blues singer. It is not necessary in this instance to embark on any deep investigation into the fine distinction between a blues singer and a jazz singer. For surely the prima facie qualifications of a blues singer are that he or she should actually sing the blues—not just occasionally but as a staple part of the repertoire. Out of the hundreds of songs which Billie Holiday recorded, only three blues numbers come readily to mind. 'Billie's Blues', 'Long Gone Blues' and 'Fine and Mellow' are all attractive pieces, the last-named being one of Billie's finest recordings in its original version. On the strength of these, some have argued that, like some other more consistent blues performers such as Jimmy Rushing and Joe Turner—and indeed, Bessie Smith herself—Billie treated popular songs as if they were blues. But this, if it means anything at all, implies a declamatory delivery and a liberal use of the flattened 'blue notes', neither of which were characteristic of her singing. The truth is that Billie Holiday had a unique singing style which she applied without discrimination to twelve-bar blues or thirty-two-bar popular songs alike.

In guessing at the origins of that style (we know she listened to Bessie Smith and Louis Armstrong but can only make assumptions about what she actually *got* from either of them), it is tempting to add the name of Lester Young to those twin influences. Billie herself gave fuel to this notion when she said, 'I don't think I'm singing. I feel like I'm playing a horn. I try to improvise like Les Young, like Louis Armstrong, or someone else I admire. What comes out is what I feel, I hate straight singing. I have to change a tune to my own way of doing it. That's all I know.' The deep platonic friendship that existed for a while between Billie and Lester has given rise to more than one misconception. Enshrined in much jazz literature is the assumption that they were drawn together by a common psychological inability to cope with the hard realities of life, two souls adrift and clinging to each other for survival. In reality, their friendship pre-dated both her capitulation to hard drugs and his decline into alcoholism and eccentricity. It marked a period when, according to all accounts, she was presenting a robust, if sometimes pugnacious, face to life's injustices and he was riding high as a star soloist in the gregarious environment of the Count Basie band. The later, unhappier times brought a rift between them which was never completely healed. Likewise, the linking of Billie and Lester stylistically ignores historical fact. Though she vaguely recalled an earlier encounter, it seems probable that they first met in the recording studios in January 1937, when the results show that, though there was an immediate rapport between them, Billie Holiday's style was fully formed and not destined to undergo further drastic change. At that time, Lester Young had been featured on no more than four recordings, made three months earlier and hardly likely to have impinged on her consciousness, even if they had indeed been issued by then.

The safest line to take in respect of Billie Holiday's stylistic origins is to say that she clearly grasped to the full the rhythmic freedom, the independence from the basic beat, which Louis Armstrong had demonstrated so miraculously. In listening as often as she could to the recordings of Bessie Smith, she would have heard, behind the 'big volume' which she could not produce, something much more important. It was the capacity to use phrasing and melodic variation to impart to a song more emotional weight than the original words and melody could possibly sustain. It was this quality in Bessie Smith's performance that induced me, in the first book, to describe her as a supreme jazz singer. Billie inherited it in full and bestowed it on every performance.

Few of the 'standard' songs which singers of Billie Holiday's generation performed were written with more than cheap and superficial sentimentality in mind. It's interesting to dwell for a moment on the way in which they actually came to be performed. After the initial recordings with Benny Goodman, Billie Holiday was brought together by John Hammond with another musician, Teddy Wilson, in whose burgeoning career he had an interest. Hammond had secured for Teddy Wilson a recording contract which enabled the pianist to make regular, informal recordings using what are known in the trade as 'pick-up bands'—*ad hoc* groups of musicians assembled from whoever happened to be currently in town. In his autobiography, *John Hammond on*

Record, the author wrote: 'It astonishes me, as I look back, at how casually we were able to assemble such all-star groups. It wasn't that we didn't know how great they were. We did. It simply was a Golden Age; America was overflowing with a dozen truly superlative performers on every instrument. And yet business wasn't that good. Compared to the kind of money that's around today, they all came for scale.'

The Teddy Wilson bands were indeed repositories of all the greatest names in jazz in the mid-Thirties. But they had, nevertheless, to conform to the rules established for hack performers by the popular music industry. Teddy Wilson described the process in an interview: 'In those days the publishers made the hits. They had what they called number one, number two and number three plugs—the songs they were pushing. We never got into the plug tunes. We had our choice of the rest. That's why many of those songs we recorded you never heard anybody sing besides Billie.' Her interpretations even of these low-grade songs didn't always meet with approval from their publishers and composers. One of the latter is said to have complained, on hearing the playback of a Holiday rendering of one of his brainchildren, 'That's a nice job, but it isn't my tune.'

And here is the irony of the situation. Many of the songs which we regard as 'standards' today owe their honoured place in posterity to the skill with which Billie Holiday—and, in similar circumstances, Louis Armstrong and Fats Waller—performed them. Her versions were not so much interpretations as transformations, which the begetters and the proprietors of the material did not always smile upon at the time. The trombonist Bennie Morton, who often worked with Billie, once recalled, 'I have seen Billie turn the melody line around completely simply because a lot of these tunes sung as written were pretty dull.'

As with other selections for these volumes, I have of necessity been arbitrary in choosing two Billie Holiday masterpieces. Many will have assumed, on seeing her name at the head of the chapter, that her historic 1939 recording of 'Strange Fruit', dramatic and startling for its time as an overt 'protest' song, would find automatic pride of place. I have set it aside not because it is a poor example of her work—quite the contrary—but because, like the blues pieces which I have also eschewed, it is not typical of her. Unlike Nina Simone in a later era, to whom she has sometimes been compared, Billie Holiday's work had no specific political or social message. The sorrow, hurt, disillusionment and bitterness which lay close to the surface of her most light-hearted material may have originated, in part, from her racial circumstances, but the feelings conveyed through her huge recorded repertoire of bitter-sweet love songs are universal.

It is into that repertoire that I have dipped for my two favourites. 'I'll Get By', a song of unusual structure by Fred Ahlert and Roy Turk, had enjoyed a modest success on its publication in 1928 and was destined to a renewed lease of life in 1945 when it struck a chord with war-weary Americans. The Billie Holiday/Teddy Wilson recording was made midway between these two peaks, in 1937, when we must presume that the publishers had it on the stock list in the hopes of a premature revivial. Happily for posterity, the principal medium of dissemination for songs in those days was the printed song copy, which was comparatively easy and cheap to store and reproduce. So a successful tune would not suffer the fleeting, butterfly existence of a modern hit song but would survive in the catalogues for many years.

Clearly, the bands of Duke Ellington, Count Basie and Benny Goodman were all in town on 11 May 1937, as star names from each—Johnny Hodges from the first, Lester Young and Buck Clayton from the second, Allan Reuss and Arthur Bernstein from the third—joined Teddy Wilson for this session, together with Buster Bailey and Cozy Cole, two of New York's most prolific session players at that time. Wilson always liked to share out the solo space among his musicians on a session, so it was no doubt the luck of the draw that relegated Lester Young to a subdued and almost inaudible supporting role on this number. Billie Holiday herself appeared on the Teddy Wilson recordings simply as the supplier of 'vocal refrain', as they used to describe it, and as such she occupied the traditional vocalist's position, taking a single chorus after the initial exposition of the tune. As we shall see, on sessions under her own name—Billie Holiday and her Orchestra—she played a fuller part, singing the opening chorus and returning again towards the end. Fortunately, her style, as fiercely concentrated as an oxy-acetylene flame, made its mark equally strikingly in either setting.

After a long, meandering introduction with Buster Bailey's clarinet to the fore, it is Johnny Hodges who takes the opening chorus of 'I'll Get By', delineating a melody that occupies the unusual span of twenty-eight bars—most popular songs of the period being thirty-two bars in length. Like these more conventional tunes, the Ahlert-Turk song is couched in an ABAC format, but the B and C sections are six instead of eight bars in length, a daring and effective innovation for its time. Likewise, there is an attractive absence of symmetry in the A sections. On the face of it, the melody consists of two complementary ascending phrases of four bars each. But the words—'I'll get by, as long as I have you Though there'll be rain'—shift the point of balance, the word 'you' clearly belonging to the first phrase although, logically, one would expect it to be the first note of the second. In the same way, the notes carrying the words 'though there'll be rain' complete the A section, providing an obvious punctuation point in the melody. But resolutely spurning the obvious, the lyric spans this junction without so much as a comma—'and darkness too'. It is a relatively rare and ingenious example of a lyric imposing subtleties on the melody line.

Johnny Hodges states the tune majestically, its ascending lines, spanning a range of ten notes in all, ideally suiting his sweeping style. But a newcomer to the tune, aware of Billie Holiday's restricted range, might well begin to wonder during the alto chorus exactly how she will negotiate it. He could scarcely be prepared for what actually happens. Benny Morton spoke of Billie 'turning the melody line around completely'. Here she stands it on its head. As written, the song, in F major, begins on the lower F and ascends, in its two opening phrases, to an upper limit of A above the octave. Billie Holiday starts her chorus on that upper A, and indeed hinges her whole variation on it, with the result that, instead of soaring aloft, all the phrases droop downwards like the boughs of a weeping willow. Furthermore, apart from two descents to a low G in which her voice falls away to vanishing point, she restricts her range to a mere six notes. In my essay on Bessie Smith in Volume One, I wrote: 'Bessie's way . . . was to restrict the range of a song to no more than five or six notes and to construct her phrases so economically that a change in direction of just one note could have a startling, dramatic or emotive effect.' Billie had absorbed that lesson completely. For a beautiful example, listen to the start of the second half of the chorus, in bar fifteen. This is a reprise of the opening phrase, in which the words 'I'll get by' were harnessed to that one nagging note a third above the upper key note. Second time around, the word 'poverty' returns to the A, but this time the third syllable drops down to the E below. It's a minute variation, made all the more effective by the unexpectedness of the interval. Both the melody and the harmony of the original tune prompt a fall from A to F—in other words, down to the key note—and in subsequent versions of the song, this is indeed what Billie does. But the casual drop to the major seventh, no doubt intuitive rather than contrived, is infinitely more effective, underlining the note of doubt which the words 'Poverty may come to me, that's true' introduce into an otherwise optimistic song.

Had it been harnessed to the original rhythmic structure of the song, Billie's drastic reshaping of the melody may have seemed like a mere evasion of the tune's inherent difficulties. But here she draws upon and, indeed, extends the notions of freedom from the basic beat implanted by Louis Armstrong. As written, the song adheres more than most to a sedate pattern of on-the-beat crotchets and minims (or quarter and half-notes). With a true jazzman's instinct, Johnny Hodges loosens this rigid skeleton with notes that anticipate and stretch across the beat. Billie Holiday cuts loose from it altogether. The very first word of the opening phrase 'I'll get by' is placed ahead of the beat, and the others do no more than hover round it. The second phrase, 'As long as I have you' is delayed by more than two beats, and then doesn't bestir itself needlessly. The art of this exaggeratedly 'laid back' phrasing, distinguishing it from mere affectation, is that the listener should not detect the point at which the performer catches up with the regular metre. The listener who expects Billie to re-orientate herself by clinging, if only for a few bars, to the beat must wait, in this instance, for ever. Like a child striding out to avoid stepping on the lines between paving-stones, she picks her way through the entire vocal chorus without once stepping fairly and squarely on the beat.

The ethereal ghostly effect that this produces is heightened by Teddy Wilson's diligent, almost fastidious, attention to time-keeping. His piano style, which so attracted John Hammond, derived principally from Earl Hines. But the two players are temperamentally different. While Hines at the keyboard has always sounded like some volatile and impetuous wayside explorer, now sauntering, now dashing off in pursuit of a fleeting idea, now tumbling head over heels in an ecstacy of *joie de vivre*, Teddy Wilson gives the impression of a man content to make a more measured progress along ordered paths. His solo following Billie Holiday's vocal is typical. Rhythmically, he has always leaned towards a two-beat feeling, the left hand, when not featuring the moving pattern of tenths which are his trade-mark, providing an oom-chah stride bass with the first and third beats emphasized. It is the somewhat precise timing of the left-hand vamping which, among other things, has attracted to Teddy Wilson such not altogether complimentary critical epithets as 'meticulous', 'elegant', 'impeccable' and 'placid'. To me, his playing is a constant joy, especially in the context of a Billie Holiday recording such as this, when the mind, in something of a turmoil after the vocal unorthodoxy, is instantly reassured by the perfect poise with which the piano takes over. Buck Clayton, of whom more in a moment, falls in with this unruffled mood by taking the per-formance out with a return to the original tune, the only way to end a record which, in three short minutes, has taken 'I'll Get By' to its emotional and structural limits and back.

Most listeners will agree that the Billie Holiday recordings in the late Thirties offered something a little bit extra whenever musicians from Count Basie's band—and especially Lester Young and Buck Clayton—were on hand. Michael Brooks, the producer of a series of Lester Young reissues on CBS called *The Lester Young Story*, put it more vividly in his sleeve note. 'There is no question that the alliance between Buck Clayton, Lester Young and Billie Holiday is one of the great romances in musical history, as if Romeo, Dante and Cleopatra met up in the recording studio, looked, listened and said the hell with Juliet, Beatrice and Antony!' In similar vein, John Hammond recalls, 'The electricity between Jo [Jones], Buck, Billie and Prez was just fantastic.' The occasions when the Basie men were on the sessions must have been somewhat unnerving for Teddy Wilson. Jo Jones, the drummer with Count Basie, has described how he and the other Basieites would try and get Wilson to abandon his rather upright, two-beat style and conform to the more pushing four-four beat which Basie used. He stood his ground, however, and it has to be said that the recordings give no hint of musical schism.

Buck Clayton was audibly in his element on the Billie Holiday sessions. Having worked with him often during the Sixties, when he showed himself to be one of those musicians of whom it can truthfully be said that he continued to improve with age, I formed the impression that he was at his happiest in medium and slow tempos, when he had the time and space to exploit his stinging attack, radiant tone, buoyant and poised swing and lyrical imagination. Louis Armstrong was his inspiration, and in his less flamboyant way, Buck, too, could invest an introductory flourish or modulating cadenza with all the authority of a call to arms.

Two 'takes' of Billie Holiday's recording of 'Back in Your Own Back Yard' have been issued, each starting with just such a commanding fanfare from Buck. My preference is for the first one, taken at a rather more taut and brisk tempo. For all the optimism and reassurance of its words, the tune, by Al Jolson and associates, is rather sad. This is no place to go into the psychology of music, but it is true to say that melodies that consist predominantly of descending phrases strike in the listener a melancholy, or at least wistful, chord. This song abounds in them, its main recurring phrase being a descent from the fifth to the tonic, like the return journey of a five-finger exercise. And there is a minor key middle-eight thrown in for good measure.

Billie Holiday needed little prompting to bring out the poignant side of any tune. The words of the song—'The bird with feathers of blue is waiting for you/Back in your own back yard'—urge us to believe that, for happiness, we need look no further than our own doorstep. The tender sadness with which Billie invests the melody imparts the rather less cosy message that we should make the best of life as it surrounds us, because it's all there is. Her approach here is quite different from the dismantling and re-assembling to which she subjected 'I'll Get By'. This tune, like the other, presents a singer of her limited range with problems. The melody accompanying the line I have written out above, keeps plunging down, in a sort of scooping figure, on the second syllable of 'feathers', again on the second syllable of 'waiting', and a third time with the words 'in your' towards the end of the line. We know from elsewhere that Billie could negotiate these sort of swooping melodic lines if she wished, but on this occasion she did not wish. Picking up on the end of Buck's introduction with a phrase that hangs in the air, she lets the melody float gently earthwards, letting the second syllable of 'waiting' rise as if momentarily caught by an upward breeze. This is the pattern that she uses in each of the corresponding sections occupying the second and last eight bars, avoiding monotony by distributing the syllables differently across the beat each time.

With the middle-eight, we find a perfect example of her way of phrasing like a jazz instrumentalist. For four bars, she places the words right across the beat. Of the words 'you can go to the East, go to the West', not one is placed squarely on the beat, and the ensuing words, 'but someday you'll come', are somehow squeezed into the remaining bars like latecomers on a crowded rush-hour Tube. But then, in striking contrast, 'weary at heart' is rapped out like a drum rhythm bang on the beat. Sing the section over wordlessly and it could come from Louis, Lester, Buck or anybody else's horn.

As for Lester Young's solo, it is hard to think of a more beautiful example of his work. As in the 'Lady Be Good' solo discussed earlier, his improvisation is totally independent from the song's original theme. Building upon the wistful mood of Billie's vocal, he unfolds a continuous line of beautifully constructed melody, starting characteristically with one of his isolated 'balancing notes'. It has sometimes occurred to me that a musician's style is often reflected in his playing stance. Louis Armstrong, for example, adopted a heraldic pose, while Coleman Hawkins in furious action looked like some medieval horseman crouched over the neck of his charger. Lester, on the other hand, with the saxophone held out at a forty-five degree angle from his body, head drooping and one hip thrown out as a counterbalance, resembled nothing so much as one of those angular, counter-poised desk lamps. Matching this image, his solos maintained a languid poise that concealed great rhythmic strength. In his second eight bars in 'Back in Your Own Back Yard,' the notes seem to lean just about as far as they can away from the beat without falling over, and yet a muscular swing is maintained. The middle-eight provides a glorious example of his melodic perversity. He seems about to play the melody as written, but turns the tables on anyone rash enough to whistle along with him by, first of all, leaving out the last note of the 'go to the East' phrase and then, in 'go to the West,' turning the 'West' note down when it should go up. Jo Jones shows his appreciation of this subtle manoeuvre with some telepathic rim-shots. And at the very end of the solo, after so much delayed across-the-beat phrasing, Lester raps out some stirring on-the-beat notes that provide a jaunty contrast. On the whole, the solo radiates a sunny mood that contrasts strongly with the equally beautiful but quite different performance in the slightly slower second 'take'. The change in tempo appears to have affected Lester's spirits in-ordinately, and his playing has an introspective, almost weary sound that foreshadows the more withdrawn style of his declining years.

There is no need for me to apply further analysis to Billie Holiday's final chorus, which repeats the general pattern of the first while lifting the tension in the most subtle way. It completes a performance which was matched on many other occasions during the same period, especially when Buck, Lester and Jo Jones were on hand. Seldom has such a close and consistent feeling of rapport been conveyed on record. To absorb just part of the eagerness, confidence and creative joy that must have crackled round the studio on that day, and then to reflect on the future that was to overtake both Billie Holiday and Lester Young, is almost too much to bear.

Roy Eldridge

WHEN OUTLINING THE COURSE of jazz history from the Twenties to the Forties, jazz historians tend to talk in terms of trumpet players. King Oliver, they will say, gave way to Louis Armstrong, who was succeeded by Roy Eldridge, who influenced Dizzy Gillespie, who spawned Miles Davis . . . It is not an altogether absurd over-simplification, any more than the tendency, after that point, to transfer the principal role to the saxophone and Charlie Parker, John Coltrane, Ornette Coleman . . . Louis Armstrong so dominated jazz in the period around 1930, making new virtuoso strides with every recording session, that his style permeated virtually every instrument in the jazz band, with the possible exception of the double-bass. It was natural, if not particularly scientific, that observers would have eyes and ears fixed on the trumpet for some time to come, if only to see what could possibly happen next.

What did happen next, in equally simple terms, was that a young trumpeter from Pittsburg called Roy Eldridge listened to Louis Armstrong on record and was not overwhelmed. 'The first time I heard any records by him was in 1927, I think,' he told in an interview reproduced in the book, *The Jazz Makers*, 'but Louis wasn't an influence on me until I saw him in person.' Over the years, critics have heard in Roy Eldridge's heated, impassioned playing the influence of Henry 'Red' Allen and, in the manner of critics, have enshrined that opinion as fact in works of jazz information. In recent times Roy has vehemently rejected any suggestion that Allen influenced him, and I hope it is not being wise after the event to say that, rhythmically and melodically, their two styles are fundamentally different. From his earliest recorded appearance, Henry Allen played in what I have called an 'impressionistic' manner, avoiding specific lines of melody and patterns of rhythm and choosing instead to build his solos out of contrasting splashes of sound, some lazily stretched across the beat, others exploding with sudden vehemence. Roy Eldridge, on the other hand, has always preferred to maintain a constant stream of improvisation that stays in close contact with both the beat and the harmonic structure of the theme. It is not surprising to hear from him that, of all the Louis Armstrong disciples with whose music he came in contact, it was Rex Stewart, with his combination of fieriness and speed, who did influence him in his early days.

But it seems that, when he did begin to play professionally in his mid-teens, he was set on a course that might well have taken him out of the Armstrong sphere of influence altogether. To anyone who ever heard the mature Eldridge either on record or in the flesh, when it has seemed after a chorus or two that steam must soon start spouting from his ears, the notion that he ever admired and emulated Red Nichols will present itself as some kind of far-fetched joke. In the Roy Eldridge that we know, it is not easy to detect even an occasional hint of the cool and calculating 'eastern' style of the white New Yorker. But we have it from his own mouth. 'I liked the nice, clean sound he was getting from the trumpet in those days. I was doing all right playing in that style until I got to St Louis.' He was already touring then as leader of his own juvenile band. 'Every Sunday, five trumpet players came down and tore me apart. I was about sixteen and I was playing smooth. They played with a guttural kind of sound. They were more or less on a Louis Armstrong kick, the way Louis used to play only more guttural. I was playing what would be called cool then and I wasn't familiar with that other style. I couldn't understand how they got around to playing like that—the lip vibrato, trills and the like. Some of the names of those trumpet players in St Louis were Dewey Jackson, Baby James, "Cookie" and "Big Ham".'

Ironically, the St Louis of a few years later would probably have given encouragement to his 'cool' style, since it became the breeding ground of a clear-cut, round-toned and relatively placid style of trumpet playing exemplified in the work of Harold 'Shorty' Baker, Clark Terry and Miles Davis. But it is hard to believe that a man of Roy Eldridge's volatile, emotional and highly competitive temperament would have thrived for long in such incompatibly 'cool' pastures. Other influences were to steer him towards the now familiar hustling style. In a word, saxophones. 'Coleman Hawkins and Benny Carter. They played so much music, Hawkins and Carter, how could you help not like them if you like music? They had, and have, distinctive sounds, voices of their own.'

It seems that, at first, the saxophones and his desire to emulate them led him astray. One of the earliest exercises which he set himself was to learn by heart the Coleman Hawkins tenor-saxophone solo in Fletcher Henderson's 1926 recording of 'The Stampede'. What emerged was a new way of playing the trumpet in jazz. Even men like Louis Armstrong and Jabbo Smith, renowned for their speed and agility, had had to bow to the trumpet's innate short-windedness in matters of phrasing. Roy Eldridge set about forming a style which could rival the continuous flow of long, far-ranging phrases, punctuated only by hastily snatched breaths, which Hawkins could produce. The result was not immediately successful. 'The cats used to listen to me and they'd say, "Well, he's nice but he don't say nothing." Consequently I didn't work. No one played as fast as I did, but the other trumpet players broke it up. I didn't. Also, I was playing fine saxophone on the trumpet. Trying to hold notes longer than they should be held, trying to get a sound that I couldn't and shouldn't get.'

Roy Eldridge's problems will not be unfamiliar to anyone who, having acquired a technique, has first tried to apply it to jazz improvisation. Clearly the vocabulary and the syntax were there, the punctuation and the construction were not. He needed an example to follow, someone to provide a revelatory insight into how to use his formidable technique in a way that, to use the jazzman's vernacular, would 'tell a story'. The example he found was one which he had already encountered and spurned. In 1932 he went to hear Louis Armstrong in person at the Lafayette Theatre in New York, '. . . and he finally upset me. I was a young cat, and I was very fast but I wasn't telling no kind of story. Well, I sat through the first show, and I didn't think that Louis was so extraordinary. But in the second show, he played 'Chinatown'. He started out like a new book, building and building, chorus after chorus, and finally reaching a full climax, ending on his high F. It was a real climax, right, clean, clear. The rhythm was rocking, and he had that sound going along with it. Everybody was standing up, including me. He was building the thing all the time instead of just playing in a straight line. I've been digging him ever since.'

Here, then, was the making of the Eldridge style which, though his period as an acknowledged trumpet king was transitory compared with the reign of Louis before him and Dizzy Gillespie after him, was to have a revolutionary effect on jazz trumpet playing. 'I started to feel that if I could combine speed with melodic development while continuing to build, to tell a story, I could create something musical of my own that the public would like.' The speed was as important as the Louis influence. Through the Thirties, there emerged a whole generation of fine trumpet players offering personal variations on the Louis Armstrong model. In extensive jazz histories more justice is done to Oran 'Hot Lips' Page, Frankie Newton, Buck Clayton, Joe Thomas, Bill Coleman, Bobby Stark, Taft Jordan and Jonah Jones than I have space for here. Though their styles had a common source, they developed such personal 'voices' that each one is instantly recognizable to the *aficionado* who hears them on records. But none of them departed far enough from the Armstrong pattern to suggest an alternative way of handling the trumpet in jazz. Were it not for the grotesqueness of associating the word 'philistine' with any creation of Louis Armstrong's, one could say that, in the mid-Thirties, the jazz world was waiting for a David to overthrow the Goliath that Armstrong's decade-long domination represented. The diminutive Roy Eldridge, ambitious, bursting with a sense of his own ability and scared of no one when it came to a musical fight, had just the temperament to fill the role.

Here it was that the influence of the saxophonists, Coleman

Hawkins in particular, played an essential part. Simply to have reproduced Armstrong's basic style but at breakneck speed would hardly have earned Eldridge a place in jazz history as an innovator. What he did was to force the trumpet itself to change its character. In Louis Armstrong's hands—and indeed the hands of his predecessors stretching back to Buddy Bolden—both trumpet and cornet had assumed the role to which the former had always been assigned in the symphony orchestra and the military band. Clarinets, flutes and piccolos, with their multiplicity of keys, were clearly designed to scamper about over a range of several octaves. The trumpet, initially confined, through the absence of any valve or piston mechanism, to the widely spaced harmonics that are found in the present-day bugle, was there to make commanding, declamatory noises, making up in dignity and martial authority what it lacked in agility. Early players such as King Oliver, Freddy Keppard and, presumably, Buddy Bolden himself, made predominant use of the cornet's open notes— that is to say, the harmonics which can be attained without recourse to the valves simply by raising or lowering the lip pressure. As jazz improvisation became increasingly adventurous, it still came more naturally for the trumpet players to construct their solos on arpeggios than to ignore the instrument's basic system of harmonics and play flowing lines based on the scales. Louis Armstrong's showcase of the mid-Twenties, 'Cornet Chop Suey', was in every sense a classic example of this. The themes themselves, written either by Louis, his wife, Lil Hardin Armstrong, or a collaboration of the two, followed the normal scalar construction of any other ragtime or popular song. But when Louis played his variations and added an introduction and a coda, they were all designed to show off his and the instrument s agility in leaping up and down arpeggios. Later, when he began to apply his talents to popular songs from the Broadway shows, it became a characteristic of his to declaim the melody of the tune in the high register while at the same time linking the notes with descending arpeggios which indicated the underlying harmonies.

In writing about both Coleman Hawkins and Lester Young here, I have mentioned the system of chorus-building known as 'running changes'. If Rex Stewart, in his role of jazz historian, is to be believed, Coleman Hawkins was inspired to pursue this line of musical thought after hearing Art Tatum some time in the late Twenties. This was the aspect of saxophone playing which attracted Roy Eldridge. An unsung jazz hero, trumpeter Cuban Bennett, is the man whom Roy acknowledges as his own inspiration in this direction. 'Cuban Bennett was Benny Carter's first cousin. He was really making his changes in those days. You could call him one of the first of the moderns . . . He played more like a saxophone did. You see, the saxophone then, or some of them, would run changes, would run through all the passing chords and things, and then do a little turn around.' To run changes, it is necessary to get completely away from the arpeggio style of playing in which, for example, the harmony is involved only at those strategic points at which the player will run up or down the key notes of the chord to emphasize it. In running changes, the player will construct a continuous line of notes which are selected intuitively to suggest, rather than state specifically, every minute change in the underlying harmony. In jazz analysis, the two methods are sometimes described as improvising 'vertically' (up and down specific chords) or 'horizontally' (along a continuous line of harmony). If we accept Rex Stewart's theory about Coleman Hawkins, we have here a fascinating line of development. With Fletcher Henderson in the mid-Twenties, Hawkins received the message as to how to swing on tenor saxophone from the example of Louis Armstrong, whose style he largely adopted. Hearing Art Tatum inspired him to change course, in a direction which Roy Eldridge eventually followed. It led Roy temporarily into a dead-end from which he was rescued by hearing—Louis Armstrong.

It is one of the great ironies of jazz history that, in extending the expressive range of the trumpet into the fleeter areas occupied by the keyed instruments, Roy Eldridge sowed the seeds of his own destruction as top man. Soon after his encounter with Louis in 1932, he began to attract the attention of other musicians. He played in a succession of popular bands—with Elmer Snowden, McKinney's Cotton Pickers, Teddy Hill and Fletcher Henderson —as well as leading small groups of his own and appearing on record in 'pick up' or *ad hoc* groups. Though he made impressive, indeed startling, appearances on record with Henderson and small groups led by Joe Marsala, Gene Krupa and Teddy Wilson, it was almost certainly through radio broadcasts that his fame spread. Some of the broadcasts by his own little band from the Three Deuces in Chicago and the Arcadia Ballroom in New York have recently been issued on obscure labels, and they show him more strongly committed to the Armstrong brand of trumpet showmanship than on records, while at the same time exploiting his technical range to the full. It is little wonder that, from the mid-Thirties onwards, he had superseded Louis Armstrong as the exemplar of modern 'hot' trumpet playing. New players and indeed, some formerly committed to the Armstrong style (Buck Clayton with Basie and Taft Jordan with Chick Webb in their fiercer up-tempo moments) began to express themselves in tumbling cascades of notes, at the same time prodding and hustling the beat in the impatient manner that later came to be identified as 'jump' style.

Two men especially presented Eldridge with early competition. One was a New Yorker of great technical facility called Charlie Shavers, six years Roy's junior but capable, as a twenty-year-old with John Kirby's Sextet in 1937, of matching the older man's technical feats. What Shavers lacked, then and in later confrontations with Eldridge in the touring Jazz at the Philharmonic shows, was the passionate intensity which has always underpinned Roy's playing. If Shavers seemed, on many occasions, to be able to match Roy phrase for phrase with greater cleanness of execution, it is because he approached the task in hand with a certain detachment. Comic quotations or passages of mock-sentimentality would often interrupt a Shavers solo in full flood—an inconceivable occurrence with Eldridge, whose notes, phrases and, indeed, actual person often seemed about to disintegrate under the intense emotional pressure.

The other trumpeter who followed Roy Eldridge's lead with even more success in matching the original was a young man called John Birks Gillespie, nicknamed 'Dizzy'. When Roy Eldridge was enjoying his reign as trumpet king at the head of his own little band in 1938–9, Gillespie was occupying his old chair in the brass section of Teddy Hill's Orchestra, whose recordings of 'King Porter Stomp' and 'Blue Rhythm Fantasy' in 1938 show how uncannily the younger man had assimilated his idol's style. Indeed, it was the chiding of other musicians about his lack of an individual style that spurred Dizzy into making the harmonic and rhythmic experiments which characterized his formative contributions to modern jazz in the mid-Forties.

The arrival of bebop in a burst of publicity, both promotional and adverse, found Roy Eldridge hoist with his own petard. Having wrenched jazz trumpet out of Louis Armstrong's grasp, so to speak, and coerced it into running changes with the headlong speed of a saxophone, he was at the mercy of anyone who came along with an even greater turn of speed and a more complex and advanced set of changes to run. In telling the story, one lapses almost without thinking into the terminology of gladiatorial conflict—'hoist with his own petard', 'wrenched from the grasp', 'at the mercy of' and so on—because, in the circumstances of the mid-Forties, a fight for survival is what it was. The situation is summed up by an often told and probably apocryphal story of a night in 1941 or '42 when Roy, an inveterate sitter-in at after-hours jam sessions, had turned up at Minton's Playhouse, the breeding ground of modern ideas. In an interview with jazz writer Ross Russell, the drummer, Kenny Clarke, recalled the incident:

'Monday night was always a free for all at Minton's. All the young musicians in town would be in the place with their horns, waiting for a chance to get up on the stand and blow. Big name stars used to drop in . . . Charlie Christian, Lester Young and especially Roy Eldridge. Roy was the king. Dizzy Gillespie had started out playing like Roy, but had gotten on the new kick, working out his ideas with Charlie Parker, Thelonious Monk, Nick Fenton and myself. Dizzy could play and his ideas were new, but try as he would, Dizzy could never cut Roy. Roy was just too much. Roy had drive and execution, and he could keep going chorus after chorus. Every time Dizzy tried, Roy gave him a lesson, made him pack. But Dizzy never quit. Then one night, Dizzy came in and started blowing. He got it all together that night. He cut Roy to everyone's satisfaction and that night Roy packed his horn and never came back.' Other even more colourful versions of the story have Roy Eldridge running off the stand in tears.

If the story is hard to swallow as a single, cataclysmic event, it does describe quite accurately the fate which overtook Roy Eldridge in the Forties. The conquest of Roy by Dizzy Gillespie is, indeed, the sort of thing which Louis Armstrong could have suffered at the hands of Roy in the mid-Thirties had he not removed himself *hors de combat* into the securer realms of show-business. We need not pursue the story any further here, other than to observe that the law of the jazz jungle is less savage and unrelenting than such stories as the above suggest. Roy Eldridge did, it is true, suffer a period of collapsing confidence in the late Forties, when all ears were on the 'new' music and it seemed to him that he must either try and conform or be left behind. This kind of bebop-inflicted shell-shock assailed many older musicians at the time, but the aspect of the situation which must have hurt him most was the cold shoulder that he received from the younger men at his beloved after-hours jousting spots. As with some other musicians in the doldrums, it was the impresario, Norman Granz, giving Roy a permanent and honoured place in his *Jazz at the Philharmonic* touring package, who did much to restore his confidence and reputation. No admirer of the young David of the mid-Thirties with his bursting enthusiasm and vitality can fail to find something heart warming in the friendly and often cheerfully erratic bouts which have taken place in the JATP arena in the Fifties and Sixties between Eldridge and Gillespie, two old adversaries reliving past and more acrimonious battles in a spirit of comradeship, in front of audiences that acknowledge each as the master that he is.

But the period with which we are concerned here is the late Thirties when Roy Eldridge was undisputed king. In 1937 his small group, in which his brother Joe played alto saxophone, made a small batch of recordings which set the seal on his ascendancy. Most Eldridge admirers, I imagine, would settle for one of three pieces—'After You've Gone', 'Wabash Stomp' or 'Heckler's Hop' —as an Eldridge masterpiece. The first-named makes fascinating comparison with Louis Armstrong's version of the same piece in 1929. Louis takes it at a stately tempo compared to which Roy's is positively headlong. The contrast between their two styles is underlined in the mid-chorus break, corresponding to the line 'You'll miss the dearest pal you've ever had' in the lyric. Eldridge has not, up to this point, diverged to any degree from the Armstrong manner, except in the overall feeling of impatience in his approach. Indeed, in the way that he follows the opening phrase ('After you've gone') with a little downward phrase to indicate the harmony, in case the accompaniment should overlook or understate it, he reproduces a familiar Armstrong trait. But when it comes to the break, he replaces Armstrong's sparse rhythmic phrases with a cascade of quavers or eighth-notes phrased, in Coleman Hawkins fashion, in pairs (DOOdle-DOOdle-DOOdle) with the first quaver in each pair heavily outweighing the second. After a vocal chorus by Gladys Palmer in which Turner Layton's melody receives rather more attentive treatment than Henry Creamer's lyrics, it is all Eldridge in two choruses that show clearly the lesson in chorus-building which he learnt from Louis. Once again, it is in the breaks, between and in the middle of choruses, that Roy Eldridge departs most drastically from the Armstrong pattern. The break that links the two choruses is absolutely astonishing, approached by a sustained note which Louis would probably have carried over the whole four-bar section in majestic fashion, but which Roy subsequently breaks up into a rapid, shifting, drumming rhythm by the combined use of fast tongueing and alternative or 'fake' fingering. The whole performance is a show-stopping *tour de force* in which each successive break involves more reckless feats of daring than the last.

Despite this formidable display, my own choice for the supreme masterpiece from this batch is 'Heckler's Hop'. In this original composition by Roy Eldridge, the Armstrong style is almost entirely superceded, except in the way in which Roy's own choruses build to a climax. The theme itself, a series of bustling riffs relieved by a 'standard' middle-eight, belongs to the saxophone rather than the trumpet. Harmonically, it offers no more challenge than most Swing Era riff themes, changing its basic chords every two bars and resembling, in this instance, other old swing vehicles such as Count Basie's 'Doggin' Around', Teddy McCrae's 'Broadway' and Charlie Shavers's 'Undecided'. Indeed, when Roy Eldridge bows out for a while after the opening chorus, the alto and piano contributions by Scoops Carry and Teddy Cole are pretty commonplace. Then Roy Eldridge makes his entry. The feeling that one gets from the first bar of his solo is not an unusual one to the jazz connoisseur. From the undistinguished and some-times turgid surroundings of the Fletcher Henderson and Paul Whiteman bands respectively, Louis Armstrong and Bix Beider-becke would often leap into clear and unequivocal solo statements that announced, in the opening notes, that the serious business of swinging was about to begin. And the rhythm section would respond eagerly as if a burden had been lifted from its shoulders. In drummer Zutty Singleton, Roy had rhythmic support well equipped to rise to the occasion. Erstwhile associate, close friend and running mate to Louis Armstrong in the heady days in Chicago of the late Twenties, Zutty's driving power could always be felt even when recording conditions obscured the detail. He was raised in New Orleans, and to the end of his days advertised the fact through a drum kit in which all kinds of accoutrements—woodblocks, ratchet, cow-bells—clustered behind a massive bass drum. In these modern times when a solo such as Roy's would inevitably have been pushed along by a riding top cymbal, it is interesting to note that Zutty stays on the snare drum throughout, emphasizing the off-beat with the tightest of press rolls and high-lighting the climactic moments with swatting rim shots.

Roy Eldridge's solo starts in a way strikingly similar to the Coleman Hawkins 'Crazy Rhythm' solo discussed earlier, with a nagging riff that seems to rally the band behind him. In the inter-view quoted above, he says of the saxophone players whom he admired and emulated, 'They might play six bars, and in the seventh would start going into the release [the cadence concluding each eight-bar section] and then the eighth would be all set up for the second eight.' The start of the 'Heckler's Hop' solo exemplifies this. The four bars of riffing lead, in bars five and six, to a natural conclusion. Had Roy cut out after the first note of bar seven and left the rhythm section to vamp through two bars, the result would have been typical of any number of swing solos. Bar nine would then have started all over again with a different set of rhythmically stimulating figures, probably ending as conclusively at the start of bar fifteen. Roy's way, learnt from such master saxists as Hawkins and Carter who were adept at composing on their feet, is to pause momentarily on the first beat of bar seven before scurrying off on a new phrase that spans the release and carries over into the second eight-bar section without paying heed to the 'natural break' at the end of bar eight. In this bridging phrase, the flow of quavers is broken up by a rhythmic device that harks back to Louis Armstrong's 'Weather Bird' *tour de force* and, at the same time, anticipates Charlie Parker and Dizzy Gillespie. In it, the emphasis is suddenly shifted from the notes that fall on the beat to those between it, while the usually strong notes are articulated so softly that they are really only suggested or 'ghosted'.

In the second eight bars, the phrases flow blithely, sounding in bars twelve and thirteen much nearer to Gillespie than Armstrong. Once again, the bridge from this section into the middle-eight is crossed effortlessly, this time by starting the first long phrase of the section a bar early, in bar sixteen. It is interesting to note that this phrase would make perfect sense if it were deferred, to start in bar seventeen. But then it would end conventionally in the fourth bar of the middle-eight, with the second phrase starting in the fifth bar after a breath taken bang in the middle of the section. By bringing the whole thing forward so that the phrases start and end in unexpected places, just as Lester Young did in 'Lady Be Good', Roy Eldridge was showing himself well versed in a practice that has often been listed among the 'innovations' of the boppers.

As always in these analyses I have to stress that niceties which take me a laborious paragraph to describe occur intuitively in an improvised solo. To make too much of them is to risk subduing the *frissons* of surprise and pleasure which they can evoke. So I will focus on just two more key points in the solo. The first occurs at the junction of the two choruses. It is to be expected that a man who learned a crucial lesson in chorus-building from hearing Louis Armstrong play 'Chinatown, My Chinatown' would at some stage in a red-hot solo ascend into the upper register. Roy does so in characteristic fashion. Over the last two bars of the first chorus he holds a top C, oscillating the note with a lip trill or shake as Louis Armstrong so often did. But whereas Louis Armstrong's notes thus sustained would float and shimmer, Roy's positively quiver with excitement as if straining at the leash. From this launching-pad he starts the second chorus with a series of short phrases stabbing at top C, then from some preparatory high F's unleashes an A with a pulverizing force that must have come straight up from the soles of his feet. Many commentators have observed over the years that there have been occasions when Roy Eldridge has generated so much high-pressure emotional intensity that he has seemed on the verge of exploding. Sometimes, especially in later years, the courageously assaulted high notes have come out as little more than a quivering hiss of steam. But in 'Heckler's Hop' everything was going Roy's way, and the top A, encouraged by some intensified thwacking of the off-beat by Zutty Singleton, squeals defiantly. It is not in any sense a display of exhibitionistic fireworks, as some contemporary critics with a suspicion of technical agility were wont to suggest. The phrase which Roy Eldridge plays is in itself constructive, raising the tension of the second chorus in much the same way that Louis Armstrong would do. The fact that it carries him way above the normal range of the trumpet gives added excitement.

To have reached such an explosive climax half-way through a chorus would present any soloist with the problem of sustaining the tension and excitement. Other trumpeters with similar technical endowments—and indeed, Roy Eldridge himself with Jazz at the Philharmonic in later years—might have succumbed to the temptation to continue belabouring the upper register, inevitably invoking the law of diminishing returns. On this occasion, fully in charge of both the instrument and himself, Roy resumes the running quavers with sustained invention. Careering again over the junction between the first and second eight-bar sections, he starts the latter with a favourite device of his, a chromatic run of quaver or eighth-note triplets from the third up to the fifth and back. It is a phrase that was to become an Eldridge trade-mark (it occurs twice, stratospherically, in 'After You've Gone') and a much abused cliché among his imitators.

In this instance, Roy shows at once the total control he has over events. In the second and fourth bars of the second eight-bar section, the flow of quavers is interrupted by two relatively long, stressed notes, the first started ahead of the beat, the second right on it. The phrase is perfectly balanced not only rhythmically but harmonically also, the notes in question being 'passing notes' (i.e. the flattened seventh *en route* to the sub-dominant chord and the flattened sixth leading back to the tonic) promoted above their station in life. The shifting of emphasis from the strong to the weak notes in a melody line became, like the stressing of weak beats, common practice among the boppers.

The hints of things to come to be found in the playing of Roy Eldridge and other giants of the Swing Era must not be exaggerated. Too much ink has been spilled in vain by jazz historians trying to trace a clear evolutionary line from Buddy Bolden to the present day. The point that should emerge from these passing observations is that, as most of its still-active founders such as Dizzy Gillespie now insist, bebop was not some sort of revolutionary manifesto, a point by point refutation of, and departure from, everything that had gone before. From the moment when, in the Twenties, Louis Armstrong demonstrated the possibilities inherent in extended solo improvisation, the use of more complex harmonies, greater rhythmic variation, new ways of starting, developing and finishing a solo, different approaches to tone production and so on were inevitable. They began to emerge at all kinds of random points during the Thirties. The idea, unfortunately embedded in many jazz histories, that the boppers invented a new music out of disgust and boredom with all that preceded them does not bear a second's investigation. Indeed, the reverse is true. They were inspired and stimulated by players such as Coleman Hawkins, Art Tatum, Lester Young and Roy Eldridge, just as those musicians acknowledged the influence of *their* predecessors.

If I seem to have turned aside from 'Heckler's Hop' rather abruptly at the point at which Roy Eldridge's two choruses end, it is because, alas, the tenor-saxophone solo which follows demonstrates that it was not *every* saxophonist who had something to teach him in terms of speed and fluency! Luckily, Roy's contribution establishes such momentum that we have hardly finished boggling at its audacity before he is back again with a reprise of the theme, a climactic coda and a casually pipped top A that seems to challenge all-comers with a defiant 'Follow that!'

Select Bibliography

Balliett, Whitney. *The Sound of Surprise* William Kimber, 1960
Bechet, Sidney. *Treat It Gentle* Cassell, 1960
Chilton, John. *Who's Who in Jazz* Chilton Book Co., 1970
——. *Billie's Blues* Quartet Books, 1975
Condon, Eddie. *We Called it Music* Peter Davies, 1948
Dance, Stanley. *The World of Duke Ellington* Macmillan, 1970
——. *The World of Earl Hines* Scribner, NY, 1977
Ellington, Duke. *Music is My Mistress* W. H. Allen, 1974
Feather, Leonard. *The Encyclopedia of Jazz* Horizon Press
Freeman, Bud. *You Don't Look Like a Musician* Balamp Publishing, 1974
Hammond, John. *John Hammond on Record* Ridge Press, 1977
Harris, Rex. *Jazz* Pelican Books, 1952
Harvey, Eddie. *Teach Yourself Jazz Piano* English University Press, 1974
Hentoff, Nat and Nat Shapiro. *Hear Me Talkin' To Ya* Peter Davies, 1955
——. *The Jazz Makers* Peter Davies, 1958
Hodeir, André. *Jazz: Its Evolution and Essence* Secker and Warburg, 1956
Holiday, Billie. *Lady Sings the Blues* Barrie Books, 1958
Hughes, Spike. *Second Movement* Museum Press, 1951
Jones, Max and John Chilton. *Louis: The Louis Armstrong Story 1900–1971* Studio Vista, 1971
Kirkeby, Ed. *Ain't Misbehavin'* Peter Davies, 1966
Lambert, Constant. *Music Ho!* Faber and Faber, 1934

Mezzrow, Milton 'Mezz' and Bernard Wolfe. *Really the Blues* Secker and Warburg, 1946

Rust, Brian. *Jazz Records 1897–1942 A–Z* Storyville Publications and Co., 1970

Schuller, Gunther. *Early Jazz: Its Roots and Musical Development* Oxford University Press, 1968

Smith, Jay D. and Len Gutteridge. *Jack Teagarden* Cassell, 1960

Stewart, Rex. *Jazz Masters of the 30's* Macmillan, 1972

Vance, Joel. *Fats Waller: His Life and Times* Robson Books, 1979

Waller, Maurice and Anthony Calabrese. *Fats Waller* Cassell, 1977

Williams, Martin. *Jazz Panorama* The Cromwell–Collier Press, 1958

Discography

'Sweethearts on Parade' *Louis Armstrong and his Orchestra*
Louis Armstrong, trumpet and vocal; George Orendorff, Harold Scott, trumpets; Luther Graven, trombone; Les Hite, alto and baritone sax, leader; Marvin Johnson, alto sax; Charlie Jones, clarinet, tenor sax; Henry Prince, piano; Bill Perkins, banjo; Joe Bailey, bass; Lionel Hampton, drums.   23 December 1930

'Handful of Keys' *Fats Waller*, piano solo   1 March 1929

'Twelfth Street Rag' *Fats Waller and his Rhythm*
Herman Autrey, trumpet; Rudy Powell, clarinet; Fats Waller, piano and vocal; James Smith, guitar; Charles Turner, bass; Arnold Boling, drums.   24 June 1935

'Crazy Rhythm' *Coleman Hawkins and his All Star Jam Band*
André Ekyan, Benny Carter, alto saxes; Alix Combelle, Coleman Hawkins, tenor saxes; Stephane Grappelly, piano; Django Reinhardt, guitar; Eugene d'Hellemmes, bass; Tommy Benford, drums.   28 April 1937

'Body and Soul' *Coleman Hawkins and his Orchestra*
Coleman Hawkins, tenor-sax solo with nine-piece band.
11 October 1939

'Knockin' a Jug' *Louis Armstrong and his Band*
> Louis Armstrong, trumpet; Jack Teagarden, trombone; Happy Caldwell, tenor sax; Joe Sullivan, piano; Eddie Lang, guitar; Kaiser Marshall, drums.   5 March 1929

'Jack Hits The Road' *Bud Freeman and his Famous Chicagoans*
> Bud Freeman, tenor sax; Pee Wee Russell, clarinet; Jack Teagarden, trombone; Dave Bowman, piano; Eddie Condon, guitar; Mort Stuhlmaker, bass; Dave Tough, drums.   23 July 1940

'Tiger Rag' *Art Tatum*, piano solo.   21 March 1933

'Tea for Two' *Art Tatum*, piano solo.   12 April 1939

'Never No Lament' (Don't Get Around much any More') *Duke Ellington and his Orchestra*
> Wardell Jones, Cootie Williams, trumpets; Rex Stewart, cornet; Joe 'Tricky Sam' Nanton, Lawrence Brown, Juan Tizol, trombones; Barney Bigard, clarinet; Johnny Hodges, Otto Hardwick, alto saxes; Ben Webster, tenor sax; Harry Carney, baritone sax; Duke Ellington, piano; Fred Guy, guitar; Jimmy Blanton, bass; Sonny Greer, drums.   4 May 1940

'Squatty Roo' *Johnny Hodges and his Band*
> Johnny Hodges, alto sax; Ray Nance, trumpet; Lawrence Brown, trombone; Harry Carney, baritone sax; Duke Ellington, piano; Jimmy Blanton, bass; Sonny Greer, drums.   3 July 1941

'Smack' *The Chocolate Dandies*
> Roy Eldridge, trumpet; Benny Carter, alto sax; Coleman Hawkins, tenor sax; Bernard Addison, guitar; John Kirby, bass; Sidney Catlett, drums.   25 May 1940

'Sweet Sue' *Dicky Wells and his Band*
> Dicky Wells, trombone; Bill Coleman, trumpet; Django Reinhardt, guitar; Richard Fullbright, bass; Bill Beason, drums.   7 July 1937

'Dickie Wells Blues' *Dickie Wells Quartet*
> Dickie Wells, trombone; Sam Allen, piano; Roger Chaput, guitar; Bill Beason, drums.   12 July 1937

'Lady be Good' *Jones-Smith Incorporated*
> Lester Young, tenor sax; Carl 'Tatti' Smith, trumpet; Count Basie, piano; Walter Page, bass; Jo Jones, drums.
>   9 October 1936

'I'll Get By' *Teddy Wilson and his Band*
> Teddy Wilson, piano; Buck Clayton, trumpet; Johnny Hodges, alto sax; Lester Young, tenor sax; Buster Bailey, clarinet; Allan Reuss, guitar; Arthur Bernstein, bass; Cozy Cole, drums; Billie Holiday, vocal.   11 May 1937

'Back in Your Own Back Yard' *Billie Holiday and her Orchestra*
> Billie Holiday, vocal; Buck Clayton, trumpet; Lester Young, tenor sax; Benny Morton, trombone; Teddy Wilson, piano; Freddy Greene, guitar; Walter Page, bass; Jo Jones, drums.   12 January 1938

'Heckler's Hop' *Roy Eldridge and his Band*
> Roy Eldridge, trumpet; Joe Eldridge, Scoops Carry, alto saxes; Dave Young, tenor sax; Teddy Cole, piano; John Collins, guitar; Truck Parham, bass; Zuttie Singleton, drums.   23 January 1937

Index